THE
FIFTEEN
MINUTE
HOUR

THE FIFTEEN MINUTE HOUR

Applied Psychotherapy for the Primary Care Physician

SECOND EDITION

Marian R. Stuart, Ph.D.
Joseph A. Lieberman III, M.D., M.P.H.

Foreword by Robert E. Rakel

PRAEGER

Westport, Connecticut
London

Library of Congress Cataloging-in-Publication Data

Stuart, Marian R.
    The fifteen minute hour : applied psychotherapy for the primary
care physician / Marian R. Stuart and Joseph A. Lieberman III :
foreword by Robert E. Rakel.—2nd ed.
      p.   cm.
    Includes bibliographical references and index.
    ISBN 0–275–94498–0 (hc : alk. paper).—ISBN 0–275–94499–9 (pb :
alk. paper)
    1. Physician and patient. 2. Sick—Psychology. 3. Psychotherapy.
4. Family medicine. I. Lieberman, Joseph A. (Joseph Aloysius).
II. Title.
    [DNLM: 1. Family Practice. 2. Primary Health Care.
3. Psychophysiology. 4. Psychotherapy. WM 420 S9315f]
R727.3.S87   1993
616′.001′9—dc20   92– 48985
DNLM/DLC
for Library of Congress

British Library Cataloguing in Publication Data is available.

Library of Congress Catalog Card Number: 92– 48985
ISBN: 0–275–94498–0
    0–275–94499–9 (pb.)

First published in 1993

Praeger Publishers, 88 Post Road West, Westport, CT 06881
An imprint of Greenwood Publishing Group, Inc.

Printed in the United States of America

The paper used in this book complies with the
Permanent Paper Standard issued by the National
Information Standards Organization (Z39.48–1984).

10 9 8 7 6 5 4 3 2 1

Contents

Foreword

Ever since family practice was established as an academic discipline with continuing comprehensive care as its hallmark, behavioral medicine has been recognized as an essential component of care. This is a departure from the traditional disease oriented biological model of medicine, which has proven to be an inadequate model for the effective delivery of primary care. It gives too little recognition to the role that emotions, expectations, fears, and stress play in every day life.

Primary care, when done well, integrates biological medicine and the psychosocial sciences into daily medical practice. Psychological and social factors are recognized and addressed as well as the physical. The mind-body approach to medicine is not a dichotomy but a dualism that family practice incorporates as *systemic family medicine*. This views the doctor-patient relationship as a complex interaction involving emotional, relational, and belief systems.

Bio-psycho-social medicine is an accurate but unwieldy term to describe comprehensive primary health care. It recognizes the patient's total life situation and the way psychological and social stress may be contributing to the problem. A primary care physician who is locked into the biologic model is much less effective than one who appropriately incorporates the psychological and social aspects of health care. This added dimension is an essential part of the comprehensive health care provided by family physicians.

The authors demonstrate in a very pragmatic and efficient way how to incorporate psychotherapy effectively into a busy medical practice. The BATHE technique, described in Chapter 6, allows busy family physicians to improve their effectiveness by incorporating the principal features of psychosocial medicine into the patient interview. Using this technique, primary care physicians can effectively and efficiently incorporate psychotherapy into every patient visit and achieve a better outcome than physicians who are stuck in the disease oriented model. Psychotherapy is not as ominous and difficult as many people feel and certainly requires less time than other forms of psychiatric care. Psychotherapy is often most effective when given frequently in small doses by a family physician who knows the patient well and enjoys the trust that comes from a long relationship.

Depression is a common problem seen in practice, and patients frequently present with a variety of somatic symptoms. It takes specific training for a primary care physician to be able to recognize and manage depression in its early stages, and family physicians trained in the bio-psycho-social model are the best prepared to recognize and treat this disorder before it results in significant morbidity or mortality. The identification of potentially serious disease in its early, undifferentiated stage is one of the most difficult tasks in medicine.

The world is becoming increasingly aware of the higher standard of medical care that can be achieved by excellent primary care. The knowledge gained by a family physician through years of continuous care contributes significantly to early and accurate diagnosis of potentially serious problems, such as depression. This is not only more economical care, it contributes to improved quality of life to a much greater degree than episodic care by a succession of unfamiliar physicians.

The interface between caring and curing, and between medical and social issues is often blurred. More than any other type of doctor, the family physician works at these undefined interfaces and utilizes this knowledge in the daily care of patients. Family practice focuses on the therapeutic benefit of an effective doctor-patient relationship. It is the formal training in interpersonal skills and the incorporation of psychosocial awareness into medical practice that allows the family physician to be so effective.

This book will be of value to all primary care physicians, especially those whose training in behavioral medicine was limited. It is especially recommended to students and residents who will be entering another discipline than family medicine, yet will be providing primary care. The more comprehensive the approach to patient care and the more complete the consideration of factors effecting a patient's health, the higher the quality of the health care provided.

Robert E. Rakel, M.D.

Acknowledgments

The authors wish to recognize and express appreciation to the many people who made meaningful contributions to this book. We would first like to thank the following physicians: Maria Auletta, M.D., Hana Chaim, D.O., Alicia Dermer, M.D., Steven Frank, D.O., Joan Gopin, M.D., Patricia Janku, M.D., Naomi Kolb, M.D., Ronald Lau, M.D., Yves Morency, M.D., Jean Plover, M.D., Andrew Sachere, M.D., Yasser Soliman, M.D., Roger Thompson, M.D., and Harvey Weingarten, M.D., for practicing our methods and contributing experiential clinical material. We would also like to acknowledge our colleagues; Robert Like, M.D., Thomas Seck, M.D., Frank C. Snope, M.D., David Swee, M.D., and Alfred Tallia, M.D., for their advice and encouragement. Special thanks to Beatrix Hamm, M.D., and Ronald Nathan, Ph.D., for their fine editorial suggestions. Finally, we would like to thank Ms. Brenda Bundy, Ms. Louise Ignoscia, Ms. Jeanne Olson, Ms. Natalie Richman, and Ms. Joan Roberts, without whose skill and support our deadlines could not have been met.

Introduction to the Second Edition

As with the first edition, this book has only one purpose: to convince you that by routinely incorporating psychotherapeutic approaches into medical practice, many problems may be solved or prevented. Consequently, your practice will become more productive and pleasurable. The book grows out of our own clinical practice and our experience in training residents and practicing physicians in the art of therapeutic talk. In the six years since the publication of the first edition of *The Fifteen Minute Hour*, we have heard from many enthusiastic practitioners from all over the United States and Canada who have assimilated our techniques into their practices. The overwhelming consensus has been that the strategies work, patients respond, physicians save time, doctor-patient relationships become richer, and everyone experiences less stress.

There are several things that this book is not: It is not a book on psychiatry in primary care. There are many good books about that subject. It is not a book dealing with mental illness, or its diagnosis. Furthermore, it is not a text on psychoanalysis. This is a book about incorporating useful knowledge from psychology and psychotherapy into medical practice in order to become more effective in dealing with the emotional overlay (or underlay) of problems that patients bring to the primary care physician.

In the intervening years since the publication of *The Fifteen Minute Hour*, research has supported many of our contentions regarding the importance of addressing the psychological components related to a patient's health status. We hope that you will master our relatively simple techniques for dealing effectively with this dimension of patient care. If you have already accepted responsibility for managing the psychosocial problems brought by patients, or if we can convince you to do so, then this book will provide you with theoretical background material that should be extremely useful. We will point out what actually works in practice to help improve patient functioning. Furthermore, we will provide specific suggestions, outlines for therapy, and particular phrases and approaches that we have developed, practiced, taught, and tested over the last fourteen years.

Our approach is not necessarily the only "true, good, or beautiful" way in which to engage patients in therapy, but it is a flexible, practical approach that is easily learned—and it works. Also, it is designed to fit into a regular fifteen minute (or shorter) office visit without requiring lengthy, extended therapy sessions.

We strongly recommend that you read this book from beginning to end. Early chapters provide the theoretical background and rationale for the subsequent chapters, which focus on how to put this knowledge into action. In essence, this is a how-to book. We aim to help you develop skills that will benefit both you and your patients by providing some tools that you can use in your practice. They are effective and require less investment of time and energy than you would imagine. We will explain these tools and exactly how to use them.

There are many schools of psychotherapy. We are not preaching a dogma, but rather invite you to explore the effects of using our techniques and empirically confirm their usefulness for yourself. We do not have the need to establish a true religion in this area. Indeed, we are quite comfortable with practical eclecticism: It works, and primary care physicians desperately need effective techniques. In essence, what we are saying is, "Try it, you'll like it."

Over one hundred years ago, John Godfrey Saxe, a Vermont lawyer and humorist, wrote the following poem. "The Blind Men and the Elephant" based on an Indian tale thought to date back thousands of years, yet it still seems most applicable today.[1]

> It was six men of Indostan
>   To learning much inclined,
> Who went to see the Elephant
>   (Though all of them were blind)
> That each by observation
>   Might satisfy his mind.
>
> The First approached the Elephant,
>   And happening to fall
> Against his broad and sturdy side,
>   At once began to bawl:

"God bless me! but the Elephant
   Is very like a wall!"

The Second, feeling of the tusk,
   Cried, "Ho! what have we here
So very round and smooth and sharp?
   To me 'tis mighty clear
This wonder of an Elephant
   Is very like a spear!"

The Third approached the animal,
   And happening to take
The squirming trunk within his hands,
   Thus boldly up and spake:
"I see," quoth he, "the Elephant
   Is very like a snake!"

The Fourth reached out an eager hand,
   And felt about the knee
"What most this wondrous beast is like
   Is mighty plain," quoth he;
" 'Tis clear enough the Elephant
   Is very like a tree!"

The Fifth who chanced to touch the ear,
   Said: "E'en the blindest man
Can tell what this resembles most;
   Deny the fact who can,
This marvel of an Elephant
   Is very like a fan!"

The Sixth no sooner had begun
   About the beast to grope
Than, seizing on the swinging tail
   That fell within his scope,
"I see," quoth he, "the Elephant
   Is very like a rope!"

And so these men of Indostan
   Disputed loud and long,
Each in his own opinion
   Exceeding stiff and strong,
Though each was partly in the right,
   And all were in the wrong!

In our opinion, different schools of psychology and psychiatry use different lenses through which to view the patient and the patient's problems. Each has something valuable to offer; each has a small piece of useful insight.

Collectively, these fragments form a practical armamentarium with which to help people suffer less, prevent physical and psychological ills, and structure satisfying lives for themselves and their loved ones.

In writing this book, we have tried to present a coherent whole. Each chapter builds on the previous one, but we have also incorporated illustrative clinical examples throughout the text. The case material is based entirely on actual encounters, although we have changed the names and altered some details in order to guarantee patient confidentiality. In this second edition, we have tried to build on the strength of the first. In making our revisions, we have considered the many thoughtful critiques and reviews of *The Fifteen Minute Hour* and have clarified and expanded important sections. In addition, we have added new case material, new concepts, and new techniques.

In Chapter 1, we discuss current trends in the delivery of health care, the outmoded medical model, and the need to employ a new structure that integrates George Engel's biopsychosocial model with an awareness of current sociological, political, and economic realities. Chapter 2 presents in detail patient reactions to stress and forms the theoretical basis for the effectiveness of the type of therapy we are promoting. We bring together research findings from a variety of sources, some of which may be new to you, and try to build a strong foundation. In Chapter 3 we discuss the qualifications and natural proclivities of primary care physicians that make them ideal psychotherapists.

In the next chapter we present, from a variety of viewpoints, what we consider to be the actual elements that induce the type of positive changes attributed to psychotherapy. We deal with elements common to all schools of psychotherapy and introduce several new concepts that simplify the process of facilitating positive changes. Chapter 5 looks at the differences between the type of psychotherapy that we are advocating and that which is generally provided by traditional mental health practitioners. Again, the second part of this chapter falls into the how-to category, as we suggest ways to take advantage of these differences as well as when and how to make referrals.

Chapter 6 focuses on how to structure the therapy, while Chapters 7 through 10 provide clear directions on just what, how, when, and with whom to do what we propose. We have expanded the material dealing with anxiety and depression, and at the request of a number of practitioners, we have added material related to working with children. Chapter 11 projects our vision of what is possible for the present and the future of medical care, given the widespread acceptance and practice of these ideas.

We hope you enjoy reading this book. Please, have fun with it. Your patients will thank you many times over.

Marian R. Stuart, Ph.D.
Joseph A. Lieberman III, M.D., M.P.H.

REFERENCE

1. Saxe, John G. *Clever stories of many nations: Rendered in rhyme.* Boston: Ticknor and Fields, 1865.

THE
FIFTEEN
MINUTE
HOUR

The Relationship between Mental and Physical Health: Implications of the New Medical Model

American medicine, although undergoing evolution, now faces changes of a magnitude that has never before been encountered. Among the many causes are the dramatic proliferation of knowledge in general; the effects of burgeoning technology; sociological changes within the community that encourage wellness and self-help programs; redirection of financial resources, with material constraints imposed on both the public and private sectors; and increased personal longevity, with its concomitant chronic illness. Individually and collectively, these phenomena are working to reshape the system of American health care delivery.

All this ferment can be distressing, foreboding, and uncomfortable for the physician; however, at the same time, it can be challenging, fortuitous and, in many ways, refreshing. Finding a successful way of adapting to the changing circumstances becomes the primary task. The physician who wishes to endure and prosper is faced with the need to acquire new skills and rethink ideas that are currently being challenged. What is critical is to meet the patients' emerging needs. The ability to clearly comprehend the scope of these needs is the central issue.

We know that the first step in solving any problem is to identify it. The simple recognition of a situation as a problem alters it. This book is largely devoted to looking at the doctor-patient relationship and patient needs from a somewhat untraditional perspective. We hope in this way to help define problems that heretofore may not have been considered by the traditionally trained physician. It is precisely in the resolution of these problems that the contemporary practitioner will gain the skills needed to practice medicine effectively in this new, and at times difficult, climate of health care delivery. There is a considerable body of literature demonstrating that patients encountered by primary care physicians commonly present with a psychiatric, or at least a behavioral, problem as the reason for seeking care.[1,2] Even in those instances where a patient is seen for an obvious biomedical problem, there frequently is an emotional overlay that needs to be addressed if the patient is to receive optimal care. One of the beauties of primary care practice is the diversity of patient problems. This also gives rise to profound challenges, particularly regarding the behavioral, and in more extreme cases, the psychiatric, aspects of this type of practice. However, effective health care mandates internists and family physicians to provide appropriate psychiatric interventions in order to diminish suffering in their patients by addressing the sources of their distress, and not just the effects.[3]

THE LIMITS OF THE TRADITIONAL, DISEASE-ORIENTED MEDICAL MODEL

In order to better understand the need for the contemporary physician to acquire new skills, we will start by looking at how that physician was trained (meaning how the practitioner acquired the current skills). Traditional medicine has long and effectively concerned itself almost exclusively with the biomedical model of illness. Medical education has perpetuated this approach with its overwhelming emphasis on tertiary care and bench research. Few professors (the role models for the next generations of physicians) ever encounter the undifferentiated patient population that is the daily fare of the medical generalist. The halls of academe have little appreciation of the role of the primary care physician who toils at the interface of the biomedical, behavioral, and social sciences. This academic model creates a structure for examining, classifying, and treating disease. In the process, this pathogenic orientation creates a dichotomous classification of people as either having, or not having, a disease. Diseases are viewed almost in isolation from their patient victims. This reductionistic approach, which literally separates the patient from the disease, has been the working model in our systems of medical education and health care delivery. It is the disease that is on center stage, and efforts are mainly directed toward categorizing it from a largely etiological and therapeutic perspectives. The disease is the raison d'être for the doctor-patient encounter, and thus, in most instances, it dictates an acute care setting.

In order to arrive at the proper etiology and thereby establish the proper therapy, the reductionistic approach is also utilized in clinical decision making. Diseases are traditionally put into large classifications and then gradually subclassified until the specific disease entity has been identified. Further, it is assumed that each disease has a specific cause for which treatment, in one form or another, is generally available. Frequently, the choice between chemical, surgical, radiological, or other treatment must be made, but always with the intention of somehow counteracting the cause of the pathology and thereby changing the natural course of the disease. The main function of the traditional physician has been to direct this process for the patient and to prescribe an appropriate therapy after an etiological diagnosis has been established.

This type of clinical reasoning lends itself particularly well to the generalist's need for a system with which to approach an undifferentiated patient population. By this, we mean the need for a model that will enable the primary care physician to deal effectively with a waiting room full of patients who have varying and unorganized signs, symptoms, and problems. Frequently, these patients have few external clues as to the nature of their particular problems. Moreover, while individually they may be suffering from a variety of problems, collectively, their problems are even less well defined. Categorization, followed by subcategorization and then sub-subcategorization, efficiently leads the physician from these broad-based, frequently ill-defined presenting problems to a manageable diagnostic entity that is then amenable to a specific therapeutic intervention. He or she is thus able to sort through a variety of data in an efficiently organized fashion and arrive at a meaningful conclusion that dictates a specific action.

There is a real problem with this scenario, however. Although it certainly works in clarifying issues for the physician, we agree with George Engel that:

The crippling flaw of the model is that it does not include the patient and his attributes as a person, as a human being. The biomedical model can make provision neither for the person as a whole nor for data of a psychological or social nature, for the reductionism and mind-body dualism on which the model is predicated requires that these must first be reduced to physico-chemical terms before they can have meaning. Hence, the very essence of medical practice perforce remains "art" and beyond the reach of science. (p. 536)[4]

It would seem that the biopsychosocial whole is greater than the sum of the biomedical parts. In spite of the fact that it may not add up properly, this model is still the preeminent way in which contemporary American medicine is practiced. A better understanding of this process can be achieved by an examination of its application in its most common form, the typical office encounter.

NATURE OF THE OFFICE ENCOUNTER

Under ordinary circumstances, patients present themselves at the doctor's office with a symptom or collection of symptoms. The physician goes through a series of physical assessments and laboratory and other evaluations, and then arrives at a working hypothesis concerning the cause of the symptomatology and the nature, therefore, of the disease. After developing a differential diagnosis and listing all the disease entities that might account for the symptoms, the physician uses the data to rule out the most serious ailments and arrives at a diagnosis that provides a label for the patient's condition. The appropriate therapy is then prescribed. Since this is commonly a pharmacologic agent, the prescription will now be generated. In fact, issuing the prescription consistently marks the end of the doctor-patient encounter. If no pathological cause can be established for the symptoms, the diagnosis is frequently made that they are some manifestation of a behavioral or emotional disorder. Again, the prescription will be employed. Now, however, the physician will more likely order a psychotherapeutic agent. Nevertheless, the encounter is still terminated in the same fashion. The implication that every disease must have a specific cause and that this cause can be pharmacologically treated is central to the process. If a definite cause for the illness cannot be ascertained, then at least the symptoms can be treated, also pharmacologically.

The office encounter is now almost complete. The patient only has to pay for the visit or sign the insurance form attesting to having received specific services.

TENSION BETWEEN THE SCIENTIFIC METHOD AND PATIENT NEEDS

Regrettably, this entire scenario frequently meets the needs of the physician far better than those of the patient. Perhaps, this is the central problem: Patients arrive at the physician's office knowing only that they do not feel well and have symptoms. After a series of maneuvers and studies, patients are informed of a purported cause for their symptoms. If this is amenable to a specific therapy, they will be fortunate enough to have their symptoms relieved and to be considered cured. The physician is gratified that the patient can, in fact, be treated, and the patient is satisfied and grateful, since the particular problem has been dealt with effectively. Far more commonly, however, the patient's symptoms are part of a much larger gestalt. Patients are complex, multidimensional human beings, and they bring a variety of problems to the physician, some of which are quite obvious, while others take the form of hidden agendas. I. R. McWhinney suggested that if the "patient is fortunate, he will find a physician who will meet these needs as well as providing the best of technical care."[5] If the underlying reasons for a patient's visit are to be discerned, the physician needs to be a perceptive student of human nature. However, if, instead, the physician simply focuses on the organic aspects that are presented, it is likely that this unidimensional view will prevent an accurate perception of the patient's problems.

The presenting problem (which the physician can frequently handle with little difficulty) may not be the main reason for the patient's visit. There is a substantial body of literature showing that people do not visit doctors simply for the relief of organic disorders but also go to the primary care physician because of life stress, psychiatric disorders, social isolation, and informational needs.[5] Even those patients who are fortunate enough to have their symptoms relieved by the physician's intervention may find this insufficient to meet all their other needs. If, on the other hand, patients have the misfortune of not even having their symptoms relieved and are instead informed that, in fact, it is "only your nerves that are causing your symptoms," they become subject to the stigma that the explanation implies. All too frequently, they are only left with a therapy that will relieve their most obvious symptoms but will not treat the underlying condition. By "turning off" the symptom (which is a signal that something is wrong), the physician removes the evidence without addressing the problem. By analogy, if we were to turn off the bell on our telephone, we would never know when someone was calling and therefore could not respond by either giving or receiving information.

INTERRELATIONSHIP BETWEEN PHYSICAL AND PSYCHOLOGICAL HEALTH

The use of the reductionistic approach can be very valuable for the patient, particularly when there is a specific physical malady to explain the symptoms. However, if the physician is to be truly a healer, this approach is far too limited to satisfy patient needs (even though it may admirably satisfy the needs of the physician). We have repeatedly alluded to the traditional biological approach in the evaluation of symptoms. Obviously, we feel this is insufficient for dealing with patient needs. A whole body of recent research substantiates the inadequacy of this approach.[6,7] These investigations indicate conclusively that the soma does not function in a vacuum, but rather, that the psyche and the soma are so closely related that imbalances or blockages in either one can produce symptoms or disease in the other. Indeed, there has been a geometric progression in the production of studies of stress-related disorders. For example, a patient's psychological response to the diagnosis or treatment of cancer can be related to the course of the disease.[8] S. Greer, T. Morris, and K. W. Pettingale found that women diagnosed as having breast cancer who express anger and hostility have a better prognosis than those who passively and helplessly accept their disease.[9] D. Spiegel and his colleagues were absolutely amazed to find that women with breast cancer who attended support groups not only had a much better quality of life (as had been expected), but survived significantly longer than women in the control group.[10] The mechanism involved in the well-known mortality risk following bereavement was first reported by R. W. Bartrop and his colleagues.[11] A prospective study published in the *Journal of the American Medical Association* replicated their study by monitoring the immune system of husbands of women with breast cancer and found a highly significant suppression of lymphocyte function to specific antigens within one month of the spouse's death. This suppression lasted for a period of fourteen months after bereavement and was not due to preexisting conditions.[12] The investigators concluded that "suppressed immunity following the death of a spouse may be related to the increased morbidity and mortality associated with bereavement" (p. 374). J. M. Weiss cited numerous experimental studies leading to an increased understanding of the mechanisms involved in the development of peptic ulcers and other gastrointestinal pathology.[13] Studies of the pathophysiological links between behavioral factors and cardiovascular disease and other life-threatening illnesses are also proliferating.[14] Other studies have focused on the role of psychosocial influences on mortality after a myocardial infarction.[15] Finally, a study in the *New England Journal of Medicine* reported finding that psychological stress not only increased the risk of contracting an infectious respiratory disease but also showed a dose-related effect.[16] If the psyche and the soma were not integrally related, none of these effects would occur. It is not our intention to bore the reader by citing research that may be either familiar or else of little interest. Instead, our wish is to heighten awareness and indicate the importance of incorporating these understandings into the day-to-day practice of medicine. In his introduction to Norman Cousins's *The Healing Heart*, the cardiologist Bernard Lown wrote:

Although most physicians would not deny that many variables, including psychological factors, influence disease, these are regarded as secondary and largely irrelevant once the basic cause is discovered. For example, when streptococcal upper-respiratory infections are controlled, psychological factors in a child's rheumatic fever are not given serious consideration. . . . Similarly, some physicians would maintain that once the biology of cancer is comprehended, the psychological factors that may govern its progress or modulate its anxiety and pain become but an irrelevant script on ancient scrolls.

The most immutable fact of life is death. It will never be annulled by artificial organs or scientific progress. The days of a human being will ever be finite, and disease and pain will always stalk life's journey. The patient will always require care, sympathetic judgment, and healing. The physician will never be relieved of the responsibility to assuage pain, promote comfort, and instill hope. But there is an additional aspect, relating to the patient's psycho-biological constitution, that has powerful self-regulating and self-healing capacities. In ignoring these intrinsic gifts for self-repair, the physician obstructs the amplification of the efficacy of his own scientific methods and impedes the very process of recovery.[17]

DECLINE OF THE RELEVANCE OF TRADITIONAL MEDICINE

Regrettably, the medical establishment's failure to recognize all that the relationship between the psyche and soma implies—by unwisely relying on the traditional approach—is resulting in meeting ever fewer of the needs of an enlightened patient population. This has caused a certain public disenchantment with the medical profession and has spurred the growth of many of the self-help and allied programs that can be seen proliferating today. If, indeed, a physician does not answer a patient's needs, the patient will seek help elsewhere, even though this decision may ultimately be to the patient's detriment.

Cults, quacks, vitamin megadoses, purges, blood lettings, extreme nutritionalism, and other fads—which are in some ways reminiscent of the Dark Ages—are flourishing today, in many ways spurred by the public's disenchantment with the inability of the medical establishment to meet their individual needs. Certainly, constructive self-help is to be encouraged. Programs to reduce stress; improve physical conditioning; do away with drug, alcohol, and cigarette dependency; and maintain ideal height-weight ratios and good physical conditioning are all to be encouraged. What is unfortunate is that much of the lead in these various areas has been taken by the lay public and not by the medical profession per se. R. B. Taylor has underscored the need for health care providers, whose scientific knowledge dictates a rational approach that promotes living wisely, to take the lead rather than leaving it to cultism or the financial aspirations of alternative interests.[18] Many components of the self-help movement, constructive as they may be, are in fact still another manifestation of public dissatisfaction with the medical profession and its perceived inability to deal with the individual patient and his or her needs.

ECONOMIC CONSIDERATIONS

The restructuring of the financial reimbursement system for medical services provides yet another incentive for contemporary practitioners to rethink the way in which they practice. Until recently, the preeminent method of paying physicians was on a fee-for-service basis. Typically, a patient would present to a physician with an illness, such as appendicitis, and a service, in this instance, an appendectomy, would be performed by the physician. A fee would then be collected from the patient or the patient's insurance carrier. With this method, high-technology services are generally compensated better than the so-called cognitive services, although both may involve equivalent time and effort on the physician's part. Such a system, of course, rewards utilization, because there is no payment unless the service is rendered. Likewise, such a system favors the more complicated services over the simpler ones, as well as the procedural services over the cognitive ones, because in both instances, the former type are more liberally rewarded financially.

It is interesting to note that patients are frequently the innocent players in this scenario, since they have little choice and virtually no expertise concerning the services they are to receive. With the proliferation of health care insurance, patients also bear little responsibility for the financial consequences of their physicians' actions. Physicians frequently find themselves in the position of being rewarded only if they "do something," and of being pressured by patients, who, because they have insurance, want something done. Right or wrong, much of the blame for rapidly rising health costs is laid on this method of reimbursement.

The Great Society of the 1960s had, as a cornerstone of its health care philosophy, a dedication to the equalization of access to medical care for all Americans, regardless of age, sex, race, economic status, or geographic location. By the mid-1970s, however, the consensus among government and other health care planners was that this grand dream was economically not feasible. Subsequently, cost containment for medical expenditures began to drive policy formation and implementation in the public sector.

More recently, industry, which heretofore had played a largely passive role in this entire process, has caught up with our government, which is cost-conscious about health care. Both parties are now concerned about the amount they must pay to support their respective entitlement or insurance programs. Rather than worry exclusively about quality of, or access to, care, government and industry, in concert, are now equally oriented to the bottom line. As a result, they are energetically supportive of any programs that can both rationalize the system and reduce health care costs, such as the Resource-Based Relative Value System for establishing fee schedules and reimbursing physicians.

For the primary care physician or generalist in medical practice, this reorientation and redirection of resources presents an opportunity to maximize efforts directed toward such things as preventive medicine and cost-effective health care. Systems providing managed care of reimbursement that do not pay on a fee-for-service basis, but rather reimburse the physician by providing the practitioner with a set monetary remuneration for a patient or family over a specified period of time, are gaining in popularity. This form of reimbursement rewards the practitioner who can minimize expenditures (such as hospitalization) and maximize wellness, thereby resulting in the conservation of those funds that are set aside for payment of other specialists or consultants for the care of each patient or family. There is an impressive and rapidly growing body of literature that documents the necessity and cost-effectiveness of providing psychological suypport to patients in hospital as well as outpatient settings.[19–24]

In this book, we present strategies that will provide effective psychosocial treatment in the context of a standard office medical practice. These strategies, coupled with good medical practice, should enable the knowledgeable practitioner to maintain a competitive position relative to other practitioners in what is becoming an overcrowded profession. As Paul Starr bluntly pointed out, "Increasingly, the gains of one physician, or group of physicians, will have to come at the expense of other physicians or providers."[25] Farsighted physicians must acquire the skills that are needed to flourish in just such a professional environment.

It therefore behooves those of us who are in the healing professions to begin to look at what we do and critically analyze how well we are providing the services for which the public seeks us out. To deal purely with the physical realm is, in almost all instances, to deal only incompletely with the patient's problems. We must be able to expand somewhat on our ability to meet the patient's needs, while at the same time conserving our resources so that we may meet the needs of all our patients.

We need to reexamine what we do and change the model, or paradigm, by which we operate. Thomas Kuhn's observations led him to suggest that there is a cycle determining scientific revolutions, which must occur periodically.[26] M. J. Mahoney described Kuhn's contribution very concisely:

According to Kuhn, "normal science" is a powerful problem-solving machine dedicated to grinding out the rich harvest of experimentation. As the machine becomes more precise and productive, however, there are increasing probabilities of encountering—or more accurately, recognizing—anomalies. These anomalous pieces of information do not fit the paradigm's conceptual categories and/or predictions and they cannot be assimilated without at least adjusting, if not overhauling, the machine.[27]

Research has brought to light phenomena that simply cannot be fit into the traditional biomedical model. Because of the new information that we have acquired about both patients and disease, it would seem that traditional medicine is at that point in Kuhn's cycle where the conceptual categories are in need of a serious overhaul. We must shift, or change, the paradigm in order to build a new structure that accommodates our current understandings and points to a more effective practice. Under the old paradigm of medicine, there are seven central concepts.

1. Patients suffer from diseases;
2. Diseases are independent and can be categorized;
3. Each disease has a cause;
4. The physician's task is to diagnose and prescribe;
5. The correct disease can be determined through a process of differential diagnosis;
6. The patient is the passive recipient of the diagnostic process; and
7. The mind and the body are separate entities, although both are involved in specific psychosomatic diseases.

We have already cited several limitations to the traditional medical model. McWhinney has pointed out three particular anomalies.[28] The first concerns the incidence of illness without disease. Studies of abdominal pain have shown that specific diagnoses were obtained in less than 50 percent of the cases. Headache, chest pain, back pain, and other illnesses, often present in the absence of clear-cut, identifiable disease. Second, there is a general susceptibility to disease that is evidenced by some individuals. Why is it that 25 percent of patients have 75 percent of the illness? If diseases truly had specific etiologies, it would seem likely that every person would have an even chance of contracting them. However, this is not the case. In subsequent chapters, we will discuss some of the factors that make people either more or less vulnerable. The third anomaly is the placebo effect, which cannot be explained using the traditional medical model. In every controlled trial, a percentage of people respond physiologically to an inert substance. The magnitude of the placebo effect varies in every study, but it actually approaches 100 percent in some instances. The difference between treatment and healing has to come from within. The mind, as an organ that processes information (beliefs), interacts with the body by producing chemical changes that initiate chain reactions. Jerome Frank wrote a provocative commentary entitled, "The Placebo Is Psychotherapy."[29] We wholeheartedly agree.

Perhaps the most important factor in developing a new and more effective medical model is a focus on the processes of the doctor-patient relationship and the patient's interaction with the environment. The role of the physician will be increasingly to mobilize the patient's own healing power. Norman Cousins underscored the effectiveness of confidence in the body's recovery potential, involvement in the treatment, and a sense of partnership with the physician as making major contributions to creating the physiological heal-ing response.[30]

It is pointedly obvious to us, and, undoubtedly, to any other well-informed primary care practitioner, that the old paradigm has, in fact, been over-whelmed, and that if a practitioner is to remain relevant, he or she must change the approach taken toward the patient. The contemporary practitioner must deal with the paradox that has resulted when training dictates the isolation of an illness by a reductionistic approach, yet patients present with multiple needs in which the disease entity may play a part of varying importance.

DEVELOPING AN INTEGRATED (HOLISTIC) APPROACH BASED ON SCIENTIFIC METHOD

Certainly George Engel's conceptualization of the biopsychosocial model presents an innovative and relevant way in which to apply the tenets of modern biology and the behavioral sciences to the patient encounter.[31] In this way, the biological bases are fully exposed and touched on, while at the same time, the psychosocial context is incorporated.

Engel believes, as do we, that the basic organic building blocks—that is, subatomic particles, atoms, and molecules, up through cells, tissues, organs, and organisms—are part of a larger system, including the family, community, and subculture, and on up through the biosphere.[32] He has further maintained that the systems are interrelated to the degree that an event impacting on any one component has an effect on all the other components. He presented clinical examples, such as the stress-related illness of an electrical engineer, that produce events in a community, such as loss of income, failure of businesses, and outward migration of the population. In this example, he also demonstrated the impact of stress on the engineer's organ systems, with the production of such signs and symptoms as lethargy, pain, and nausea. In another example, Engel referred to a case of severe physical and mental retardation caused by radiation-induced mutation, and he demonstrated how this impact will, at the subatomic particle level, lead to arrested development in tissues, organs, and systems; cause emotional trauma at the family level; and produce an overall resource strain at the biosphere level.

In both the examples, Engel cited many other effects that result from an adverse impact sustained predominantly at just one level in this system. We join with him in questioning the wisdom of dissecting out certain levels, such as the cellular tissue, and organ systems, for study in a reductionistic and isolated fashion. This is a characteristic style of the medical profession, which tends to leave the balance of the effects on the total system to other disciplines.

There is a massive and evolving body of literature that substantiates the anecdotal observations of most practitioners who deal with patients from day to day. It has been repeatedly noted that many events that are far removed from the organ and tissue levels will nonetheless have profound effects on components of the system. Therefore, to study and treat these components in the abstract, and only in the biomedical context, is a form of undertreatment that is every bit as damaging to the patient as undertreatment in any other form.

In developing a new, more relevant paradigm of medicine, McWhinney has suggested incorporating the following concepts:

1. More attention must be paid to health promotion and disease prevention;
2. We must keep separate disease categories, but recognize the effects of interactions and disease susceptibility;
3. We must pay more attention to nonorganic factors such as environmental and relationship characteristics when determining the etiology of disease;
4. The role of the physician is to mobilize the patient's own healing powers;
5. Physicians must develop advanced communication skills in order to diagnose and treat patients (rather than diseases);
6. Physicians must develop skills to determine the meaning of illness for the patient; and
7. The body, mind, and spirit are integrated.[28]

To put these principles into practice, we plan not only to investigate the patient's psychosocial setting and to integrate the psychosocial context into our understanding of the illness, but we also expect to intervene by supporting the patient and by tapping into his or her own resources in a constructive fashion, thereby optimizing the outcome.

The traditional reductionistic approach to medical practice has had as its end point an understanding of how a particular disease developed in a given patient. An often-quoted aphorism attributed to Sir William Osler states, "It is much more important to know what sort of patient has a disease than what sort of disease a patient has." Still, that does not tell us exactly what should be done about either the patient or the disease. Our intention here is to clearly spell out for the practitioner how to use this information to potentiate a patient's own resources and thereby improve the outcome. In the following chapters we will discuss practical interventions that can be used to achieve these ends.

SUMMARY

In light of the dramatic proliferation in medical knowledge, technology, and costs of care; sociological changes within the community that encourage wellness and self-help programs; redirection of financial resources to include prospective payment plans; and autonomous decisions and actions regarding their treatment on the part of the patient population, the primary care physician is urged to reassess and discard the traditional reductionistic, disease-oriented medical model. The typical office encounter has generally met the needs of the physician more fully than the multidimensional needs of the patient. Recognizing the interrelationship between physical and psychological health, the true inseparability of the psyche and the soma, and the tension between the scientific method and patient needs, the practitioner is urged to focus on the process of the doctor-patient relationship. There is a need to incorporate the insights from George Engel's biopsychosocial model in order to develop communication skills that will help foster a therapeutic encounter designed to support the inherent strength of the patient and promote his or her own healing powers.

REFERENCES

1. Barsky, A. J. Hidden reasons some patients visit doctors. *Annals of Internal Medicine*, 1981, *94* (part 1), 492–498.

2. Barrett, J. E., Barrett, J. A., Oxman, T. E., & Gerber, P. D. The prevalence of psychiatric disorders in a primary care practice. *Archives of General Psychiatry*, 1988, *45*, 1100–1106.

3. Eisenberg, L. Treating depression and anxiety in primary care: Closing the gap between knowledge and practice. *New England Journal of Medicine*, 1992, *326*, 1080–1084.

4. Engel, G. L. The clinical application of the biopsychosocial model. *American Journal of Psychiatry*, 1980, *137*, 535–544.

5. McWhinney, I. R. The meaning of holistic medicine. *Canadian Family Physician*, 1980, *26*, 1097.

6. Dantzer, R. Stress and disease: A psychobiological perspective. *Annals of Behavioral Medicine*, 1991, *13*, 205–210.

7. Ader, R., Felton, D. L., & Cohen, N. (Eds.). *Psychoneuroimmunology*. 2d ed. San Diego, Calif.: Academic Press, 1991.

8. Derogatis, C. R. Abeloff, M. D., & Melisaratos, N. Psychological coping mechanisms and survival time in metastatic breast cancer. *Journal of the American Medical Association*, 1979, *242*, 1504–1508.

9. Greer, S., Morris, T., & Pettingale, K. W. Psychological response to breast cancer: Effects on outcome. *Lancet*, 1979, *13*, 785–787.

10. Spiegel, D., Bloom, J., Kraemer, H. C., & Gottheil, E. Effect of psychosocial treatment on the survival of patients with metastatic breast cancer. *Lancet*, 1989, *2*, 888–891.

11. Bartrop, R. W., Lazarus, L., Luckherst, E., Kiloh, L. G., & Penny, R. Depressed lymphocyte function after bereavement. *Lancet*, 1977, *1*, 834–836.

12. Schleifer, S. J., Keller, S. E., Camerino, M., Thornton, J. C., & Stein, M. Suppression of lymphocyte stimulation following bereavement. *Journal of the American Medical Association*, 1983, *250*, 374–377.

13. Weiss, J. M. Behavioral and psychological influences on gastrointestinal pathology: Experimental techniques and findings. In W. E. Gentry, (Ed.), *Handbook of behavioral medicine*, pp. 174–221. New York: Guilford Press, 1984.

14. Smith, T. W. Hostility and health: Current status of a psychosomatic hypothesis. *Health Psychology*, 1992, *11*, 139–150.

15. Ruberman, W., Weinblatt, E., Goldberg, J. D., & Chaudhary, B. S. Psychosocial influences on mortality after myocardial infarction. *New England Journal of Medicine*, 1984, *311*, 552–559.

16. Cohen, S. C., Tyrrell, D. A. J., & Smith, A. P. Psychological stress and susceptibility to the common cold. *New England Journal of Medicine*, 1991, *325*, 606–611.

17. Lown, B. Introduction. In N. Cousins, *The healing heart: Antidotes to panic and helplessness*, pp. 12–13. New York: Norton, 1983.

18. Taylor, R. B. Health promotion: Can it succeed in the office? *Preventive Medicine*, 1981, *10*, 258–262.

19. Smith, G. R., Jr., Monson, R. A., & Ray, D. C. Psychiatric consultation in somatization disorder: A randomized controlled study. *New England Journal of Medicine*, 1986, *314*, 1407–1413.

20. Ackerman, A. D., Lyons, J. S., Hammer, J. S., & Larson, D. B. The impact of coexisting depression and timing of psychiatric consultation on medical patients' length of stay. *Hospital and Community Psychiatry*, 1988, *39*, 173–176.

21. Levenson, J. L., Hamer, R. M., & Rossiter, L. F. Relation of psychopathology in general medical inpatients to use and cost of services. *American Journal of Psychiatry*, 1990, *147*, 1498–1503.

22. Frasure-Smith, N. In-hospital symptoms of psychological stress as predictors of long-term outcome after acute myocardial infarction in men. *American Journal of Cardiology*, 1991, *67*, 121–127.

23. Strain, J. J., Lyons, J. S., Hammer, J. S., Fahs, M., Lebovits, A., Paddison, P. L., Synder, S., Strauss, E., Burton, R., Nuber, G., Abernathy, T., Sacks, H., Nordlie, J., & Sacks, C. Cost offset from a psychiatric consultation-liaison intervention with elderly hip fracture patients. *American Journal of Psychiatry*, 1991, *148*, 1044–1049.

24. Guthrie, E., Creed, F., Dawson, D., & Tomenson, B. A controlled trial of psychological treatment for the irritable bowel syndrome. *Gastroenterology*, 1991, *100*, 450–457.

25. Starr, P. *The social transformation of American medicine*. New York: Basic Books, 1984, p. 424.

26. Kuhn, T. S. *The structure of scientific revolutions*. Chicago: Universtiy of Chicago Press, 1962.

27. Mahoney, M. J. Open exchange and epistemic progress. *American Psychologist*, 1985, *40*, 29.

28. McWhinney, I. Time, change and the physician. Plenary Address to the Society of Teachers of Family Medicine, 16th Annual Spring Conference, Boston, Mass., May 1983.

29. Frank, J. D. The placebo is psychotherapy. *Behavioral and Brain Sciences*, 1983, *6*, 291–292.

30. Cousins, N. *The healing heart: Antidotes to panic and helplessness*. New York: Norton, 1983.

31. Engel, G. L. The need for a new medical model: A challenge for biomedicine. *Science*, 1977, *196*, 129–136.

32. Engel, G. L. The biomedical model: A procrustean bed? *Man and Medicine*, 1979, *4*, 257–275.

CHAPTER 2

How Patients React to Stress

Neither illness nor health can be understood as a purely personal event but rather must be seen in the context of family and cultural ties. At any given time, the patient and his or her health are influenced by a multitude of factors, including past experiences, the present situation, and expectations for the future.[1]

The purpose of *The Fifteen Minute Hour* is to outline simple interventions available to primary care practitioners that will have a major impact on patients' experiences of their illnesses and their lives. The physician can minimize the benefit of the "sick role," foster growth, provide social support, and help both patients and their families set realistic expectations for their illnesses and their lives.[2] When we consider the social context as part of the treatment, we enhance the restoration and maintenance of healthier functioning in our patients.

STRESS AND SOCIAL SUPPORT

Our understanding of the stress response as a nonspecific physical reaction comes originally from Hans Selye, who saw stress as a biological mobilization for the action required to adapt to change.[3] There are many ways to define stress; in fact, stress has been defined not only as a response, but also as both a cause and even an effect of a response to perceived threat.[4] Although the reaction of the automatic nervous system to perceived danger or demand is often thought of as a standard process (achieving the physiological readiness for fight or flight), many factors mediate the relationship between stress and illness. On an individual or psychological level, these factors include personality traits, coping styles, and the availability of social support. Personality traits, by definition, are set patterns, while coping styles vary in effectiveness. In contrast, social support is a resource that can be mobilized rapidly by concerned others.

Just as every part of the human organism is involved in maintaining homeostasis, so also each person strives to maintain a personal steady state while interacting with other people. Some people are more skilled than others in communicating their needs and having them met. Every person records in memory both the subjective experience and an interpretation of these interactions. This recorded information is then used to develop expectations for subsequent encounters and becomes part of the person's "story." The story and the expectations the individual then bases on it will affect his or her style of interacting with others, causing these personal expectations to act as self-fulfilling prophecies. In later chapters, we will discuss how to elicit and help people modify them.

Social support can be understood as a psychological mechanism that provides positive information to help people reassess or redefine perceptions regarding themselves, their situation, or the quality of their interpersonal relationships. The information may be about the individual, about the relationship, or about solutions to a problem. It is the positive quality of the social support that aids the person in developing more positive expectations toward others, and in subsequently behaving in such a manner as to realize these expectations.

A Practical Model

A useful model for understanding how people respond to events is expressed in the formula, *person plus stress yields reaction.*[5] *Person* refers to the patient's characteristics: demographic data, genetic predisposition, cultural heritage, family influences, previous coping mechanisms, personality structure, value system, personal story based on beliefs about the past, the present, and the future, and the expectations generated by the story.

Stress in this model refers to the demands being experienced by the person. These demands can be internally or externally generated. Internal demands include psychological stress that is self-induced through having unrealistic expectations, and also physiological stress such as hunger, thirst, illness, or sleep deprivation. External demands may include the demands of other people (which will then be internally processed) or such environmental stressors as noise, heat, pollution, or combinations thereof. Stress can be chronic or acute: It can consist of a major event or result from the accumulation of daily irritations and petty annoyances that demand the person's attention.[6] Stress is increased or diminished by the social support available.

Finally, *reaction* refers to the person's response to the particular stress. The primary care physician is consulted because the patient has become uncomfortable with these reactions, which may be manifested through a variety of physical or emotional symptoms. Sometimes, the physician can intervene to reduce the stress, for example, by asking family members to make certain adjustments or by writing an excuse to relieve pressures at work. However, it may be more constructive to suggest ways to modify the patient's perception of the stress or to help him or her develop stress management techniques. In this way, the physician helps the patient to moderate the *reaction*. The stress remains the same. However, the perception of the stress changes, and the patient reacts differently. Objectively, nothing has changed, but subjectively, everything is different.

HELPING PATIENTS COPE WITH STRESS RELATED TO THE MEDICAL OFFICE VISIT

An appointment with a physician may be stressful for the patient because negative past experiences with doctors may cause him or her to anticipate unpleasant experiences and therefore arouse the fight-or-flight response. Since at this point neither fight nor flight is appropriate, unpleasant bodily sensations are experienced.

The patient goes to the doctor because of a physical complaint or the anxiety attached to it. Current perceptions based on previous encounters with physicians will predetermine his or her specific expectations. The patient may feel anxious in anticipation of having to respond to certain demands, such as requests for personal information or permission to examine parts of his or her body: these are perceived as demands for physical and emotional exposure. There is really nothing that a physician may not look at, touch, or ask about. There may also be demands to accept the physician's authority, to please him or her, to follow instructions, or to be a "good patient." The patient may feel stressed in the dependent role, due to having no control in this situation. An illustration of this response is provided by recent studies of the "White-Coat Hypertension Response," which have consistently shown that approximately 40 percent of patients have systolic or diastolic blood pressure readings in the office setting that are at least ten points higher than readings taken at home.[7,8]

The Medical Appointment as a Source of Stress

The sources of stress related to the office visit can be divided into three basic categories: Almost all patients come to doctors because of pain or anxiety about a symptom or illness, and thus they experience a basic level of stress right from the start. The second category of stress has to do with logistics. It concerns requirements for the patient to make an appointment, take time off from work, arrange transportation, arrive and wait in the examining room, and finally, provide payment. The third category concerns the interpersonal elements of the visit. Patients may feel stressed as they anticipate questions, scoldings, praise, instructions, and ultimately the diagnosis that the physician may voice. There are certain "demand characteristics" that have to do with being a "good patient."[9] Some of this is learned behavior on the patient's part. This learning is greatly influenced by family or cultural perceptions of the appropriate role. Since the physician's expectations regarding the patient's behavior and the patient's expectations regarding the physician's behavior may not always coincide, more stress can be created.

By recognizing the effect of the situation on patient behavior, the physician can help relieve much of the stress and anxiety being experienced. A recent article in the *Journal of the American Medical Association* cited the effectiveness of empathic understanding in calming anxious patients.[10] There are key phrases that physicians can use to address the patient's response to a stressful situation, make it overt, and legitimize or normalize it. Just recognizing a situation as a problem changes it. By saying, "It must be difficult for you to get here in the middle of your busy day," or, "You have had to wait a long time and must be quite impatient," the physician helps the patient relax.

In general, unfortunately, if physicians do address the issue at all, instead of focusing on the patient's experience and providing empathy, they generally explain why they were detained, citing emergencies or situations involving other patients whose needs were more acute. This underscores the physician's importance while minimizing that of the patient. The resulting decreased level of patient self-esteem makes it more difficult for him or her to cope, thereby increasing the stress.

When we acknowledge that a patient has a right to be annoyed or upset by having to wait, and that this is a reasonable response to the situation, we have provided him or her with our support. One element of support is approval (or at least acceptance) of another person's behavior. In giving support, we also give relief. Our aim is to alleviate the patient's psychological distress. Thus, it is preferable to recognize and accept reactions rather than explain them. As Fritz Perls emphatically stated, the *what* and *how* are important, not the *why*.[11] It may make little sense to us that patients feel a particular way. Therefore, rather than trying to talk them out of how they feel or understand why they feel a certain way, we acknowledge those feelings and deal with them in a practical, therapeutic, and time-effective manner.

Many issues determine patient expectations in the doctor-patient relationship. These include the patient's illness stories,[12,13] their requests,[14] and various explanatory models of illness growing out of their cultural heritages.[2,15] A full discussion of these elements is beyond the scope of this book, but they are all factors that we would subsume under the *person* element of our operational model, *person plus stress yields reaction*. When anxiety is the reaction, whether to the stress of a prospective examination or to other life stressors, it is most important to avoid saying, "You have no reason to feel anxious." If the patient really had no reason to feel anxious, he or she would not feel that way. Instead, we recommend saying: "I can understand that you would feel anxious in this situation. Let's see what we can do to make you feel better."

WHY PATIENTS ADAPT DIFFERENTLY TO STRESS

When their mental health is poor, individuals are more likely to develop disease and are much less tolerant of physical symptoms.[16] The correlation between illness and stressful life events has been generally accepted. In 1951, T. H. Holmes, T. Treuting, and H. G. Wolff first documented the effects of life situations and the accompanying emotional reactions on patients with hay fever.[17] Holmes and R. H. Rahe went on to standardize their schedule of recent life events, which has been widely used in research.[18] However, many people under stress do not succumb to disease. They seem to resist diseases developed by others and to prosper both physically and mentally, even under traumatic conditions. What makes them different?

The "Salutogenic" Model

Aaron Antonovsky, in his carefully researched *Health, Stress, and Coping*, examined a variety of research in order to determine what factors protect people from the consequences of stress.[19] He suggested that it is useful to switch from a pathogenic to a salutogenic model when studying people's reactions to stress. In determining why some individuals stay healthy regardless of what happens to them, Antonovsky first listed a variety of generalized resistance resources, such as biogenetic constitutional factors, knowledge and intelligence, education, access to money, and a rational, flexible, and farsighted coping style. Then he pointed to a global orientation to the world which is held by those persons who seem most immune to stress-related illness. Antonovsky called this a "sense of coherence," which seems to insulate a person from negative health consequences, even from stressful events that cause disease in more vulnerable people. The sense of coherence is basically a psychological orientation in which individuals are able to make sense out of different aspects of their lives, thus weaving their experience into a coherent whole. They are able to put the pieces of their lives together, and thus they maintain a basic faith that, generally "things will work out as well as can reasonably be expected," which they consider to be acceptable. This sense of coherence is an important concept that can be therapeutically applied, as will be discussed in Chapters 5 and 8.

It seems important to connect aspects of our experience into a coherent whole, just as it is important to feel connected to other people. The loss of this sense of connection is quite likely a critical factor in feeling and becoming vulnerable. The mechanism that may be involved in this phenomenon was first proposed by J. Cassel, who suggested that the subjective interpretation, or personal experience, of an ill person produces a loss of connection.[20] It is interesting to note that S. C. Kobasa has developed the concept of hardiness and has specified qualities in people under stress who do not succumb.[21] Hardy personalities exhibit the "four C's": commitment, challenge, control, and connection. These people find some way to make a meaningful commitment to the task, retain a sense of perceived control by focusing on their own behavior, redefine situations as a challenge, and connect with other people in supportive ways. Based on hardiness scores, Kobasa, S. R. Maddi, and S. Courington were able to predict differences in illness response among executives stressed by similar life changes.[22] It is the body's (hormonal) response to the perceived loss of control that may make a person vulnerable, by compromising the immune system. Epidemiological evidence is accumulating suggesting that psychological distress may play a causal role in both morbidity and mortality.[23]

A LOOK AT THE DATA

Now we wish to look at several sets of research findings. First, we will examine a prospective longitudinal study that related mental and physical health.[16,24–25] Next, we will discuss both theoretical and empirical data indicating that every person has at least two levels of functioning. Finally, we will show how functioning under stress is related to the concept of locus of control.[26]

A Longitudinal Study of Adaptation

In his book *Adaptation to Life*, George Vaillant described the details of the lives of a large number of the subjects of the Grant Study of Adult Development, a comprehensive prospective study that has so far followed over more than two hundred initially healthy college men for over forty years.[24] The initial data was collected through repeated physical examinations and by interviews and comprehensive questionnaires for the longitudinal monitoring of psychological, social, and occupational adjustments. All important life events were followed. Among other characteristics to be carefully studied were the types of symptoms that the subjects developed under stress. This research clearly demonstrated the connection between healthy psychological and healthy physical functioning. Further, after carefully analyzing his data, Vaillant concluded that there was little evidence to support the existence of specific mental diseases, only evidence of maladaptive reactions to stress.

Vaillant found that people change over time, generally maturing psychologically as they grow older. He also found that some people are healthier than others. Under favorable circumstances, mental health develops and is correlated with robust physical health. This also generally predisposes the person to success in the work environment. Both physical and mental health depend on successful adaptation. In a later report published in the *New England Journal of Medicine*, Vaillant reported that poor physical health accompanied, and was followed by, poor mental health.[16] Conversely, poor mental health (i.e., poor adaptation to stressful life events) was a clear predictor of subsequent poor physical health. In the most recent follow-up, after forty-five years of the study, psychosocial factors that were evaluated before age 50 were examined in relation to physical health, mental health, and life satisfaction at age 65.[25] Interestingly, the extent of tranquilizer use before age 50 (hardly the best response to managing stress) was the most powerful negative predictor of both physical and mental health. Paradoxically, a warm, supportive childhood environment made an important independent contribution to predicting physical health only.[25]

Vaillant, in fact, defined health as *successful adaptation*. It is successful adaptation to problems, not the absence of stressors, that determines healthy functioning and growth. Vaillant found that individual traumatic incidents did not generally have dramatic effects on the quality of people's lives. Rather, in general, people's lives seemed to have a relatively stable course.[24]

By studying the reactions of the Grant study subjects to the stressors inherent in their lives over a forty-year period, Vaillant determined a range of adaptive mechanisms, which can also be labeled defense mechanisms. He proposed four lines of defenses: psychotic, immature, neurotic, and mature.

Defense mechanisms such as delusional projection, denial, and distortion, which are part of the psychotic level, are normal for individuals under the age of 5. Immature mechanisms, such as projection, hypochondriases, and acting out, are common in healthy 3- to 15-year-olds. The neurotic defenses outlined by Vaillant are intellectualization, repression, and reaction formation, which are commonly seen in "healthy individuals ages three to ninety, in neurotic disorder, and in mastering acute adult stress" (p. 384).[24] Mature mechanisms, such as altruism, humor, suppression, anticipation, and sublimation, are normal in healthy individuals aged from 12 to 90. Under stress, however, people may switch to less mature mechanisms. When overwhelmed by demands from the internal or external environments the individual will temporarily abandon the mature defense mechanisms and make a retreat to more primitive defenses. This may be labeled regressing, or, under severe conditions, decompensating.

Extreme stress always causes individuals to regress from their characteristic coping mechanisms to poorer or less mature ones. Use of these more primitive coping mechanisms results in less successful adaptation and, therefore, erodes mental and physical health. The most important finding, according to Vaillant, is not that stress kills us, but that ingenious adaptation to stress, which he calls good mental health or the use of mature coping mechanisms, facilitates survival.[24] Vaillant's work provides support for the themes that are central to this text:

1. Mental and physical health are inextricably linked.
2. Individuals use different coping mechanisms under stress than under normal circumstances;
3. In general, individuals have consistent coping patterns. At a particular level of maturity, they use specific patterns under normal circumstances and other, less functional ones when severely stressed.
4. It is most important to support people who are under stress in order to return them to the use of their more adaptive defenses.

A Holistic Theory of Neurosis

Vaillant comes out of a psychoanalytic school of psychiatry. We shall now look at a psychiatrist with a very different orientation, who provides interesting theoretical support for the conclusions of the Grant study.

Andras Angyal's work is not well known in the medical community. Angyal was a successful analyst who proposed a theory and treatment of neurosis which he labeled a holistic method.[27] His theory is useful because it provides a plausible explanation for the uncomfortable phenomena that people experience when they are under overwhelming stress. Angyal also provides direction for producing relief.

Angyal's theory of human nature and personality posits that two systems, one healthy and one neurotic, vie for dominance in human personality. All persons have a need to feel competent, or, as Angyal put it, all experience a drive for autonomy. There is also a companion need to belong, which Angyal calls the need for "homonymy." This is essentially a feeling of connectedness. The healthy system develops through the experience of having one's basic needs met, that is, feeling personally competent and also feeling accepted by the significant others in one's life. The healthy system is based on both feeling loved (connection) and feeling effective as an autonomous person (competence). The world of the healthy personality is a reasonably safe and loving place.

Conversely, the neurotic system builds on experiences of feeling incompetent, rejected, or resentful. It registers only unfulfilled needs. Angyal suggested that since no life, however unfortunate, consists only of trauma, the raw data processed by the two systems is basically the same. Thus, according to Angyal, we actually live in two separate worlds. Both are complete systems, and they vie for dominance. We never live in the world proper, but rather, we create our own map of the world, and the map is not the same as the actual territory.[28,29] Moreover, we have now learned that we really have two different maps, which we use under different circumstances.

.We either relate to the world with positive expectations, using our healthy map, or with fear and discomfort, using our neurotic map. When the neurotic system is engaged, the world seems threatening, hostile, and withholding, and our main aim is to protect ourselves and escape danger. We feel as though the world is too large and we are very small and inadequate. When caught up in neurosis, we feel angry, anxious, and isolated. This belief system makes it impossible for us to feel safe or optimistic. Danger appears to be every-where. Until our healthy self has been reengaged, we cannot feel hope or confidence.

The role of the supportive person is to restore the sense of trust in the world that is represented by the healthy personality system. When the actions of the physician create an environment that makes the patient feel competent and connected, the healthy system will be reengaged.

Research from Experimental Psychology

Although expressed in different language, physiological experimental psychology has demonstrated specific responses in subjects under stress. As people become overaroused (tense and overstimulated), they filter out parts of current experience: coping mechanisms become more primitive in several ways, including reversion to more dominant, first-learned behaviors. When recently learned behavior is not available, the responses that would be most appropriate to the situation are temporarily blocked and cannot be utilized. Moreover, novel stimuli are treated as though they were similar to previously experienced ones. When having to cope under highly aroused conditions, people revert to automatic behavior that has been done so often it requires no conscious thought.[30] On the other hand, when levels of arousal are brought back to a comfortable level, problem solving again becomes effective. The recently learned material again becomes part of the behavioral repertoire, increasing the variety of options available, and mental health is restored.

The connecting thread between these viewpoints confirms our personal clinical experience that facing unmanageable stressors puts people on a "tilt" condition. For many people there are degrees of diminishing functioning under stress, and perhaps even a peak of efficiency before the decline sets in, but there appears to be a threshold that precipitates behavior characteristic of overstressed (overaroused) functioning for every individual. Having passed this threshold, people engage their neurotic map of the world and then act as though that were the only reality they knew. For the physician, the primary therapeutic task is to provide support that will restore these people's equilibrium and refocus them in their healthier orientation. K. E. Weik pointed out that by labeling a problem as minor rather than serious, people's arousal level can be lowered. He suggested that this is particularly beneficial when "people don't know what to do or are unable to do it."[31] More will be said about this in Chapter 6.

Internal or External Locus of Control

Locus of control is a critical concept in understanding people's reactions to stressful circumstances and designing appropriate interventions.[26] Although all people have both a healthy level of functioning, which is engaged when the individual feels safe or in control, and a neurotic level, which is engaged when the person feels unsafe or out of control, the feeling of safety is a purely subjective one and is affected by a person's locus of control. Locus of control is an important construct that few physicians apply with awareness, yet a growing body of literature indicates that it influences people's health-related behavior.[32,33] In connection with achieving a feeling of safety, individuals with an internal locus of control feel safe when they have the resources (information, power, and time) to handle a situation, whereas individuals with an external locus of control feel safe when a trusted authority figure has taken charge and told them what to do or when family or community resources have been recruited for their support. The implications for medical practice and for dealing with patients and others under stress are obvious.

The physician who understands the issues involved in these three areas of research—the relationship between psychological and physical well-being, the regression to more primitive functioning whenever defenses are overwhelmed, and the basis of security on either an internal or an external locus of control—will be able to make effective interventions at critical times with little investment of time, energy, or effort.

Application to Illness Behavior

The effects of acute illness constitute a high degree of stress. People's behavior under these circumstances can be better understood by reviewing the normal developmental process by which human beings mature. Chris Argyris, writing from the point of view of organizational psychology, specified five dimensions of individual development.[34] As people mature, they move along a continuum from being passive to being active; from dependence to independence; from requiring immediate gratification of their needs to being able to delay gratification for long periods; from concrete thinking to abstract thinking; and from having few abilities to having many. At any given time, each person functions at a specific level on each of these dimensions. The more highly developed or mature the individual, the higher the level of functioning along each axis can be expected to be. This was confirmed by Vaillant's findings. In circumstances of acute stress, all people will temporarily regress along each of the five dimensions, though not necessarily to the same extent on each axis.

Acute illness is an acute stress and causes an acute regression in functioning. People who are ill generally become more passive and dependent, want their demands met instantly, become more concrete in their thinking, and have fewer abilities to help themselves. This can try the patience of the caregiver, but the situation can be more easily handled if it is anticipated and perceived as transitory. In chronic illness, unfortunately, the regression often becomes permanent. If a physician is aware of this phenomenon, efforts can be made to alleviate further stress on all care providers. This can be done by helping them to set realistic expectations for the patient and the course of the illness while providing support to maximize the patient's return to the premorbid levels of functioning.

RESULTS OF BEING OVERWHELMED

The subjective feeling of being overwhelmed contributes to an objective inability of individuals to function at optimum levels. The resulting perception of inadequacy lowers the individual's sense of self-esteem. These feelings can be transient, lasting only several seconds, or they may constitute the individual's general phenomenological experience. These negative experiences of the self may be specific to particular situations that are symbolically threatening, or they can be precipitated and maintained by traumatic life events or by an accumulation of daily hassles.[6] In actuality, if the patient perceives the event or accumulation of events as dangerous or demanding, the stress is, by definition, real. William James first suggested that emotions and their effects on our bodies are objective phenomena that are determined through the subjective experience:

Our natural way of thinking about these . . . emotions is that the mental perception of some fact excites the mental affection called the emotion, and that this latter state of mind gives rise to the bodily expression. My theory on the contrary, is that the bodily changes follow directly on the perception of the exciting fact, and that our feeling of the same changes as they occur IS the emotion. Common sense says, we lose our fortune, are sorry and weep; we meet a bear, are frightened and run; we are insulted by a rival, are angry and strike. The hypothesis here to be defended says that this order of sequence is incorrect, that the one mental state is not immediately induced by the other, that the bodily manifestations must first be interposed between, and that the more rational statement is that we feel sorry because we cry, angry because we strike, or tremble because we are sorry, angry or fearful, as the case may be. Without the bodily states following on the perception, the latter would be purely cognitive in form, pale, colorless, destitute of emotional warmth. We might then see the bear, and judge it best to run, receive the insult and deem it right to strike, but we should not actually feel afraid or angry.[35]

When we feel basically in control of our responses to the events happening in our lives (appropriately choosing to flee, fight, or "flow"), we function at an effective level. As long as the demands of the external environment (the situation and other people) and internal environment (physiological state and expectations for the self) are experienced as manageable, we will continue to function at our customary level. Once the tolerance for comfortable adaptation has been exceeded, however, we will begin to use a different coping style. At the extreme, M.E.P. Seligman has shown that once people are convinced that events are completely beyond their control and that their behavior will in no way affect the outcome of a particular situation, they behave in a stereotyped manner which he labeled "learned helplessness."[36] This is an emotional sequence that involves going through a fear-protest stage to a helpless-depressed stage. The less in control a person feels, the more primitive the defenses to be called into play. Ineffective as this appears to be, it is a person's best effort to survive when in an overwhelmed state.

Each of us can usually identify when we are feeling overwhelmed by observing our behavioral repertoire. We go on tilt and are momentarily unable to do anything about it. Sometimes our awareness can help us engage strategies to restore our equilibrium. In many cases, however, our perception of our behavior and our inability to control or modify it exacerbate the feelings of being overwhelmed. When we lose faith in our power to manage at all, we fall into a dependent mode and look to be taken care of. When there is no one to do this, or we do not trust the person who is in charge, we will become despondent and helpless.

Research has shown that over time, this type of stress can contribute to a compromise of the body's defense systems, subsequently leading to disease.[37-39] At first, patients are simply aware of symptoms such as muscle tension, which may be experienced as back, neck, or head pain. Patients may become aware of a rapid pulse, abdominal pain, breathing difficulties, blurred vision, a full bladder, diarrhea, sweating, or a tight throat, or they may have trouble swallowing. Other, less noticeable bodily reactions triggered by the sympathetic nervous system–mediated stress-response syndrome may result in elevated blood pressure, elevated lipid levels, changes in blood sugar, and ultimately, the compromise of various organ systems.

THE CRISIS INTERVENTION MODEL

Although patients often experience chronic stress, acute episodes can be triggered by a personal crisis. A crisis may be thought of as an environmentally produced situation to which the individual must respond, such as a disaster, an accident, the loss of a job, or the death of a loved one. There are also the normal developmental crises (also called transition points) in the life cycle. A situation may be experienced as a crisis because the individual perceives the event as threatening to him- or herself in some highly significant way. Physicians generally define a crisis as a clinical syndrome involving emotional upset, increased tension, unpleasant affect, the breakdown of coping mechanisms, and disorganized functioning. A crisis may be thought of most simply as the time of greatest change or potential change. During a crisis certain decisions must be made because the previous status quo no longer holds, and consequently, some adaptive behavior is required. Crisis is a time when the decisions that are made will affect the subsequent options available. However, it is also a time when, because of the emotional overlay, an individual is least capable of thinking clearly or solving problems effectively.

In explaining the effectiveness of crisis intervention, Gerald Caplan suggested that each person generally functions within a specific range of effectiveness and personal satisfaction.[40] We have seen this empirically demonstrated in the Grant study.[16,24] There is a continuum of functioning, from people who are generally very ineffective to those who are well adjusted and adapted and who enjoy living. In general, people are quite static in their level of functioning, regularly fluctuating within a given range as they experience manageable life stress. In a crisis, when there is an overwhelming amount of emotional distress, the individual is unable to process information objectively, preventing effective problem solving. Since a crisis is defined as the time of greatest change, regardless of the nature or degree of adaptation required, crisis, by definition, is time-limited.[40] Some resolution will undoubtedly occur within a time span of four to six weeks. The individual is generally open to receiving help because of the clearly experienced need, having temporarily moved down on the dependency scale.

If the resolution of the crisis is favorable, the individual will function at a higher level of adjustment. New coping skills have been learned, and confidence in the self and others, enhanced. Conversely, if there is no help available, or if the individual is not able to solve the problem successfully, with or without help, the crisis will still be resolved, but at the cost of a subsequent lower level of functioning. People will move down the scale in all five of Argyris's dimensions.[34]

As we have suggested, during a crisis, an individual experiences increased dependency feelings, wishes to be helped, and signals this to the environment. One of the most efficient ways of signaling for help in our society is to develop an illness, whether an acute ailment or the exacerbation of a chronic condition. The visit to the physician is a cry for help, and for the relief of symptoms. It affords the physician an opportunity to intervene effectively at a time when an individual in crisis is open and highly suggestible.

The Goal of Crisis Intervention

Crisis intervention aims at very specific outcomes. There are four objectives: The first is the prevention of dire consequences. In a crisis, the individual is forced to deal with new situations just at a time when his or her ability to solve problems has been compromised. The intervening person can suggest that no decision be made that is not absolutely crucial, and that those issues that must be resolved should be explored carefully with a disinterested person.

The second objective is to return the individual to the premorbid level of functioning. This can best be done by providing support. Expanding the behavioral repertoire and enhancing self-esteem are the two other objectives of crisis intervention that follow from a successful resolution of the crisis.

The physician can provide relief of the symptoms and empathy for the subjective experience of distress. The physician can also be supportive by providing information and explanations, by exploring options, or by simply pointing out that options exist. Most of all, the physician can encourage new behavior that will help the patient manage the crisis and regain a better level of functioning after his or her psychological and physical equilibrium have been restored.

APPLICATION TO THE OFFICE SETTING

Some patients at first seem reluctant to discuss their psychological condition when they seek medical treatment. The following example is quite typical of our practice.

Mrs. Z is a 53-year-old school teacher who has come to the office for the second time. Her presenting complaint is a sinus problem; she reports having had congestion and severe recurrent headaches for the past three days. Mrs. Z has a history of chronic sinusitis, but this time, she says the symptoms have persisted for longer than usual. Mrs. Z is a well-dressed, reserved white female who appears somewhat anxious to get out of the office. When asked about her current life situation, she reluctantly admits that she is working two jobs and is separated from her husband, but she states that everything is under control. She refuses to give any details of her current situation, and when asked how she feels about her separation, she denies having any problems and says she does not want to talk about it. The physical exam is normal. The physician then explains to her that sometimes stress and emotional problems have a way of lowering bodily resistance and making physical symptoms persist longer or prove more difficult to treat. If these problems are not recognized and dealt with, a person's physical health will be compromised. The physician simply presents this explanation to help the patient make sense out of both her current situation and her reaction to it. Deciding to give the patient a few minutes to think about it, he leaves the room to get a prescription. When he returns, he notices that the patient appears much more relaxed. She says: "Doctor, I really didn't mind you asking me questions about my separation and so forth. It was good that you did. I really have to start dealing with all that stuff." The doctor then schedules her for an appointment the following week, primarily to talk about her psychosocial situation. Mrs. Z leaves, feeling much better.

We have tried to show that the physician usually sees patients at a time when they are feeling vulnerable. Interventions at this time are very effective, both in restoring a patient's equilibrium and in promoting constructive change. Specific techniques and a detailed rationale will be discussed in subsequent chapters. The physician is in a unique position to help the patient at an opportune time and is equipped with a variety of valuable skills, which will be discussed in the next chapter.

SUMMARY

The stress response is a biologically programmed mobilization for adaptive action in response to changes in the external or internal environments. A model—*person plus stress yields reaction*—is offered to help specify the point of intervention. A person with particular characteristics (personality variables) who is subjected to particular environmental demands will have a particular reaction. The visit to the physician is usually triggered by discomfort with the reaction. Patients also experience stress in regard to the office visit and their interaction with the physician. This can be reduced by specific strategies.

In general, there is a relationship between illness and adaptation to life events. Mental health potentiates physical well-being. Some people are characteristically healthier than others. Drawing from a variety of sources, we present two central concepts: First, individuals generally function at a specific level of adaptation, and second, individuals under severe stress, including physical illness, temporarily regress to lower levels of functioning. People with an internal locus of control primarily need to feel competent, while those with an external locus of control primarily need to feel connected to a caretaker they trust.

When individuals are in a state of feeling overwhelmed, they will be unable to function at optimum levels. They go on tilt and engage their neurotic map of the world. Social support, which provides information regarding an individual's basic acceptability and competence, is crucial at this time.

The crisis intervention model is useful in specifying the time-limited nature of acute stress. Crises generally resolve within four to six weeks. By providing support, crisis intervention aims to prevent dire consequences, return the individual to a premorbid level of functioning, and enhance his or her self-esteem and subsequent coping abilities. If physicians understand these mechanisms and can provide a supportive response, the results will be therapeutic for their patients and rewarding for the practitioners.

REFERENCES

1. McWhinney, I. R. Beyond diagnosis: An approach to the integration of behavioral science and clinical medicine. *New England Journal of Medicine*, 1972, *287*, 384–387.

2. Kleinman, A., Eisenberg, L., & Good, B. Clinical lessons from anthropologic and cross-cultural research. *Annals of Internal Medicine*, 1978, *88*, 251–258.

3. Selye, H. *The stress of life*. New York: McGraw-Hill, 1957.

4. Selye, H. The evolution of the stress concept. *American Scientist*, 1973, *61*, 692–699.

5. Stuart, M. R., & Mackey, K. J. Defining the differences between crisis intervention and short term therapy. *Hospital and Community Psychiatry*, 1977, *28*, 527–529.

6. DeLongis, A., Coyne, J. D., Dakof, G., Folkman, S., & Lazarus, R. S. Relationship of daily hassles, uplifts, and major life events to health status. *Health Psychology*, 1982, *1*, 119–136.

7. Lerman, C. E., Brody, D. S., Hui, T., Lazaro, C., Smith, D. G., & Blum, M. J. The white-coat hypertension response: Prevalence and predictors. *Journal of General Internal Medicine*, 1989, *4*, 226–231.

8. White, W. B., Schulman, P., & McCabe, E. J. Average daily blood pressure, not office blood pressure, determines cardiac function in patients with hypertension. *Journal of the American Medical Association*, 1989, *261*, 873–877.

9. Orne, M. T. On the social psychology of the psychological experiment with particular reference to demand characteristics and their implications. *American Psychologist*, 1962, *17*, 776–783.

10. Bellet, P. S., & Maloney, M. J. The importance of empathy as an interviewing skill in medicine. *Journal of the American Medical Association* 1991, *266*, 1831–1832.

11. Perls, F. S. *Gestalt therapy verbatim.* Moab, Utah: Real People Press, 1969.

12. Brody, H. *Stories of sickness.* New Haven, Conn.: Yale University Press, 1987.

13. Kleinman, A. *The illness narratives.* New York: Basic Books, 1988.

14. Mechanic, D. Response factors in illness: The study of illness behavior. *Social Psychiatry* 1966, *1*, 11–20.

15. Lazare, A., & Eisenthal, S. A negotiated approach to the clinical encounter I: Attending the patient's perspective. In A. Lazare (Ed.), *Outpatient psychiatry*, pp. 157–171. Baltimore, Md.: Williams and Wilkins, 1979.

16. Vaillant, G. E. Natural history of male psychologic health: Effects of mental health on physical health. *New England Journal of Medicine*, 1979, *301*, 1249–1254.

17. Holmes, T. H., Treuting, T., & Wolff, H. G. Life situations, emotions and nasal disease: Evidence on summative effects exhibited in patients with "hay fever." *Psychosomatic Medicine*, 1951, *13*, 71–82.

18. Holmes, T. H., & Rahe, R. H. The social readjustment rating scale. *Psychosomatic Medicine*, 1967, *11*, 213–218.

19. Antonovsky, A. *Health, stress, and coping.* San Francisco: Jossey-Bass, 1979.

20. Cassel, J. The contribution of the social environment to host resistance. *American Journal of Epidemiology*, 1976, *104*, 107–123.

21. Kobasa, S. C. Stressful life events, personality, and health: An inquiry into hardiness. *Journal of Personality and Social Psychology*, 1979, *37*, 1–11.

22. Kobasa, S. C., Maddi, S. R., & Courington, S. Personality and constitution as mediators in the stress-illness relationship. *Journal of Health and Social Behavior*, 1981, *22*, 368–378.

23. Somervell, P. D., Kaplan, B. H., Heiss, G., Tyroler, H. A., Kleinbaum, D. G., & Obrist, P. A. Psychologic distress as a predictor of mortality. *American Journal of Epidemiology*, 1989, *130*, 1013–1023.

24. Vaillant, G. E. *Adaptation to life.* Boston: Little, Brown, 1977.

25. Vaillant, G. E., & Vaillant, C. O. Natural history of male psychological health, XII: A 45-year study of predictors of successful aging at age 65. *American Journal of Psychiatry*, 1990, *147*, 31–37.

26. Rotter, J. B. Generalized expectancies for internal versus external control of reinforcement. *Psychological Monographs*, 1966, *80* (1, whole no. 609).

27. Angyal, A. *Neurosis and treatment: A holistic theory.* New York: Wiley, 1965.

28. Korzybski, A. *Science and Sanity*, 4th ed. Lakeville, Conn.: International Non-Aristotelian Library Publishing Company, 1958.

29. Bateson, G. *Mind and nature: A necessary unity.* New York: Dutton, 1979.

30. Staw, B. M., Sandlelands, L. E., & Dutton, J. E. Threat-rigidity effects in organizational behavior: A multilevel analysis. *Administrative Science Quarterly*, 1981, *26*, 501–524.

31. Weik, K. E. Small wins: Redefining the scale of social problems. *American Psychologist*, 1984, *39*, 41.

32. Wallston, B. S., Wallston, K. A., Kaplan, G. D., & Maides, S. A. Development and validation of the health locus of control (HCL) scale. *Journal of Consulting and Clinical Psychology*, 1976, *44*, 580–585.

33. Janz, N. K., & Becker, M. H. The health belief model: A decade later. *Health Education Quarterly*, 1984, *11*, 1–47.

34. Argyris, C. *Intervention theory and method: A behavioral science view.* Reading, Mass.: Addison-Wesley, 1970.

35. James, W. *The principles of psychology*, vol. 2. New York: Holt, 1913, pp. 449–450.

36. Seligman, M. E. P. *Helplessness: On depression, development, and death.* San Francisco: Freeman, 1975.

37. Christie-Seely, J. Life stress and illness: A systems approach. *Canadian Family Physician*, 1983, *29*, 533–540.

38. Dantzer, R., & Kelley, K. W. Stress and immunity: An integrated view of relationships between nervous and immune systems. *Life Sciences*, 1989, *44*, 1995–2008.

39. Watson, D., & Pennebaker, J. W. Health complaints, stress and distress: Exploring the central role of negative affectivity. *Psychological Review*, 1989, *96*, 234–254.

40. Caplan, G. *Principles of preventive psychiatry.* New York: Basic Books, 1964.

CHAPTER 3

The Psychotherapeutic Qualifications of the Primary Care Physician

Since primary care represents a comprehensive and personal approach to patient care, physical and psychological problems must be addressed in an integrated manner. Many times, emotional problems manifest as physical problems and, conversely, physical problems have emotional consequences. Adequate treatment is not possible without confronting the psychological aspects. Whether or not the physician invites or even desires to provide it, patients often expect help with emotional problems along with their physical ailments. The physician thus becomes a psychotherapist almost by default.

THE REALITY OF BEING ON THE SPOT

Are primary care physicians really qualified and competent to practice psychotherapy? The good news is that patients seem to think they are. There is an impressive literature showing that patients clearly consider their personal physician as their primary source of mental health care.[1-3] A recent study showed that patients with psychosocial problems confided in their primary care physician more often than any other type of professional. The type of problems included depression, anxiety, bereavement, marital problems, problems with children, and other practical problems, as well as coping with chronic illness. Nearly all the patients (95%) reported that the contact was helpful.[4]

Now the bad news: Many physicians do not know they are qualified and have the skills to do psychotherapy, and therefore they do not attempt the simple interventions that can be so highly effective. They often do not even ascertain that there is a problem. Studies have shown that although almost 60 percent of mental health care is provided in primary care settings, primary care providers fail to recognize up to two-thirds of their patients who are manifesting an emotional disorder.[5,6] In one study, primary care providers failed to recognize six out of seven patients who had depressions and fifteen out of eighteen with anxiety disorders; they also missed all four drug or alcohol abusers.[7] Our technique increases the probability of identifying and treating a much greater proportion of these problems, using psychotherapy along with the appropriate medication.

Although the literature is sparse and controversial, there have been several studies commenting on the efficacy of psychotherapeutic techniques in primary care.[8–12] There seems to be general agreement that the provision of psychotherapy by the primary care physician is considered appropriate by both patients and physicians, but controlled randomized trials are difficult to conduct. In one successful study, psychotherapy proved acceptable to both physician and patient, but the rigid protocol, which required exactly eight half-hour sessions, no psychiatric referrals, and no medications other than benzodiazepines, cramped the physician's style. Moreover, the eight-week limit proved ineffective in meeting the needs of patients with persistent psychological symptoms.[8]

Another structured program, which was designed to teach practitioners a specific behaviorally oriented treatment for depression, was also unsuccessful.[9] Physicians may or may not be successful with existing modalities of therapy, but they seem to agree on the need to develop specific techniques and to train primary care physicians to manage patients' psychological problems.[8–12] This is precisely what we would like to address.

Patients do talk to their physicians about their personal problems. However, many are disappointed when the physician, after listening for a while, cuts them off without any acknowledgment or resolution. Our experience with residents has shown that they frequently do not know what to say next or feel that the physician has spent enough time listening. After letting the patient ventilate for some time and nodding at seemingly appropriate places, the physician will generally return abruptly to the business at hand: specifically, the physical symptoms, which fall into the "safe," biomedical arena. In spite of this conduct, it is our impression that many patients feel much better after talking to their doctor, even though the physician may not be aware of the therapeutic process in the interaction or its impact on the patients.

Norman Cousins has written much about the importance of the therapeutic interaction with the physician in promoting the patient's feelings of being cared for and in potentiating his or her healing.[13] In general, without the awareness of inherent skills and particular strategies, physicians have a hard time dealing with the emotional aspects of patients' lives or illnesses. In a recent study, physicians expressed moderate self-confidence in the ability to prescribe medication for depression, panic disorder, and chronic anxiety, but rated their ability to treat these disorders psychotherapeutically much lower.[14] The simple techniques described in this text are designed to enhance both skills and confidence.

Writing in the *New England Journal of Medicine*, W. W. Benjamin commented that with the half-life of current medical knowledge at about five years, and with medical technology growing exponentially, many physicians feel overwhelmed when trying to keep up scientifically.[15] Benjamin pointed out that since the true healing skills are those of communication and caring, physicians should instead affirm the healing power of their words. He wrote:

The Greeks divided their healers into three categories: the "knife" doctor, the "herb" doctor, and the "word" doctor. Whereas the Greeks held them in balance, the low status today of the "word" doctors—the psychiatrists—indicates that we believe words are cheap if not useless. We are action oriented and get paid for performing procedures rather than for being—for doing rather than for talking. Western medicine, following the Cartesian dualism between mind and body, has become largely a somatic business. Words have been left behind in the rush to master chemistry. Emotions have been minimized in the reductionist effort to understand cells and genes.

All physicians, whatever their specialty, can improve their therapy of the word. . . . The emotional condition of a patient is as basic as any single factor in the treatment of disease. (p. 596)[15]

Since the publication of the first edition of *The Fifteen Minute Hour*, many practitioners have noted an improvement in their therapy of the word and in their competence to address the emotional conditions of their patients.

The separation of mind and body has become an anachronistic paradigm (as suggested in Chapter 1). Since all physical illness has an emotional component, the physician is called upon to respond in some way. Applying the techniques described in this text will help practitioners respond empathically, efficiently, and comfortably. This will effectively promote the patient's sense of well-being. It is the healing dialogue between the physician and the patient that constitutes the essence of psychotherapy.

PSYCHOTHERAPEUTIC QUALIFICATIONS OF THE PRIMARY CARE PHYSICIAN

What are the characteristics of a therapeutic relationship? Let us look at a few of the more obvious factors.

Trust

The sine qua non of any therapeutic relationship is trust. Trust can be thought of as an assessment that a person is both competent to fulfill a promise and sincere in the desire to do so.

When patients have confidence in the physician's skill, integrity, and character, they will feel free to expose personal aspects of their lives in order to receive help. They can expect that the information they share will be respected, understood, responded to, and kept confidential. In a sense, the physician creates a safe environment. Patients may not be aware of the exact text, but they know that the physician is bound by the Hippocratic Oath:

Things that I may see or hear in the course of the treatment or even outside of treatment regarding the life of human beings, things which one should never divulge outside, I will keep to myself holding such things unutterable (or "shameful to be spoken").[16]

Trust implies that patients feel assured no harm will come from disclosing to the physician data about themselves, their lives, or their significant others. There is also the expectation that the physician will use his or her available training and skill in the patient's interest. In other words, the patient believes in the physician's ability and sincere desire to care and provide help. Trust also implies the patient's expectation of not being rejected or abandoned. In primary care, an open-ended relationship, built over time, helps build the patient's confidence.

In order for trust to develop, a past history of successful encounters with this or other physicians is essential. Success, in this connotation, suggests that patients were able to get their needs met in previous encounters with physicians. Thus, they had positive experiences. It is, of course, possible that trust can exist without previous personal experience. In many cases, a significant other person who is trusted (e.g., a mother) tells someone (e.g., her son), "The doctor will take care of it." This provides trust by association.

These factors, singly and in concert, denote trust. The patient expects to feel safe in the presence of the wise physician, who is assumed to be capable of, and committed to, providing personal, ongoing, quality care and who will respect the patient's confidentiality.

Continuity

In primary care, an assumption is made that the physician's commitment to the patient has no defined end point.[17] The continuity of the relationship is thereby established. The personal physician does not treat the patient for just one illness episode, but rather expects to follow him or her and attend to his or her ongoing medical care. If the physician has known the patient and his or her family over time, this will simplify the communication of particular aspects of any situation.

When the physician is familiar with the family structure, cultural background, and orientation toward health care, and when he or she already knows many of the factors involved in a patient's personal situation, little time will be required to be brought up to date. Moreover, the physician will know from the history of this particular patient's "care-seeking behavior" whether he or she tends either to exaggerate or deny the severity of situations. Further, because of the continuity in the relationship, the physician can anticipate and follow critical transitions in the patient's life and can intervene in a timely and convenient fashion.

The salient point is that the relationship is preestablished. Even in a group practice, health maintenance organization (HMO), or other prepaid plan, the patient "belongs." Records are kept and provide continuity even if a different physician is in attendance. There is an expectation of consistent care and follow-up in the particular office, even if with a different physician. Thus, the patient will not fear being abandoned or rejected.

Nurturance

Competent adults are capable of taking care of themselves and others who are dependent. However, when feeling low, besieged, or overwhelmed by physical or mental stressors, everyone experiences a need to be nurtured. Adults and children, physicians and patients, all are vulnerable to the same forces. The more our resources feel depleted by the forces impinging on us, the more dependent we become. When this happens, nurturance from others becomes an emergent need.

Physicians, by profession, are seen as healers who provide care and nurturance on demand. This expectation is held by the patient, and it is generally met. By conducting a patient-centered interview, physicians can focus the interaction directly on the patient's needs.[18,19] Patients feel better after seeing the physician. As discussed in Chapter 1, the patient always receives something from the interaction. The prescription, completed form, or doctor's "note" may become the symbol of the nurturance that the patient seeks, but the caring may be found entirely in the process. In any case, the patient asks for help and is open to receive whatever the physician is willing to provide. Since there is a positive expectation, there will be little resistance to experiencing the positive impact of quality caring. The patient assumes that the physician's training, intelligence, experience, and general wisdom will be devoted to the task of alleviating his or her pain.

THE ISSUE OF POWER

Although physicians are generally very aware of their power to affect life and death through the medical decisions they make, especially in the hospital setting, few physicians have been exposed to the literature on social power. Consequently, they tend to have little awareness of their impressive potential to influence certain aspects of their patients' attitudes and behavior.

What Is Social Power?

Social power has been defined as the potential of one person to change the beliefs, attitudes, or behavior of another.[20] Changing a patient's beliefs, attitudes, or behavior is the central function of psychotherapy. Basically, power can be defined as the potential or ability to satisfy needs. If we can satisfy our own needs, we have personal power. That means we can muster sufficient personal resources to get what we want, and we do not have to depend on other people. If we are in a position to satisfy other peoples' needs, or if they believe that we can satisfy them, they give us power. This type of power, which is generally referred to as social power, enables one person to influence the behavior, thoughts, and feelings of another.

There is No Free Lunch

Social exchange theorists see all human relationships in terms of potential payoffs.[21] Using this framework, all interpersonal relationships are seen as exchanges of behavior between people. Great stress is placed on the ability to provide rewards that cause behavior to be repeated. This commonsense approach suggests that people only relate to others because they get something from the interaction. The individuals who have commodities to trade also have power.

Expertise is seen as a highly valued commodity.[22] In this connection, N. Postman pointed out that, to a large extent, the authority of adults over children derives from their position as the principle source of knowledge (expertise).[23] Francis Bacon was thus quite accurate when he asserted, "Knowledge is power."[24]

Physicians have a great deal of knowledge at their disposal. This is a commodity that they can use to relieve the distress of their patients. This is, however, only one source of the physician's power. Before we examine the many other power resources at the physician's disposal, it will be useful to distinguish between the concepts of attributed and manifest power.

Manifest versus Attributed Power

When we say that we "give someone power," it generally implies that we hold them in high esteem and allow them to influence our behavior, beliefs, and attitudes. Social psychologists distinguish between attributed power and manifest power. Power is attributed to someone who is believed by others to have the potential to meet their needs. (Whether this is actually the case is totally irrelevant.) Manifest power, on the other hand, means that the ability to mobilize or withhold resources has been clearly demonstrated.

Physicians have both types of power. First, they are given a great deal of attributed power. Patients respect physicians (and sometimes fear them), believe them to have extensive knowledge in many areas (some of which may actually be outside the physician's area of expertise), and expect to be influenced by them. Physicians clearly have manifest power, which they demonstrate through ordering tests or hospitalizations, dispensing prescriptions, writing excuses, filling out insurance or disability forms, providing reassurance, doing procedures, reporting seizure disorders (which means taking away people's drivers' licenses), and reporting sexually transmitted or other contagious diseases, to mention only a few examples.

Types of Social Power

Although there are many ways in which to look at social power, the work of J.P.R. French, Jr., and B. H. Raven clarifies the power base that operates in the physician-patient relationship.[20] French and Raven analyzed a large body of empirical research on the outcome determinants of social power, that is, the psychological changes induced through the relationship between an influencer and an object. Not surprisingly, they found that the more important the relationship, the stronger the base of the power that can be exerted by the influencer. However, they distinguished five specific types of power: reward, coercive, legitimate, referent, and expert. Having multiple types of power in a relationship increases the power base. Although there are other categories of power (including consistency power), it will be useful to look at the particular categories which we have cited.

Reward power, the first type of social power distinguished by French and Raven, depends on the ability to provide symbolic or material rewards: giving people what they want or need. In a physician-patient interaction, this might be attention, time, approval, or advice. It can mean providing relief from pain or anxiety. It can also mean responding favorably to requests for medication, tests, or procedures, or filling out administrative forms.

Coercive power depends on the ability to respond to a person's behavior in a punitive way: to create negative or uncomfortable consequences. Coercive power is efficient in situations where one has a captive audience, but it is detrimental to the quality of relationships. Behavior that changes in response to coercion will revert back to its natural form when supervision has been removed. Coercive power is omnipresent in the physician's potential for giving disapproval, denying requests, prescribing aversive protocols, refusing to see patients or answer phone calls, and withholding permission for desired activities. The ineffectiveness of coercive power, in the absence of supervision, may well account for the dismal rate of patient compliance with medication regimens, especially when dissatisfied with their relationships with their physicians.[25-27]

Referent power has to do with the person's desire to identify with another. The desire to identify is heightened by the attractiveness of the power source. There is a clear parallel here with work by H. C. Kelman, who studied attitude change.[28] Kelman identified the positive feelings generated by the thought of associating oneself with a person or a group, and thus connected by shared beliefs, as the most powerful and lasting way in which to influence a person. Attitude or behavior change induced by this *affective* influence becomes internalized, and is sustained even in the absence of supervision. Changes induced through referent power generally become self-maintaining quite rapidly. People want to be the way the "role model," "mentor," "hero," or "rescuer," would want them to be. They want to do what is required. It makes them feel good, which is reinforcing and futher promotes positive behavior.

It can be seen that referent power can help assure compliance in the outpatient setting. When the patient admires the physician and wants to both like and be liked by him or her, pleasing this attractive source of power is rewarding. The internalization mechanism causes the patient to feel competent and virtuous when following directions. It also potentiates the feeling of being connected. When thinking in terms of "my doctor," the patient's self-esteem is raised by the perception of the relationship. The mechanism is not one of internalizing the values, but of a feeling of oneness or a desire for such an identity. It is part of the feeling of belonging, which we discussed in the previous chapter. The perception that "My doctor wants to see me" or "My doctor says I'm doing well," really makes patients feel good.

Legitimate power derives from perceptions that another person has an institutionalized right to exert influence. This type of power is attributed to the physician by a patient through the act of initiating a consultation. Since payment for service is also a part of the contract, even if a third party is involved, the legitimacy of the physician's power over the patient is confirmed. By contracting to pay for the advice given, the patient acknowledges the legitimacy of the physician's right to give instructions. This right, in fact, becomes an obligation that the patient has instigated.

The more legitimate the power is perceived to be, the less resistance there is to the influence being exerted. It is important to understand that the legitimacy derives from internalized values, whereby the patient accepts the physician as a valid authority with a right to prescribe standards. If the patient has ambivalent feelings toward authority due to a history of conflicts with coercive or overdemanding authority figures (such as parents, teachers, or bosses), there may well be a tendency to thwart the authority of the physician. Many patients do have some problems with authority, so compliance is not always assured, regardless of the legitimacy of the power. In subsequent chapters we will discuss ways in which the physician can avoid power struggles smoothly.

The last type of power outlined by French and Raven[21] is expert power. Unquestionably, patients accept the physician as an expert in medical matters and are, therefore, most vulnerable to being influenced. The physician's word on psychological or social matters will also rarely be questioned, regardless of the actual level of the physician's knowledge. The patient attributes the expert power to the physician. The less sure people are about an issue, the more open they are to being swayed by others' opinions. The more under stress a person feels, the more open he or she will be to help and suggestions. The more difficult a matter is to understand, the more persuasive the arguments of an expert are found to be. Conversely, when people hold firm beliefs or simplistic understandings, these must first be explored and acknowledged before counterarguments can be effective.

It is interesting to note that information accepted from an expert power source becomes totally independent of that source and is absorbed into the person's cognitive structure. French and Raven identified a "sleeper effect" that occurs when information is at first not accepted by subjects because the source has a negative connotation (an expert perhaps, but not one that is attractive or admired).[20] Unfortunately, we have all experienced the power of negative advertising in political campaigns. Distorted unfavorable allegations about candidates are often accepted even by supporters, because these allegations have been repeatedly heard and the "facts" have been separated from their source. In experimental studies, subjects consistently forget the source of a communication faster than the content. This explains the power of rumors.

Physicians have tremendous potential for correcting erroneous or harmful psychosocial information that was previously internalized by patients. This information has become part of the belief system—the story in operation, thus affecting the patient's thoughts, attitudes, and behavior.

Perhaps a hated authority figure has convinced a patient that he or she is not important as a person. This erroneous information results in poor self-esteem, a sense of helplessness, and a worldview devoid of reinforcing experience. The physician's expressed interest in the patient is incongruent with this view. Since the physician is generally seen as a source of social power, the therapeutic effect of intentionally made, supportive statements cannot be minimized.

Conversely, physicians have the power to undermine patients' self-esteem and self-confidence. By talking down to the patient or discounting the patient's concerns, the physician reinforces the patient's low self-opinion. How particular evaluations or instructions are communicated becomes critical. For example, if a patient is concerned about a particular symptom such as a vague pain, the physician's offhand instruction, "Don't worry about it," not only discounts the patient and the patient's experience, but becomes an order that the patient cannot follow. This further lowers the patient's self-esteem and exacerbates anxiety. If, however, the physician says, "I have examined you and I see no cause for concern," or, "I'm not worried," then the patient can infer that the condition is truly benign. The statement on the part of the physician regarding the physician's concern taps into feelings of identification. The patient feels, "O.K. My doctor is an expert on the matter. The doctor says it will go away by itself, so it can't be serious. I won't worry."

People change their beliefs when they are convinced by information that, though differing from their current understanding, presents a convincing picture based on the qualifications of the source providing the new information. However, people change their beliefs only when they feel it is safe to do so, and when they are ready.

Final Words on Power

We have tried to convince you that the physician is at once a powerful, attractive, and credible source of information and, therefore, has great potential for effecting behavioral change in patients. The ability to manipulate others affords a measure of power and control that some physicians find uncomfortable. Writing about mental health professionals, J. W. Cone pointed out that although some clinicians may have some conflicts regarding issues of power and control, they appear to be unaware that they already hold a powerful upper hand in relationship to their clients.[29] Since this power already exists, Cone suggested that its random, noncontingent, "unknowing" use has to be more frightening than the intentional application of the power in the service of the patient. This is precisely our point. The rich sources of power inherent in the doctor-patient relationship are a given. Our purpose is to raise the physician's level of awareness so that this power can be applied judiciously and skillfully toward the goal of making the patient feel better.

BUILDING ON EXISTING SKILLS

Every physician who knows how to talk with, and listen to, patients has the basic tools with which to provide psychological support. Essential skills in the medical interview consist of establishing rapport, eliciting information, clarifying the patient's problems, and then communicating the diagnosis and management plan. Talking with patients is primarily a theme-centered conversation, which is focused on the patient's concerns. This is the essence of the patient-centered interview.[18,19]

Physicians are perhaps most skilled in the data collection aspect of the consultation. In our view, when gathering information dealing with the psychosocial aspect of the patient's problems, questions must be designed to help the patient become aware of the affective state being experienced. This includes an awareness of current stressors, their reactions, major concerns, and options available for dealing with the situation. It also includes an assessment of what resources the patient can muster to initiate action, if appropriate, to reach some resolution.

This is not a psychiatric interview. We do not advocate initiating a workup or an in-depth analysis of the patient's coping mechanisms. Although we would certainly expect that the physician would become aware of any major depressive or anxiety symptoms at this point, we are not interested in deriving a categorical, differential diagnosis of mental disease. Instead, we assume that the patient is distressed and propose that the process of inquiry be structured so as to give the patient the opportunity to bring to awareness and reassess the situation in a more productive way. We are looking to normalize the patient's reaction. With this in mind, the data collection phase of the interview is specifically goal-oriented, utilizing previously learned skills.

When physicians gather data, they usually approach the patient in a logically organized way, asking: "What is troubling you?" "When did it start?" "What did you notice first?" "Please, describe the symptoms." "What makes it better?" and similar questions. Information is gathered, prioritized, and synthesized. When unexpected data is elicited, time is taken for reflection.[30] The physician attempts to get a comprehensive view, to avoid premature closure, and to diagnose the problem. Having done this, the doctor explains the findings, communicates the management plan, and reassures the patient. These communication skills are all that is required to adequately treat the psychological aspects of the patient's problems. What is involved is simply a conscious, focused, deliberate application of the therapeutic agent: the physician. This is accomplished through the medium of therapeutic talk, which helps the patient to identify problems, recognize when they started, and understand how these problems make the patient feel and what is required to fix them. It is the quality of the interaction between the doctor and the patient that promotes a positive effect on the patient's self-image and view of the world and helps the patient modify the story.

Communicating a Caring Attitude

The relationship between a *person* and the *other* (a unique individual who is genuinely valued) is the most powerful therapeutic tool there is. How we relate to the other and the quality of the time we spend is often communicated most clearly in the nonverbal rather than the verbal parts of the interaction. Physicians are aware of the value of eye contact, the powerful messages carried by body language, and the positive effect of active listening techniques. It is the quality of the time given the patient that determines the therapeutic effect, and not the absolute amount of time which the physician spends. Does the physician pay attention, show interest, and concentrate? Every well-trained doctor should have these skills. These techniques have generally been *overlearned* and become automatic, having been performed repeatedly. When providing psychological support (as stated earlier), it is important to efficiently organize the data collection in order to clarify the problem for the patient. It is the patient who needs to understand the situation in order to have power to affect it. It is not useful for the physician to probe for details about how the situation evolved. It may satisfy the physician's curiosity, but it is not therapeutic. It is not important to gather information about matters that the physician cannot control. It is, however, extremely useful for the patient to gain awareness about the response that is generated by the situation and to recognize the legitimacy of that response. Applying the formula *person plus stress yields reaction*, the physician focuses on the reaction (which may well be the patient's presenting problem). In this case, reassurance consists of acknowledging to the patient that the symptoms, to include the emergent emotional state, are appropriate. Patients then do not have to be upset about being upset or angry about being angry. Similarly, they do not have to worry about being worried or be depressed about being depressed. The physician has diagnosed the situation as being a stressor and has pronounced the patient's reaction as logical and normal given the patient's perception. This is experienced by patients as highly supportive. In Chapters 6–10 we will discuss ways to help patients modify their perceptions and reactions to stressors, but the first step is *always* to accept the patient's reaction.

Giving the patient this type of positive attention has an added therapeutic effect: The healing is in the relationship. Focusing on the psychosocial aspect of the patient's problems communicates genuine caring about the patient as a person. For most of us, attention from significant others is interpreted as a confirmation of our sense of worth and belonging. Children will do almost anything to get attention. We all know that if a child cannot get attention through some positive action, we can expect that child to act in some provocative fashion. Even a reprimand or a slap is felt to be better than no attention at all. It seems that there is a driving need to be attended to, even in negative ways. We need to feel connected to others, to be seen and acknowledged. By responding to the psychological needs of the patient in a positive and deliberate way, the physician therapeutically connects with the patient. By focusing the patient on potential solutions to problems or at least legitimizing the patient's current reaction, the physician enhances the patient's sense of autonomy and competence.

Perhaps there are those who will still question the physician's qualifications for doing psychotherapy. The simplest answer is that the opportunity exists. When patients feel bad enough to consult a physician, they may not even be aware of the specifics of what made them feel better but only know that they feel better after the visit.

DETERMINING THE CONTEXT OF THE VISIT

Probably the most important question that any practitioner asks about a patient's visit (in other than an acute, life-threatening episode) is, "Why is the patient coming now?" Mr. Jones has had a sore throat for two weeks. He denies any fever. He has no cough or other symptoms. His throat is slightly erythematous. What made him decide to come today? He does not seem to be that sick. It would seem that he has felt at least this bad for the past two weeks. The best way to find out what Mr. Jones is most concerned about is to ask him, "What are you afraid is going on?" It is also important to get some idea of what is actually going on in his life. What level of stress is he dealing with? How well are his coping mechanisms working? Does he have adequate social supports? Information about his symptoms in the absence of the context of his current life situation is almost meaningless. The greatest danger lies in getting caught up in the details of Mr. Jones's experience. Many physicians are reluctant to explore the psychosocial aspects of a patient's problem because they have experienced the time-consuming nature of this process. Patients, when encouraged to talk, often consume great amounts of the physician's time without coming to any resolution. The physician feels battle-weary and behind schedule without the satisfaction of having successfully "treated" anything specific.

The problem to be solved concerns eliciting background information quickly and efficiently without having the patient feel cut off. We have devised a simple protocol for the exploration of the psychosocial context, which has specific goals. These limited goals include:

1. Raising the patient's awareness of the concomitant events which might be affecting his or her health status;
2. Focusing the patient on the emotional state that is being experienced;
3. Guiding the patient into specifying one aspect of the problem that is most troubling;
4. Focusing on the manner in which the patient is handling the experienced stress; and
5. Providing an empathic response, which makes the patient feel validated.

We ask four basic questions. What is going on? How do you feel about it? What troubles you the most? How are you handling that? Then we give the patient a response showing we have understood that there is a problem and that the patient is handling it just as well as can be expected under the circumstances. It is crucial that the physician give this type of empathic response. As we pointed out previously, providing no response or making an abrupt change of subject may leave the patient feeling dissatisfied, even though there was an opportunity to ventilate about a problem. When the patient expresses concerns about some issue, the physician *must* respond (if the physician wishes to be therapeutic). The phrase, "That must be very difficult for you," is extremely useful. We suggest that any time a physician is at a loss for words after having been presented with some complicated, or painful, problem, the automatic reply, "That must be very difficult [or hard, painful, tiring, or discouraging] for you," is always appropriate. Coming from a powerful, attractive, knowledgeable source, such as the physician, it makes the patient feel affirmed.

Although the situation is tough, at least the response is reasonable. If this *is* a difficult situation, as understood by the doctor, the patient feels much better and less subjectively out of control. Perhaps he or she is not as incompetent, worthless, or helpless as he or she had imagined. Moreover, perhaps it is not true that "Nobody cares," since the doctor obviously does. Hope is rekindled. The patient is no longer demoralized. Tolerance for symptoms will be enhanced and the healing capacity of the body will be facilitated.[31,32]

Often patients will go into great detail about their situations. By paraphrasing the patient's concerns and reactions to the problem, the physician demonstrates careful listening and indicates that the patient has been understood. This will often cut down on the amount of repetition in the patient's story. The physician can also interject that it is obvious that the situation is difficult. Mentioning that it will be important to hear the outcome in follow-up allows the patient to move on. These easy-to-learn techniques constitute the essence of psychological support. The following is a clinical example:

A 24-year-old woman visited the office, complaining of a sore throat and a mild earache which she had had for ten days. The chart showed that there had been several previous visits for minor complaints and some evidence of mild postpartum depression. Her youngest child was presently 12 months old. There were two older children in the home. Questioning by the physician elicited no particular acute stress, just a general lack of enthusiasm. Asked about the progress of the baby, the patient brightened somewhat. The physician then suggested that taking care of an active 1-year-old, especially at this time of the year, when she was not feeling well herself, must be very difficult. The patient gave a deep sigh. "Oh, how I wish that there was someone to take care of me." "I can understand that," said the physician. He put his hand on her shoulder and guided her to the exam table. She smiled and relaxed.

We are not implying here that this simple interaction solved the patient's problems or cured her "mild depression." We are rather pointing out that as a result of the interaction, the patient obviously felt better, as shown by her affect. We assume that she interpreted the physician's comments as indicating that her response to her problems was reasonable and that therefore, she was seen as a reasonable person. This lifted her spirits and her self-esteem.

SUMMARY

In order to provide comprehensive and personal medical care for patients, psychological as well as physical symptoms must be addressed. Many patients already consider their physician to be their primary source of mental health care. The true healing skills are those of communication and caring. Primary care physicians who establish relationships of trust, continuity, and nurturance with their patients already have a base for practicing psychotherapy.

Social power is defined as the potential to influence the beliefs, attitudes, or behavior of another person. Physicians have both manifest (demonstrated) and attributed (assumed) power. Social power can be divided into five types: reward, coercive, legitimate, referent, and expert. Since physicians are powerful, attractive, and credible sources of information, they have the potential to influence patients' behavior and effect a permanent attitude change. This power base can be used, with awareness, to make patients feel better about themselves and their world.

Physicians already have the necessary interviewing skills, such as data collection, organization, information synthesis, and communication, which can be used to establish quality relationships demonstrating interest and attention. By establishing the context of the patient's visit and providing an empathic response, the physician can help to mitigate the patient's distress.

REFERENCES

1. Regier, D. A., Goldberg, I. D., & Taube, C. A. The de facto U.S. Mental Health services system: A public health perspective. *Archives of General Psychiatry*, 1978, *35*, 685–693.

2. Lee, S. H., Gianturco, D. T., & Eisdorfer, C. Community mental health center accessibility. *Archives of General Psychiatry*, 1974, *31*, 335–339.

3. Locke, B. Z., & Gradner, E. P. Psychiatric disorders among the patients of general practitioners and internists. *Public Health Reports*, 1969, *84*, 167–173.

4. Corney, R. H. A survey of professional help sought by patients for psychosocial problems. *British Journal of General Practice*, 1990, *40*, 365–368.

5. Shapiro, S., Skinner, E. A., Kessler, L. G., Von Korff, M., German, P. S., Tischler, G. L., Leaf, P. J., Benham, L., Cottler, L., & Regier, D. A. Utilization of health and mental health services: Three epidemiologic catchment area sites. *Archives of General Psychiatry*, 1984, *41*, 971–982.

6. Von Korff, M., Shapiro, S., Burke, J. D., Teitlebaum, M., Skinner, E. A., German, P., Turner, R. W., Klein, L., & Burns, B. Anxiety and depression in a primary care clinic: Comparison of diagnostic interview schedule, general health questionnaire, and practitioner assessments. *Archives of General Psychiatry* 1987, *44*, 152–156.

7. Borus, J. F., Howes, M. J., Devins, N. P., Rosenberg, R., & Livingston, W. W. Primary health care providers' recognition and diagnosis of mental disorders in their patients. *General Hospital Psychiatry*, 1988, *10*, 317–321.

8. Brodaty, H., & Andrews, G. Brief psychotherapy in family practice: A controlled prospective intervention trial. *British Journal of Psychiatry*, 1983, *143*, 11–19.

9. Stepansky, P. E., & Stepansky, W. Training primary physicians as psychotherapists. *Comprehensive Psychiatry*, 1974, *15*, 141–151.

10. Pierloot, R. A. The treatment of psychosomatic disorders by the general practitioner. *International Journal of Psychiatry in Medicine*, 1977–1978, *8*, 43–51.

11. Pincus, H. A., Strain, J. J., Houpt, J. L., & Gise, L. H. Models of mental health training in primary care. *Journal of the American Medical Association*, 1983, *249*, 3065–3068.

12. Schwab, J. J. Depression in patients of internists. *Journal of Psychiatric Treatment and Evaluation*, 1983, *5*, 429–437.

13. Cousins, N. *The healing heart: Antidotes to panic and helplessness*. New York: Norton, 1983.

14. Von Korff, M., & Myers, L. The primary care physician and psychiatric services. *General Hospital Psychiatry*, 1987, *9*, 235–240.

15. Benjamin, W. W. Sounding board: Healing by the fundamentals. *New England Journal of Medicine*, 1984, *311*, 595–597.

16. Edelstein, L. The Hippocratic Oath: Text, translation and interpretation. *Supplements to the Bulletin of the History of Medicine*, no. 1. Baltimore, Md.: Johns Hopkins University Press, 1943.

17. McWhinney, I. R. *A textbook of family medicine*. New York: Oxford University Press, 1989.

18. Levenstein, J. H., McCracken, E. C., McWhinney, I. R., Stewart, M. A., & Brown, J. B. The patient-centered clinical method 1. A model for doctor-patient interaction in family practice. *Family Practice*, 1986, *3*, 24–30.

19. Brown, J. B., Stewart, M. A., McCracken, M. C., McWhinney, I. R., & Levenstein, J. H. The patient centered clinical method 2. Definition and application. *Family Practice*, 1986, *3*, 75–79.

20. French, J.P.R., Jr., & Raven, B. H. The bases of social power. In D. Cartwright & A. Zander (Eds.), *Group dynamics: Research and theory*, 3rd ed., pp. 259–269. New York: Harper and Row, 1968.

21. Homans, G. C. *Social behavior: Its elementary form*. New York: Harcourt Brace, 1961.

22. Collins, B. E., & Raven, B. H. Group structure: Attraction, coalitions, communication and power. In G. Lindzey & E. Aronson (Eds.), *The handbook of social psychology*, 2nd Ed., Vol. 4., pp. 102–204. Reading, Mass.: Addison, Wesley, 1969.

23. Postman, N. *The disappearance of childhood*. New York: Delacorte Press, 1982.

24. Bacon, F. Meditationes sacrae. Cited in J. Bartlett, *Familiar Quotations*, 13th Ed., p. 118. Boston: Little, Brown, 1955.

25. Becker, M. H. Patient adherence to prescribed therapies. *Medical Care*, 1985, *23*, 539–555.

26. Meichenbaum, D., & Turk, D. *Facilitating treatment adherence: A practitioner's guidebook*. New York: Plenum, 1987.

27. Brody, D. S. An analysis of patient recall of their therapeutic regimens. *Journal of Chronic Diseases*, 1980, *33*, 57–63.

28. Kelman, H. C. Compliance, identification and internalization: Three processes of attitude change. *Journal of Conflict Resolution*, 1958, *2*, 51–60.

29. Cone, J. W. Formal models of ego development: A practitioner's response. In N. Datan & L. H. Ginsberg (Eds.), *Life-span developmental psychology: Normative life crises*, pp. 89–98. New York: Academic Press, 1975.

30. Schon, D. A. *Educating the reflective practitioner*. San Francisco: Jossey-Bass, 1987.

31. Cassel, J. The contribution of the social environment to host resistance. *American Journal of Epidemiology*, 1976, *104*, 107–123.

32. House, J. S., Landis, K. R., & Umberson, D. Social relationships and health. *Science*, 1988, *241*, 540–545.

CHAPTER 4

Basic Principles and Strategies of Psychotherapeutic Change

The goal of this chapter is to be explicit about what we mean by psychotherapy. In our many workshops based on *The Fifteen Minute Hour*, physicians often tell us that they feel uncomfortable with the word *psychotherapy*. They prefer the word *counseling*. The distinction we make is that when we say *counseling*, we refer to giving patients suggestions or advice, whereas psychotherapy implies that we are using specific techniques with the intention of possibly modifying how patients view themselves, their world, and their options. We want physicians to be aware that using words can be like doing procedures that affect the patient's view of reality.

As we have pointed out in earlier chapters, psychological factors predispose the patient to illness and affect recovery from illness. Therefore, therapy designed to decrease psychological pain or dysfunction becomes a critical part of all good medical treatment. Psychotherapy is the treatment of emotional, behavioral, personality, or psychiatric disorders, primarily by communication with the patient, as an alternative or in addition to treatments utilizing chemical or physical measures. Psychotherapy can be understood as a process that uses a variety of verbal and nonverbal messages to empower patients, enable them to trust themselves and others, validate feelings, enhance the sense of self-esteem, diminish feelings of isolation or depression, and develop a sense of purpose and act on it. We will identify specific techniques that particularly lend themselves to the practice of primary care.

Psychotherapy consists of the things we say (and the way in which we say them) that make the patient feel better. Our interaction with the patient, the therapeutic talk, has an ameliorating effect on the patient's distress. Different schools of psychiatry and psychology will claim that training and supervision in their particular method of psychotherapy is the critical factor in precipitating the change in self-image, worldview, emotional response, or overt behavior that is associated with a successful outcome in psychotherapy. We maintain that there are certain universal influences that can be tapped and used therapeutically, and that understanding these dynamics and applying them intentionally potentiates healing.

It is important to remember that we all make assumptions about the nature of the world based on our personal experiences, starting in early childhood. Much of this process is outside the level of awareness. Then, as one talented psychotherapist put it:

We perpetuate these conditioned ways of perceiving the world through repetitive stories we tell ourselves about "the way things are." These kinds of stories are mental fabrications, judgments or interpretations that put what is happening into a familiar framework. Usually we do not recognize these stories as our own invention; instead, we believe that they represent reality.[1]

Psychotherapy can affect the stories that patients tell themselves about who they are. These are stories that patients believe and that place limits on subsequent experiences.

PSYCHOTHERAPY MEANS EDITING THE STORY

The more neurotic a person is, the more distorted his or her worldview, and the more limited his or her story. According to A. Maslow, neurotic persons are not only relatively inefficient but also absolutely inefficient, since they do not perceive the real world as accurately or efficiently as do healthy persons.[2] Without accurate information, they cannot make good judgments, attain their goals, or even manage their anxiety. Perhaps the simplest definition for psychotherapy is the process by which we fix patients' maps of the world so that they can figure out the direction to go in order to get what they want.

Research has overwhelmingly demonstrated the effectiveness of psychotherapy over placebo or no-treatment approaches, but there is little evidence that demonstrates the actual superiority of one type of therapy over another.[3-5] However, certain approaches seem to lend themselves more effectively to specific types of clinical situations.

Our major concern is to define and modify those therapeutic features that work, regardless of the "brand name." The most effective techniques are generic. Since we are concerned with what works and how to do it, we must be very specific about what we want to accomplish. Just exactly what are our goals?

THE GOALS OF THERAPY

Most simply put, the goal of psychotherapy is to make the patient feel better; that is, to lower levels of distress and combat feelings of being overwhelmed. As pointed out in Chapter 2, when patients feel overwhelmed by the circumstances of their lives or their reaction to those circumstances, they develop a wide range of somatic and psychological symptoms. The most common symptoms from which patients suffer are anxiety and depression.[3,6] These symptoms develop because of patients' interpretations of their situation (their stories about the situation), not because of the situation proper. However, regardless of etiology, the experience of the symptoms further compromises a patient's coping ability.

Patients Go on "Tilt"

When patients' coping abilities become overextended, they cease functioning effectively, a condition we label "tilt." The goal of psychotherapy is to make the patient feel better so that he or she can function better and go off tilt. Feeling better in this connotation relates to the patient's emotional or mental state.

Specifically, we are concerned with patients' *perceived* personal power to deal with the circumstances of their lives. The sense of control has been shown to be the key factor in maintaining physical and mental health.[7] When people perceive themselves to be in control, whether they actually are or not, they function better. Perceived control has been shown to have a direct effect on autonomic reactivity and immune response.[8] Perceived control enables a person to function better in response to demands from both the internal and external environments. At the least, it improves coping, which also helps to restore the person's equilibrium, resulting in greater feelings of competence and belonging. Basically, our therapeutic goal is to help patients regain their sense of competence so that they feel empowered to affect the course of their lives.

When the Patient Is Back in Control

Once the patient feels better, he or she will be able to function better not only in the realms of interpersonal relations such as job performance, but will also be more effective in mobilizing the body's defenses in response to existent or potential disease.[7,8] The patient will also have an enhanced sense of well-being, sleep better, have a healthier appetite, and maintain a more reasonable flow of energy. In contrast to the vicious cycle of demoralization, depression, and compromised immune response leading to disease and further demoralization, the body's healthy defenses will be engaged, leading to an enhanced sense of personal competence and improved ability to resist disease.[9]

Often the psychotherapeutic intervention will cause patients to make positive changes in their assumed worldview, meaning that it will allow them to edit their stories and add new chapters. This altered belief system then precipitates new ways of thinking and behaving that result in more satisfactory experiences, providing a natural reinforcement mechanism and instigating a benevolent circle.[10] A third-year resident described the following case:

The patient is a 62-year-old white male whom I had been seeing routinely for blood pressure checks. He has a history of hypertension and peptic ulcer disease. He is a rather stoic person who generally keeps his feelings to himself and, as I found out, somatizes and develops symptoms. After seeing him several times for vague and persistent abdominal discomfort, I persisted in knowing what was going on in his life. He mentioned problems at work and at home and then unexpectedly added that the combination had made him impotent. When I asked him how that made him feel, he at first denied that it had any effect, but then complained of headaches. Questioned about what troubled him the most, the patient said it was his impotence because he could not satisfy his wife, even with her reassurance that "it doesn't bother her." I then asked how he was handling the stress. He replied that he gets up and "walks it off." After assuring the patient that this must be very difficult, I taught him some progressive relaxation techniques to help manage his stress and, after tapering all medications that could contribute to his impotence, referred him to a urologist. The interesting thing is that in all subsequent visits he has expected to be questioned about his stressors and considers it part of his treatment. Unfortunately, at present he is still impotent and refuses a prosthesis, but there are no more complaints of abdominal pain or headaches.

Supportive Therapy

Traditionally, a broad distinction has been made between supportive psychotherapy and explorative psychotherapy. Supportive therapy is designed to restore premorbid or optimal functioning, while explorative therapy is concerned with uncovering personality patterns to understand the etiology of disorders. Techniques promoted by proponents of supportive therapy include abreaction (catharsis: giving the patient a chance to talk about the problem), dependency (being there for the patient), exploration of symptomatology, encouragement of new, more productive behavior, and efforts at resolution through clarification. Basically, to be effective, all psychotherapy must be supportive.

Explorative Therapy

In explorative therapy the patient's behavior and feelings are examined from a historical perspective. Jerome Frank has pointed out that if we mean by cure that we can eradicate the cause of illness, the "features of the patient's illness that psychotherapy can cure directly would be those caused by stress-producing distortions in the patient's assumptive world. Since the patient is an open psychobiological system, correction of these distortions would inevitably be reflected in changes in the neurophysiology of the central nervous system" (p. 17).[10]

We cannot stress too strongly that insight or understanding alone have no practical benefit. P. Watzlawick, J. H. Weakland, and R. Fisch, in the book *Change: Principles of Problem Formation and Problem Resolution*, made the following point:

Everyday, not just clinical, experience shows not only that there can be change without insight, but that very few behavioral or social changes are accompanied, let alone preceded, by insight into the vicissitudes of their genesis. It may, for instance, be that the insomniac's difficulty has its roots in the past: his tired, nervous mother may habitually have yelled at him to sleep and to stop bothering her. But while this kind of discovery may provide a plausible and at times even very sophisticated explanation of a problem, it usually contributes nothing towards its solution (p. 86).[11]

In a brilliant footnote, these authors argued as follows:

Such empirical findings . . . [must be] thought through to their logical conclusions. There are two possibilities: 1) The causal significance of the past is only a fascinating but inaccurate myth. In this case, the only question is the pragmatic one: How can desirable change of present behavior be most efficiently produced? 2) There is a causal relationship between the past and present behavior. But since past events are obviously unchangeable, either we are forced to abandon all hope that change is possible, or we must assume that—at least in some significant respects—the past has influence over the present only by way of a person's present interpretation of past experience. If so, then the significance of the past becomes a matter not of "truth" and "reality," but of looking at it here and now in one way rather than another. Consequently, there is no compelling reason to assign to the past primacy or causality in relation to the present, and this means that the reinterpretation of the past is simply one of many ways of possibly influencing present behavior. In this case, then, we are back at the only meaningful question, i.e., the pragmatic one: How can desirable change of present behavior be produced most efficiently? (p. 86).[11]

Thus, contrary to conventional wisdom, *why* someone is behaving in a particular manner is irrelevant. What is important is to help the person to change it. (In some cases, very intellectual types may feel that they must understand why before they can bring themselves to change—but in the final analysis, it is their decision to make a change that is effective, not understanding why they behaved the way they did in the first place.)

FIVE ELEMENTS SHARED BY PSYCHOTHERAPEUTIC TECHNIQUES

The field of the psychotherapies includes a wide variety of modalities and orientations. There is long-term, short-term, individual, group, and family therapy. In any of these modalities, the orientation could be psychoanalytic, client-centered, gestalt, transactional, dynamic, cognitive, reality-oriented, behavioral, rational-emotive, neurolinguistic, or eclectic, to mention only a few. Regardless of theoretical orientation, there are basic principles and strategies that are associated with the therapeutic change process.[12] These are the generic forces that we wish to engage in the therapeutic interaction.

The Expectation of Receiving Help

Common to all psychotherapeutic modalities is the initially induced expectation that the therapy will be helpful. Jerome Frank has repeatedly pointed out that patients seek therapy because they are feeling helpless, hopeless, and demoralized.[13,14] He has specifically defined the demoralization commonly experienced by patients as "a state of subjective incapacity plus distress. The patient suffers from a sense of failure, loss of self-esteem, feelings of hopelessness or helplessness and feelings of alienation or isolation. These are often accompanied by a sense of mental confusion, which the patient may express as a fear of insanity" (p. 19).[10] The expectation that help is imminent helps to lift the patient from the depths of demoralization.

The Therapeutic Relationship

The second general principle associated with all psychotherapeutic modalities is the patient's (or client's) participation in a therapeutic relationship. This relationship exists for the sole purpose of fostering the well-being of the patient. A contract (or understanding) is made in which another person agrees to engage with the patient in a manner that fosters the expression of feelings and concerns in an accepting atmosphere. This contract for caring and concern is the core of therapy. It is the nature of the relationship that determines the efficacy of the healing process, whether we are discussing the classical analyst who listens and occasionally interprets, the Rogerian therapist who gives nonjudgmental reflections to the client, or the reality therapist who expects the patient to honor commitments and make no excuses. Regardless of theoretical orientation, it is the connection—the special relationship with the practitioner, who communicates that he or she understands the patient, takes the patient seriously, and is devoted to the patient's welfare—that is the generic healing component.

Obtaining an External Perspective

The third factor found in all psychotherapies is giving patients the opportunity to obtain an external or new perspective on their problems. By bringing their perceptions of their situation to a person who is not directly involved, patients are exposed to alternative interpretations, made aware of potential options, and learn something about how other people might react to a similar situation. The external perspective affords patients an opportunity to check their possibly inaccurate perceptions of reality. For example, if the listener does not get upset when hearing about the outrageous situation that the patient describes, perhaps there is some hope after all.

Encouraging Corrective Experiences

All psychotherapeutic modalities encourage corrective experiences. The definition of the corrective experience may vary according to the theoretical orientation of the practitioner, but until insights are put into practice and in some way change how patients relate to themselves, their world, and the significant others in their lives, there is no healing. The physician acts as a cheerleader, encouraging patients to think and behave in new ways that result in a sense of enhanced well-being. This is the essence of a corrective experience: Patients are coached to react to situations in less destructive ways. The benefits of this improved behavior include gaining greater satisfaction from their interactions with others, which then promotes further gains.

The Opportunity to Test Reality Repeatedly

The last principle common to all psychotherapies is the opportunity to test reality repeatedly. Patients' judgments of others, including others' intentions, are often quite inaccurate. They are part of the story that the patients constantly repeat. An objective listener can confirm the reasonableness of the patients' reactions, challenge the accuracy of patients' conclusions, or suggest alternate explanations. By examining their possibly faulty assumptions, patients are able to get a more accurate view of personal patterns of behavior, strengths, and vulnerabilities. Emotional and behavioral limitations will be reexamined. Certain goals that may previously have been judged as unattainable—not on the map—may now be seen as possible. Conversely, through repeated reality testing, unrealistic expectations tend to become more reasonable, and hence more likely to be satisfied. Often, patients need repeated confirmation that the experience of making changes can be difficult, painful, and slow.

STARTING WHERE THE PATIENT IS

Before we look at specific psychotherapeutic techniques, we would like to discuss four theoretical areas that provide important guidelines for understanding and modifying patients' reactions to their circumstances.

Language and the Story

In *The Structure of Magic*, R. Bandler and J. Grinder made understandable and teachable the language skills used by some of the world's most talented therapists.[15] The founders of Neurolinguistic Programming (NLP) then explained how people create their maps (or stories), which, if too limiting, may result in the need for a therapist's help.

The basic premise is that there is an irreducible difference between the actual world and our experience of it. Each of us creates a representation of the world, which then governs our behavior. Since no two people have the same experience, we all have different models of the world. Bandler and Grinder examined the process by which these models are built.

All information about the world is processed through our various senses, particularly the visual, auditory, and kinesthetic modalities. In order to process this information effectively, we tend to organize it in specific ways, sorting likes, and creating categories. In attending to the world, each of us chooses a predominant sense and communicates this in the descriptive language we use. The visually oriented person will "see what you mean" and the auditory dominant person will "hear you," while the kinesthetic person will "feel" that he or she understands. Bandler and Grinder found that the most successful therapists automatically responded in the same mode as the patient. When talking with patients, it is useful to listen for their predominant orientation, whether visual, auditory, or kinesthetic, and practice matching it.

We return to the map. Why is it that some people are able to respond creatively and cope productively with most of life's problems, whereas others generally perceive few options in any situation? Bandler and Grinder deduced that the second group must be using an impoverished map. In the face of the multifaceted, rich, and complex world, these linguists wondered how it was possible for people to maintain such limited models, even when they caused them so much pain. Bandler and Grinder described three perceptual mechanisms that tend to block growth and the integration of new experience: generalization, deletion, and distortion.

Generalization is an ability that is necessary for organizing information and coping with the world. At any given time, the overwhelming amount of information received by our senses must be sorted into manageable categories. To generalize from the experience of being burned that touching a hot stove is painful has survival value, but to generalize that stoves are dangerous, and therefore must be avoided, is a limiting view. Having been discouraged from expressing negative feelings as a child, a person may generalize that it is bad to express any feelings. If it is bad to express feelings, this may generalize to the belief that having feelings is bad, period.

Based on early generalizations, people tend to delete (that is, selectively filter out) experience that counters established views that they have acquired. For example, people block themselves from hearing messages of caring that conflict with generalizations they have made about their own self-worth. People who think of themselves as stupid will not hear being told that they are smart; on the contrary, they will think that the other person must really think they are awfully dense to expect them to believe such nonsense. Hence, we recommend that the clinician say, "Wow, that was a difficult problem," instead of, "Gee, you did that well."

The third modeling process involves distorting sensory data to conform to preexisting notions. People hear and see what they expect to hear and see. Given a variety of experience, people will notice only those aspects that confirm their sense of themselves and the universe. The process of therapy challenges the generalizations, deletions, and distortions inherent in the patient's experience of reality, and thereby introduces changes into their models of the world.

Language is used to organize the story about what is happening in the world and how the patient feels about it. Language affects how the patient represents past experiences in the present, including rules about which behaviors are acceptable and which are not. Language also structures what patients tell themselves about the future and what is likely to happen. Language is also the medium for making corrections in the story.

In challenging generalizations, absolutes, such as *always*, *never*, *everyone*, and *no one*, need to be questioned, for example: "You're absolutely always in pain?" "No one has ever accepted your ideas?" "You've never done anything right?"

Deletions are expressed through leaving gaps in expressions. In challenging deletions, it is useful to get patients to specify missing information. When a patient says, "I'm afraid," the physician must respond, "Of what, *specifically*, are you afraid?" The response to "I'm not good enough," is, "In *what way* are you not good?" or "Specifically, *for what* are you not good enough?" Another possible challenge would be, "How good is good enough?"

Distortions often occur when patients change verbs into nouns such as changing relating to relationship, or deciding into decision. Bandler and Grinder pointed out that turning a "process" into an "event," which is then seen as unchangeable, is limiting, guilt-producing, and destructive.

Patient: "I really regret my decision."

Response: "What stops you from changing your mind now?"

Patient: "My relationship is a disaster."

Response: "Is there a way you can respond to your partner in a different way:?"

In challenging models, the physician not only questions absolutes, but also imposed limits (the *can'ts*, *shoulds*, *musts*, and *impossibilities*, using "Why not?") and imposed values (the rights, wrongs, goods, and bads). In general, the goal is to help the patient create a richer representation of possibilities.

Models of Anxiety

Patients commonly present with symptoms of anxiety, a pervasive sense of apprehension, nervousness, and irritability, which are often accompanied by a variety of physical manifestations. Often, anxiety is a response to a conflict, part of which may be out of consciousness.

A useful way to understand anxiety comes from Dollard and Miller's formulation, first published in 1950, which is still relevant though rarely familiar to physicians.[16] J. Dollard and N. E. Miller suggested that there are three models of anxiety, that is, three prototypes of situations that precipitate feelings that people experience as anxiety: approach-approach, avoidance-avoidance, and approach-avoidance on the same pole.

In the approach-approach condition, a patient has two desires, or options that are available, and a choice must be made. As the patient gets closer to one, the other gets further away. Since the patient wants both, anxiety is generated. Sometimes these are specific situations, such as choosing between security or more pay, or between a vacation or a new car. Often, the definition of self is involved, for example, maintaining a desirable self-image, such as being a good mother versus an effective businesswoman (role strain).

Mrs. Jones comes to the office complaining of a pinched nerve in her neck. She has had trouble sleeping and is really in pain. After inquiring into what is presently going on in her life, we find that she has been offered a wonderful job in a travel agency but that she really wants to be home for her husband and children. Now that her neck has started to trouble her, she no longer has to make a decision. In an approach-approach conflict, pointing out the dynamics in the situation and the fact that either way, the outcome is positive (as the patient will get something she wants) is often sufficient to reduce the anxiety.

In the avoidance-avoidance condition, the patient is caught between two negative situations. Both situations arouse fear or other unpleasant emotions: As the patient runs from one negative pole, the other gets closer. This generates high levels of anxiety and usually will immobilize the patient at dead center.

Mr. Brown hates his job. He has to drag himself to work every morning. He is thinking about quitting, but there is high unemployment in his town and every time he thinks about his financial situation, his ulcer starts to hurt. He is also doing a good job of criticizing himself for not being able to make a decision. Often, just giving the patient permission to stay at dead center is therapeutic. It is all right to be stuck for a while. Other effective techniques include desensitization through relaxation, providing support (evoking a positive response coupled with the negative stimulus), or helping the patient see the situation in a different light. Perhaps Mr. Brown can make some changes in his job, plan to start a business in town, or think about moving to a more desirable area. Even knowing that there are other choices and then making a decision to stay can be very therapeutic. Any of these techniques will reduce the perceived negativity of the pole.

Perhaps the most interesting model is approach and avoidance on the same pole. This situation is extremely common. It occurs when someone is attracted to a situation that also represents danger. When this occurs, the experience is such that as a person gets more distant from the object, the perception of the attractiveness increases. At close range, however, the fear becomes dominant. This gradient of anxiety is unfortunately a very common experience in personal relationships.

Charles has met a woman whom he really admires. He wants to get close to her, but at the same time, he is afraid of intimacy. When he is not with her, her desirability is very strong; as he gets closer, however, his fear becomes overpowering. His anxiety and the conflict about what he wants thus become crippling. Charles moves back and forth, never able to make a commitment and never really going away. He has all kinds of somatic complaints, and every time the woman gets close, he picks a fight with her about something, perhaps her lack of sympathy for his suffering. It has been our experience that both physician and patient gain from understanding and identifying this model. It is very useful: It creates an "Ah Ha!" reaction of understanding that somehow makes the situation easier to bear. Then, the patient can decide whether to tolerate the fear and overcome the anxiety in order to get what he or she wants.

Explanatory Style

We have been talking about the importance of patients' stories (their accounts of their experiences) in influencing their subsequent perceptions. Now there is a growing body of research which empirically establishes the connection between peoples' explanations of why something happened, to their subsequent emotional and physical state. Martin Seligman and his colleagues, building on his work on learned helplessness,[17] conducted an innovative series of studies that determined that having a "pessimistic explanatory style" was not only associated with depressive symptoms but was also a risk factor in predisposing individuals to subsequent depressions when faced with negative situations.[18] This research focused on the explanations given for the occurrence of bad events in peoples' lives. Using data from interviews, questionnaires, and a technique of content analysis of verbal explanations (CAVE) that accommodates to using historical data such as diaries, letters, transcripts, and other records, these researchers were able to tie explanatory style to health outcomes and longevity.[18–20]

Explanatory style encompasses three dimensions: (1) whether it is internally or externally caused (personal responsibility or attributed to others or circumstances); (2) whether the cause is stable or unstable (this is something that will always be this way or this is something that happened now); and (3) whether it is global or specific (this is something that happens with everything or only in this type of situation). Table 1 illustrates the range of stories to explain why a checking account might have been overdrawn using these dimensions.

Consistently using explanations that are internal, stable, and global puts people at risk for both morbidity and mortality. Optimists live longer than pessimists.[21] They stay healthier.[22] Those Grant study subjects (see Chapter 2) who exhibited the pessimistic explanatory style during their college days had significantly more cardiac pathology thirty-five years later than did their more optimistic colleagues.[23] Recently, pessimistic explanatory style has even been directly linked to decreased cell-mediated immunity in an elderly population.[24]

The importance from a psychotherapeutic standpoint is that it is only when all three negative factors are present that the individual feels helpless, hopeless, and overwhelmed. Explanatory style is a fairly stable trait.[25] Although only habitual use of the pessimistic explanatory style has been

Table 1
Examples of Stories Explaining Why My Checking Account Is Overdrawn

EXPLANATORY STYLE

	INTERNAL		EXTERNAL	
	STABLE	UNSTABLE	STABLE	UNSTABLE
GLOBAL	I'm incapable of doing anything right.	I've had the flu for several weeks. I let everything go.	All institutions chronically make mistakes.	Around the holidays everything gets fouled up.
SPECIFIC	I always have trouble figuring my balance.	The one time I didn't enter a check, my account gets overdrawn.	This bank has always used antiquated techniques.	I'm surprised! My bank has never made a mistake before.

Source: Peterson, C., & Seligman, M. E. P., Causal explanations as a risk factor for depression: Theory and evidence, Psychological Review, 1984, 91, p 349. Copyright 1984 by the American Psychological Association. Adapted by permission.

shown to lead to negative health consequences, interventions that consitenly focus on challenging this destructive manner of thinking can be highly beneficial. For therapeutic purposes, then, it is profitable to listen to peoples' explanations for the bad things that happen to them and to challenge internal, stable, and global causation. Is something really their fault, or did external factors or other people influence the event? Does this really happen all the time and is it likely to continue, or will this change in the future, and what can be done to facilitate that change? Does this really happen in all areas of the patient's life or is this an area of particular weakness? Posing these questions helps the patient to move out of the internal, stable, global box (see Table 1) and is a powerful psychotherapeutic technique.

Sometimes it is necessary to correct patients' stories. The word *yet* is a very important therapeutic tool. When a patient makes a statement about the inability to do something, the physician can counter with, "You have not been able to do that yet," or, "Up to now, this has been difficult for you." These simple statements imply that is is not a stable situation. Thus, the patient is out of the box. This is psychotherapy.

When the physician consistently corrects the notion that problems have a stable quality by implying that they can be solved at some future time or that there were other factors involved that are out of the patient's control, and that there are other aspects of the patient's life that are highly successful in spite of the fact that there may be problems at work, patients may be encouraged to develop a more hopeful explanatory style.

The Sense of Self-Efficacy

In treating dysfunctional behavior, we have found that cognitive processes, which we have termed stories, determine and maintain habitual functioning. Successful change depends on changing habits, which is performance-oriented meaning that it relates to doing something. Albert Bandura first postulated the concept of self-efficacy as a way of explaining the reciprocal relationship between performance and the cognitive assessment of the likelihood of success. Peoples' beliefs in their ability to succeed at a task determines whether behavior is initiated, how much effort is expended, and how long that effort is sustained when obstacles or adverse reactions are experienced.[26] These beliefs are based on past performance, vicarious experience, physiological and psychological states, and feedback regarding the current performance. The concept of self-efficacy is very useful for understanding and predicting behavior, and also for providing a strategy to induce change. There is a diverse and rapidly expanding medical literature documenting the relationship between self-efficacy and COPD (Chronic Obstructive Pulmonary Disease),[27] return to work after angioplasty,[28] coping with pain,[29] and quality of life of cancer patients,[30] to mention only a few. The bottom line is that patients' predictions of what they will do are the most reliable indicators of what will transpire. If patients think that they are able to do something, they will try. If they fail at first, they will continue to try because they believe, based on their past experiences, that it is only a question of time until they succeed. Conversely, if patients have a low sense of self-efficacy and do not expect to be able to succeed, they may nonetheless try, but the amount of effort will be limited, and on encountering difficulties, the tendency will be to give up since their expectation is of failure anyway.

There is little sense in prescribing a nicotine patch to help patients stop smoking until those patients believe they can kick the habit, redefine themselves as nonsmokers, and develop healthy activities to substitute for the smoking urge. The sense of self-efficacy is not just a cognitive estimate of potential performance based on perceptions of past accomplishment, but is directly instrumental in enhancing performance.[31]

Bandura's work is valuable because it points to mechanisms that can positively affect the sense of self-efficacy. These include structuring successes so that the efficacy expectation is modified, providing vicarious experiences, creating supportive environments, and using verbal persuasion to change patients' views of the tasks or of themselves.

Traditional concepts of mental health have proposed that well-adjusted individuals have a relatively accurate perception of themselves and their ability to control important aspects of their lives. There is now an impressive body of literature suggesting that having positive illusions about one's self, personal control, and the future not only enhances performance, but results in a wide range of positive mental health outcomes.[32] This, too, can be seen as evidence that people's stories are the basis of self-fulfilling prophecies.

In summary, in a therapeutic relationship, positive information, which the physician provides about the patient or about a task, can affect the patient's sense of self-efficacy and encourage him or her to engage in successful behavior change. This positive outcome will further enhance the sense of self-efficacy. This, too, is psychotherapy. It changes the story that the patient tells about what can be accomplished.

USEFUL TECHNIQUES FROM A VARIETY OF SOURCES

Having outlined the major generic therapeutic components common to all psychotherapeutic interventions and sketched some interesting models explaining mechanisms involved in patients' dysphoric experiences, now we will focus on therapeutic pearls from a variety of orientations. There are clearly some things that work better than others, some techniques that are easier to learn than others, and some approaches that lend themselves more comfortably to a therapeutic encounter within a fifteen minute framework.

Psychodynamics in Brief

In general, people are simpler than insight schools give them credit for, but more complex than behavioral models suggest. By simpler, we mean that a limited number of supportive techniques are highly effective, and by complex, we imply that people's reactions are determined by a multitude of factors that are both in and out of awareness.

The unique contribution of psychodynamic theories is in pointing out the hidden agendas that pervade interpersonal relationships and the effect of maladaptive personal responses that are influenced by past experiences and projected onto current relationships. The way in which patients define themselves (as loving, hateful, or inadequate) is an ongoing process, a story that they are telling themselves based on judgments they have made. Some of this process is purely symbolic and unconscious, while some is within the patient's awareness. Since much of this behavior is demonstrated in relation to the physician, an opportunity is created to bring these dynamics into focus and to challenge the accuracy of the story.

The Healing Relationship

From Carl Rogers we have learned the value of relating to patients in a nonpossessive, accepting way, of expressing our caring by providing accurate empathy.[33] The accepting physician creates an environment that facilitates the exploration of various possibilities for change.

Empathic understanding is communicated to the patient through techniques of paraphrasing, summarizing, reflecting feelings, and responding authentically. According to Rogers, however, these techniques are relatively unimportant except as a channel for communicating positive regard and accurate empathy. There can be no therapeutic change without acceptance, understanding, and empathy.

Changing Behavior

The evolution of behavior therapies since Bandura first conceptualized psychotherapy as a learning process in the early 1960s has been nothing short of phenomenal.[34] In a review of 252 empirical studies of psychotherapy in the three decades from 1967–1968 to 1987–1988, H. Omer and R. Dar documented the striking evolution away from theory to pragmatic, clinically oriented research.[35]

The popularity of behavioral approaches to therapy can be attributed to their utility in helping patients find solutions for their problems in living. Relaxation, desensitization, visualization, assertiveness training, and bio-feedback all stem from behaviorism in that patients practice and learn new ways to manage themselves, their anxiety, and their behavior. We have modified and incorporated many of these approaches into *The Fifteen Minute Hour.*

Cognitive-Behaviorists have shown that thinking is a behavior that can be modified and that modes of thinking affect the origin, maintenance, and change process related to various human problems.[36,37] People are often unaware that how they think about a situation directly influences how they feel about it. Albert Ellis has recently pointed out that when we think about our goals, even the process of planning steps that we can take to further these goals results in positive feelings.[38]

Ellis continues to underscore the importance of identifying the rigid, dogmatic, and powerful demands and commands constituting the irrational beliefs that most of us hold regarding how the world is supposed to be. He pointed out that it is important to "dispute" statements such as: "It's awful" (meaning totally bad or more than bad), or "I can't bear it" (meaning, survive or be happy at all).[38] A. T. Beck has very successfully used these techniques to help severely depressed persons counter the negative thoughts and evaluations of self, others, and circumstances that trigger and maintain depressive syndromes. D. H. Barlow combined cognitive techniques with various forms of relaxation training in the treatment of panic and other anxiety disorders.[39] These techniques are powerful, especially when promoted by a physician. We have simplified and incorporated them, as will be seen in Chapter 9.

Expecting Patient Follow-Through

According to William Glasser, patients develop symptoms and engage in irresponsible behavior because their lives are out of control and they choose not to feel the painful emotions that this triggers.[40] Often, these painful emotions are converted to physical pain in various parts of the body. When patients do not feel worthwhile to themselves and others (competent) or loved (connected), they need the warmth, kindness, and strength of a physician who will support them while holding them responsible for changing their behavior. Using Glasser's approach (Reality Therapy), the physician acts as a coach, becoming involved with the patient, focusing on current behavior and encouraging the patient to evaluate it, and planning alternate behavior.[40] The patient is expected to make a firm commitment for follow-through. If a plan is reasonable, no excuses are accepted. However, there is also no punishment.

The physician simply insists that the commitment be honored. Patients become aware that there are consequences in real life for failure to carry out commitments. The therapeutic relationship, however, remains one of respect, caring, and involvement through setting reasonable expectations and monitoring results. Applying these principles combines the best of theory and pragmatic application. Moreover, it really works.

PUTTING THERAPY INTO THE PRACTICE SETTING

Having outlined the critical elements of the therapeutic encounter and identified the mechanisms that create the need for therapy, we need to specify exactly how to translate this understanding into primary care practice.

PLISSIT

Any encounter that inspires the patient's hopes for improvement, be it one visit or several, is therapeutic. For the primary care physician, however, it is useful to have a protocol in mind for guiding the level of intervention. A mechanistic, but practical and effective, hierarchial system was first introduced by J. S. Annon in a context of sex therapy.[41] This four-step process triggered by the acronym PLISSIT (*P*ermission; *L*imited *I*nformation; *S*pecific *S*uggestions; and *I*ntensive *T*herapy) is easily remembered and simple to apply.

In a potential therapeutic situation in which the patient is concerned with certain reactions to a particular circumstance, the levels of intervention go from permission giving to offering limited information, making specific suggestions, and developing a contract for intensive therapy.

P Stands for Permission

Regardless of what else transpires in the therapeutic session, it is always appropriate to give patients permission to feel what they feel. This simple intervention does more to restore patients' equilibrium than almost anything else the physician can do. When patients become aware that the world or other people are not as they want them to be, or that they are not handling situations as well as they want to, they feel badly. When the physician reassures the patient that his or her reaction is normal under the circumstances, the patient will feel better. He or she will recognize that it is permissible to be depressed and need not be depressed about being depressed. For example, a patient may have lost his temper and yelled at his wife. The physician assures him it is all right to get angry, especially when one is under stress. Under the circumstances, that can happen. However, the patient needs to let his wife know that he is sorry. It is important to give people permission to feel the way they feel, because if they could feel any other way at that particular time, they would. Regardless of the reaction, the physician's acceptance makes the patient feel more comfortable with the emotional state being experienced.

LI Stands for Limited Information

The second level of intervention is to provide a small amount of essential information that explains the emotional state being experienced. This helps patients set realistic expectations for themselves and others. For example, a patient in a situation of crisis is told that in general, when people experience great amounts of stress, they react by feeling overwhelmed, confused, less capable of making decisions or solving problems, have trouble sleeping, and so forth. This normalization helps get the patient off tilt. The patient feels as though under the circumstances, the reaction is appropriate after all. Information processing is a high-order coping skill. By offering accurate and pertinent information in small enough amounts for the patient to assimilate, the physician is supporting the patient's sense of competence.

SS Stands for Specific Suggestions

Specific suggestions can be given to the patient to examine options, talk to friends, get into a self-help organization, take time out, keep a journal, or any other specific strategy that helps to engage the patient's healthy functioning self and promote constructive coping behavior. These suggestions must be tailored to fit into the patient's current life-style, and must not present yet another overwhelming demand. Often it is useful to ask the patient, "What one thing could you do that would make you feel a little better?" or, "What can you do to get more information before you make that important decision?" The physician's interest and confidence that the patient is competent and in control helps to foster this behavior.

IT Stands for Intensive Therapy

Intensive therapy as it applies to the primary care setting implies that the physician makes a commitment to work with the patient over time. Appointments are scheduled and the physician contracts to offer support for the patient for a specific time in order to resolve a particular life problem. By engaging in a therapeutic contract with the patient, all the criteria specified in the section on the five essential elements of psychotherapeutic techniques are fulfilled. Positive expectations that help is forthcoming are instigated. A therapeutic relationship is established, and an external perspective for the patient's problem becomes available. Corrective experiences are encouraged, and the patient is given the opportunity to test reality repeatedly. The physician agrees to be there to share in the process with the patient.

SUMMARY

Psychotherapy means the treatment of emotional, behavioral, personality, or psychiatric disorders, primarily through communication with the patient. Psychotherapy is the process of helping patients edit their stories. The actual therapeutic features are generic to the process of making the patient feel better, that is, less overwhelmed.

Supportive therapy focuses on the patient's strength, while exploratory therapy aims to understand the etiology of feelings. It is more important to help patients change their reactions than to understand the reaction's source. Common elements among psychotherapeutic techniques include: (1) the expectation of receiving help, (2) participation in a therapeutic relationship, (3) obtaining an external perspective on problems, (4) the encouragement of corrective experiences, and (5) the opportunity to test reality repeatedly.

In general, people are simpler than insight schools give them credit for, but more complex than behavioral models suggest. Carl Rogers's contribution relates to the value of accurate empathy and nonpossessive caring in a therapeutic relationship. Behavior therapies underscore the importance of human learning in the process of modifying behavior. Anxiety presents in approach-approach, avoidance-avoidance, and approach-avoidance conflicts. A pessimistic explanatory style predisposes patients to morbidity and mortality. The sense of self-efficacy determines whether patients will initiate, maintain, and succeed at a new behavior. Cognitive therapy is based on modifying irrational beliefs that affect how people react to situations. Language is used to record and classify our perceptual experience of the world. Through processes of generalization, deletion, and distortion, people build impoverished maps or models of the world, which then limit their perceived options. The therapeutic process challenges these generalizations, deletions, and distortions in order to create a richer representation of possibilities. Through the creation of a warm and understanding relationship, the physician encourages the patient to accept responsibility for becoming more effective.

In determining levels of intervention, the acronym PLISSIT can be used to structure interventions from simple permission giving to offering limited information, making specific suggestions, or entering into a contract for intensive therapy.

REFERENCES

1. Welwood, J. *Journey of the heart: Intimate relationship and the path of love*. New York: Harper Collins, 1990, p. 25.

2. Maslow, A. H. Self-actualizing people: A study of psychological health. *Personality*, 1950, *symposium 1*, 11–34.

3. Smith, N. L., Glass, G. V., & Miller, T. I. *Benefits of psychotherapy*. Baltimore, Md.: Johns Hopkins University Press, 1980.

4. Shapiro, D. A., & Shapiro, D. Meta-analysis of comparative therapy outcome studies: A replication and refinement. *Psychological Bulletin*, 1982, *92*, 581–604.

5. Prioleau, L., Murdock, M., & Brody, N. An analysis of psychotherapy vs. placebo studies. *The Behavioral and Brain Sciences*, 1983, *6*, 275–310.

6. Sloane, R. B., Staples, F. R., Cristol, A. H., Yorkston, N. J., & Whipple, K. *Psychotherapy versus behavior therapy*. Cambridge, Mass.: Harvard University Press, 1975.

7. Rodin, J. Aging and health: Effects of the sense of control. *Science*, 1986, *233*, 1271–1275.

8. Laudenslager, M. L., Ryan, S. M., Drugan, R. C., Hyson, R. L., & Maier, S. F. Coping and immunosuppression: Inescapable but not escapable shock suppresses lymphocyte proliferation. *Science*, 1983, *221*, 568–570.

9. Kiecolt-Glaser, J. K., & Glaser, R. Psychosocial moderators of immune function. *Annals of Behavioral Medicine*, 1987, 9, 16–20.

10. Frank, J. D., Therapeutic components in all psychotherapies. In J. M. Myers (Ed.), *Cures by psychotherapy: What effects change?*, pp. 15–27. New York: Praeger, 1984.

11. Watzlawitz, P., Weakland, J. H., & Fisch, R. *Change: Principles of problem formation and problem resolution*. New York: Norton, 1974.

12. Goldfried, M. R. Rapproachment of psychotherapies. *Journal of Humanistic Psychology*, 1983, *23*, 97–107.

13. Frank, J. D. Psychotherapy: The restoration of morale. *American Journal of Psychiatry*, 1974, *131*, 271–274.

14. De Figueiredo, J. M., & Frank, J. D. Subjective incompetence, the clinical hallmark of demoralization. *Comprehensive Psychiatry*, 1982, *23*, 353–363.

15. Bandler, R., & Grinder, J. *The structure of magic I: A book about language and therapy*. Palo Alto, Calif.: Science and Behavior Books, 1975.

16. Dollard, J., & Miller, N. E. *Personality and psychotherapy*. New York: McGraw Hill, 1950.

17. Seligman, M.E.P. Learned helplessness. *Annual Review of Medicine*, 1972, *23*, 407–412.

18. Peterson, C., & Seligman, M.E.P. Causal explanations as a risk factor for depression: Theory and evidence. *Psychological Review*, 1984, *91*, 347–374.

19. Peterson, C., Bettes, B. A., & Seligman, M.E.P. Depressive symptoms and unprompted causal attributions: Content analysis. *Behavior Research and Therapy*, 1985, *23*, 379–382.

20. Peterson, C., & Seligman, M.E.P. Explanatory style and illness. *Journal of Personality*, 1987, *55*, 237–265.

21. Seligman, M.E.P. *Helplessness: On depression, development and death*. San Francisco: Freeman, 1975.

22. Kamen, L. P., & Seligman, M.E.P. Explanatory style and health. *Current Psychological Research and Reviews*, 1987, *6*, 207–218.

23. Peterson, C., Seligman, M.E.P., & Vaillant, G. E. Pessimistic explanatory style is a risk factor for physical illness: A thirty-five year longitudinal study. *Journal of Personality and Social Psychology*, 1988, *55*, 23–27.

24. Kamen-Siegel, L., Rodin, J., Seligman, M.E.P., & Dwyer, J. Explanatory style and cell-mediated immunity in elderly men and women. *Health Psychology*, 1991, *10*(4), 229–235.

25. Burns, M. O., & Seligman, M.E.P. Explanatory style across the lifespan: Evidence for stability over fifty-two years. *Journal of Personality and Social Psychology*, 1989, *56*, 471–477.

26. Bandura, A. Self-efficacy: Toward a unifying theory of behavioral change. *Psychological Review*, 1977, *84*(2), 191–215.

27. Wigal, J. K., Creer, T. L., & Kotses, H. The COPD Self-Efficacy Scale. *Chest*, 1991, *99*(5), 1192–1196.

28. Fitzgerald, S. T., Becker, D. M., Celkentano, D. D., Swank, R., & Brinker, J. Return to work after percutaneous transluminal coronary angioplasty. *American Journal of Cardiology*, 1989, *64*, 1108–1112.

29. Jensen, M. P., Turner, J. A., & Romano, J. M. Self-efficacy and outcome expectancies: Relationship to chronic pain coping strategies and adjustment. *Pain*, 1991, *44*(3), 263–269.

30. Cunningham, A. J., Lockwood, G. A., & Cunningham, J. A. A relationship between perceived self-efficacy and quality of life in cancer patients. *Patient Education and Counseling*, 1991, *17*(1), 71–78.

31. Bandura, A. Recycling misconceptions of perceived self-efficacy. *Cognitive Therapy and Research*, 1984, *8*, 231–255.

32. Taylor, S. E., & Brown, J. D. Illusion and well-being: A social psychological perspective on mental health. *Psychological Bulletin*, 1988, *103*, 193–210.

33. Rogers, C. The necessary and sufficient conditions of therapeutic personality change. *Journal of Consulting Psychology*, 1957, *21*, 95–103.

34. Bandura, A. Psychotherapy as a learning process. *Psychological Bulletin*, 1961, *58*, 143–159.

35. Omer, H., & Dar, R. Changing trends in three decades of psychotherapy research: The flight from theory into pragmatics. *Journal of Consulting and Clinical Psychology*, 1992, *60*, 88–93.

36. Beck, A. T. *Cognitive therapy and emotional disorders*. New York: New American Library, 1979.

37. Ellis, A. *Reason and emotion in psychotherapy*. New York: Lyle Stuart, 1962.

38. Ellis, A. The revised ABC's of Rational-Emotive Therapy (RET). *Journal of Rational-Emotive and Cognitive-Behavior Therapy*, 1991, *9*, 139–172.

39. Barlow, D. H. Long-term outcome for patients with panic disorder treated with cognitive-behavioral therapy. *Journal of Clinical Psychiatry*, 1990, *51* (suppl. A), 17–23.

40. Glasser, W. *Reality therapy: A new approach to psychiatry*. New York: Harper and Row, 1965.

41. Annon, J. S. *Behavioral treatment of sexual problems: Brief therapy*. New York: Harper and Row, 1976.

CHAPTER 5

Differences in Approach to Therapy between Primary Care Physicians and Psychiatrists

Obviously, there are major differences in both process and outcome between therapeutic interventions that are useful in primary care and traditional treatment as provided by psychiatrists or other mental health professionals. In this chapter, we explore these differences from several angles. After we look at patient expectations and reactions, we examine key aspects of the doctor-patient relationship. Next, we delineate the physician's investment in the patient's problems, and last, we recommend some specific therapeutic approaches that are particularly accessible in the therapeutic structure of primary care.

There is an old story about a secretary who went to work for a psychiatrist. After only a few short weeks, she resigned. When asked about why she quit the job, she reported to her friends:

I just couldn't win. He was always analyzing everything I did. If I got to work late, he said it was because I was hostile. When I got to work early, he wondered why I was anxious. Those days I got to work on time, he accused me of being compulsive.

Psychiatrists deal with a selected sample of humankind and learn what they know about people through this interaction with their patients.[1] On the other hand, primary care physicians see a different spectrum of patients presenting with undifferentiated problems. Psychiatrists are trained to look for psychopathology and to describe and classify the observed phenomena according to the appropriate category in the American Psychiatric Association's *Diagnostic and Statistical Manual of Mental Disorders, Third Edition, Revised* (DSM IIIR).[2] Devising a coherent theoretical explanation for the etiology of the symptom is usually part of the diagnostic process. Although in psychiatry the process of making a diagnosis is considered to be part of the treatment, this activity often intimidates the patient.

Regardless of other presenting problems, we believe it is part of the primary care physician's task to look for and treat patients' psychological distress. Psychosocial information should be gathered in a therapeutic manner, generating minimal, if any, additional stress for the patient.

PATIENT FACTORS

When a physician refers a patient for psychiatric treatment, whether to a mental health center or an individual practitioner, an acknowledgment of the appropriateness of the referral is generally followed by a request to have the patient call personally to set up the initial appointment for evaluation. It is accepted practice to consider the patient's taking action to seek help as the first positive step in the therapeutic process.

Referral Completions Are Not Automatic

Patients may be reluctant to admit that they need psychiatric treatment. The idea of defining themselves as mental patients is an impediment to seeking help. A study of CHAMPUS (Civilian Health and Medical Program of the Uniformed Services) utilization data showed that from 1982 to 1987, visits for outpatient behavioral health treatment increased by 35 percent, but psychiatrists' share of the market dropped from 36 percent to less than 22 percent, while treatment by primary care physicians doubled.[3] Even when referrals are made, patients often do not follow through.[4] Studies show that somewhere between 15 and 75 percent of patients who are referred for psychotherapy fail to keep initial appointments.[5] Those patients who are most resistant to completing referrals also make more medical visits, generally presenting with difficult-to-explain somatic symptoms.[6] Even when referral is successful, 30 to 60 percent of psychiatric patients in outpatient clinics drop out after only two to five sessions.[7] The reported attrition rate for private psychiatrists is almost as high.[8] Although there is some evidence that even a single session of psychotherapy can be very effective because of the ego-strengthening function that is implied in such brevity of treatment,[9] when patients are referred and it is not their idea, not only is the dropout rate high, but a study by C. L. Bowden and his colleagues found that about half the patients dropping out were feeling worse than when starting treatment.[10] It is therefore clear that referrals must be considered carefully.

Every employment application asks whether a person has been treated for a mental or emotional disorder. Once treatment by a psychiatrist or other mental health professional has been obtained, patients have two choices: to lie about their medical history or to identify themselves as mental patients. Mental patients are often seen as people who have been, or are, suffering from a type of disorder that carries a social stigma. Politicians whose histories reveal treatment for depression or other emotional conditions frequently become unacceptable to the public. It is not having been depressed that marks the flawed candidate; rather, it is a record of having been diagnosed and treated for an affective disorder, a mental disease. Although in some social circles comparing notes about what one's analyst has to say may be an accepted cocktail party sport, many middle- and lower-class patients are intimidated by the prospect of a psychiatric consultation.

Referrals Carry a Price Tag

Thomas Szasz is probably the best known critic of psychiatric labeling, but others have also pointed out that psychiatric labeling can sometimes be used in pejorative ways as a form of social coercion.[11–13] Certainly, when treatment is proposed before the patient has recognized the need, this can be initially deflating to the patient's already fragile self-esteem. The damage done to the sense of self-worth must first be restored before any positive therapeutic effect can take place.

It is not our intention to discount the value of psychiatry or psychotherapy as generally practiced. We are talking about treating a different patient population. Psychiatrists are specialists, trained to treat pepole who are seriously ill, and they may well be wasting their talents treating those who are less disturbed. Every case of chest pain does not warrant referral to a cardiologist. Even when referral is indicated, many patients experience serious impediments to receiving psychiatric treatment. Some of these obstacles are financial, some are logistical, and some have to do with the patient's reluctance to pursue treatment.[14] In spite of these factors, in our view, the primary care physician can make some very important and effective psychotherapeutic interventions. Furthermore, interventions that can be made by the primary care physician are different in several respects from those generally employed by psychiatrists. Let us look at some of these differences.

Treatment of Symptoms without Psychiatric Labeling

The first major difference is that the primary care physician can treat the patient's emotional reaction to whatever environmental stress is being experienced without labeling the patient as a mental patient. The patient receives the help that is asked for (relief of symptoms) and does not have to deal with the idea of seeing a "shrink." Actually, it has been our experience that after working with the primary care physician on the emotional overlay attached to various physical problems, patients will often request a referral to a mental health practitioner in order to extend their work of self-exploration. One of the most beneficial aspects of the therapeutic relationship with the primary care physician may be to prepare a patient for needed in-depth psychological treatment.[15] When patients start to experience the benefits that result from increased levels of personal awareness and control, they often overcome the reluctance to engage in psychiatric treatment. However, for many patients, the timely intervention by the physician restores normal functioning or even improves it to such an extent that the need for further treatment is precluded.

Small Doses of Therapy at a Time

The second major difference between psychotherapy as practiced by the primary care physician and the psychiatrist is that the patient receives small doses of psychotherapy as a part of the regular medical treatment. Every part of the interaction with the physician is potentially therapeutic. We have gone to great lengths to point out the amount of social power that is attributed to physicians. Because of this power, the personal exchanges, both verbal and nonverbal, that occur during the normal office visit can have a tremendous impact on the patient. Since each of us has an assumptive map, a mental representation of ourselves and our world based on personal history as we have recorded it (our story), our perception of ourselves can be influenced by how we see ourselves treated by significant others with whom we come in contact.[16–18] If our story line has been that we are not at all important and that no one cares about us, and if then, over time, we are repeatedly treated well by an important person, after some initial discounting and disbelief, we may change our assumptive map and edit our story. As the weight of evidence countering our preconceived notions of ourselves increases, we are able to make a change in our self-image. It may actually take the form of a paradigm shift (as explained in Chapter 1).

Small repeated doses of psychotherapeutic messages can actually be more effective, in terms of being heard, believed, and integrated, than a large dose at any one time, which may be more difficult to swallow and to assimilate. People learn by repetition over a period of time, but only when it is psychologically safe for them and when they are ready to learn.

The Patient Does Not Feel Rejected

The third major factor to be considered in providing psychological treatment personally rather than making a referral, even when appropriate, is that often the patient may interpret the referral as a rejection. When a patient's self-esteem is at a low point and the physician responds by apparently pushing him or her away to see someone else, this can confirm the patient's view that "no one can or wants to help." If the patient feels comfortable with and trusts the physician, there is a natural reluctance to start over with someone new. Being referred may play into the patient's self-deprecating pathology. In contrast, the physician's commitment to helping the patient is interpreted as an indication that the situation may be far less serious than the patient had assumed, and that he or she is worthy of help. Naturally, there will be times when a referral must be made because the physician feels overwhelmed. We will discuss this in Chapter 6.

The Body and the Mind Are Not Separated

Especially in the case of psychosomatic illness, rather than exploring all the organic elements before trying to convince the patient that psychological treatment is indicated, possibly making the patient feel inadequate and raising resistance, we treat physical and psychological components of the problem concurrently, which may, over time, convince the patient of the connection. This moves the patient in a positive direction toward combatting the underlying problem. Writing in the *New England Journal of Medicine* about functional gastrointestinal disorders, J. E. Lennard-Jones pointed out that it is essential to make the psychosocial history part of the initial inquiry "because a sudden interest in possible psychological factors after investigations have given normal results can arouse hostility in the patient."[19] Patients with psychosomatic problems who are referred to psychiatrists after a full exploration of their somatic complaints are notorious for seeking further medical opinions and proving refractory to psychiatric treatment.[20,21] Nor is the focus on purely organic problems necessarily benign. J. A. Harrington has pointed out that physicians often unwittingly precipitate or perpetuate emotional illness in patients. "Every psychiatrist sees patients who have been in the hands of three or four different specialists, all of whom are said to have told the patient something different. Such patients are hard to treat because they have lost faith."[22]

PHYSICIAN-PATIENT RELATIONSHIP

There are several distinct differences in the relationship between a patient and a primary care physician and a patient's relationship with a psychiatrist. The relationship with the primary care physician has continuity over time and is predicated on receiving whatever care is necessary to keep the patient healthy and functioning at optimum levels. Patients' emotional responses are a logical concomitant of their physical condition, and can be treated as such. In contrast, a relationship with a psychiatrist is specifically focused on eradicating some mental aberration or personality defect that is interfering with the patient's ability to function. This interference must be serious enough to overcome the patient's resistance to psychiatric treatment.

The Effects of the Psychiatric Evaluation Process

The initial psychiatric interview is structured so as to establish rapport with the patient while determining the etiology and extent of the patient's psychopathology. The psychiatrist will draw inferences from the behavior of the patient toward the interviewer. Many people, not only psychiatric patients, feel very uncomfortable when they know that they are being analyzed and evaluated. As a result, they may become defensive. Patients who are sharing information about various aspects of their functioning with the primary care physician may feel much more sanguine about disclosing personal information. This is especially true when the information is elicited in a series of visits.

Knowledge of the Family

The primary care physician often has had contact with various members of the patient's family. If the physician already knows the circumstances of a patient's family constellation and has had personal contact with the cast of characters involved, it becomes easier to empathize with the patient's experience. "Yes, I know Mary can be difficult to deal with. What can you do to make her feel more secure?" can be a powerful intervention coming from someone who has had dealings with Mary. The patient already trusts the physician, while the psychiatrist is an unknown who is suspect simply because of being cast in the role of psychiatrist, that is, as an evaluator and analyst.

The Gift of Caring

Perhaps the most crucial difference in the character of the primary care physician–patient relationship as opposed to the psychiatrist-patient relationship is that in the former, whatever psychological support is received is seen as a bonus. Although it may not always be intuitively obvious, there is a difference between psychological support that is received and that which is given. Unfortunately, we are often unreceptive to the positive messages that are directed at us. It is necessary to be open to hearing supportive statements. If self-esteem is exceedingly low, being told by another person that we are perfectly capable and will be all right is interpreted as false reassurance and a further confirmation that no one understands how dreadful we feel and how awful everything is.

A patient seeks psychiatric treatment in order to feel better. The patient expects the psychiatrist to be helpful and provide support. Instead, however, the psychiatrist may stress the patient in order to uncover pathology and obtain pertinent information so as to make an accurate diagnosis before prescribing pharmacological treatment. A physician is expected to provide medical diagnosis and treatment. Increasingly, studies are documenting the importance of physicians also providing for the socio-emotional needs of patients, with outcomes related not only to patient satisfaction but also to patients' subsequent health.[23-25]

Willard Gaylin, in his insightful book *Caring*, in which he discusses the importance of finding outlets to express the caring impulse (which is biologically programmed into the human species), makes the following point which helps to clarify the impact of the physician's interest in the psychological adjustment of the patient:[26]

We are generally touched by behavior that does more for us than we might have expected, [and] we are hurt by behavior that does less for us than we feel we have a right to expect. It is my feeling that in most senses of the usage, being touched and feeling hurt are polar phenomena. I am touched by your solicitude and hurt by your lack of solicitude; touched by the fact that despite a limited acquaintance, you remembered my birthday; hurt by the fact that even though you are my spouse, you had forgotten. If being touched is preeminently visualized in terms of the delighted and somewhat unexpected caring attitude of an individual, feeling hurt is the absence of such an attitude where we feel entitled to it and where we have every reason to expect it. In that sense we can see where we are more likely to be hurt by those who are close to us and touched by casual friends. In both cases there is an unexpected and unwarranted quality. Those who know us slightly honor us with their affection or attention, as those who know us well abuse us by failing to show that they care. To feel hurt occurs with a failure in caring. This, then, represents our vulnerability through attachments, or need to feel cared for. (p. 152)[26]

If the psychiatrist fails to give the expected support or appears to be cold and distant, the patient feels hurt. On the other hand, the physician's interest in the psychological aspect of the patient's condition is received as a gift of caring. The patient is generally touched, and this touch is healing. The bonus for the practicing physician is that the patient responds positively to the physician, increasing compliance and resulting in satisfaction for both parties.

THE PHYSICIAN'S VIEW OF THE PATIENT

The primary care physician has the special opportunity and responsibility to relate to the patient from both a physiological and a psychological perspective. Our approach to the patient is based on the assumption that the basic biological unit reacting to the demands from environment encompasses the body, mind, and spirit in dynamic interaction. This is hardly a revolutionary idea. Over thirty years ago, John Nemiah, a noted professor of psychiatry at Harvard Medical School, wrote as follows:

The practitioner who limits himself, whether it be to the confines of physiology or psychology, does so to the detriment of his patient. The art and practice of medicine requires on the part of the doctor an awareness that human life is a process lived in a constantly changing world which requires, for survival, a constantly adaptive response. . . . Rational treatment is based on helping the patient return to health by combatting the forces upsetting the balance—whether physiological or psychological.[27]

It is the role of the primary care practitioner to understand that the mind and body together constitute the complete unit of the individual, who is integrally influenced by stimuli from the external and internal environments. By engaging the patient psychologically, while at the same time "laying on hands" in the process of examining the body, the physician has the unique power to help the patient correct the disturbance in homeostasis that has precipitated the visit to the doctor.

The psychiatrist, on the other hand, is more narrowly focused on the psychodynamics of the personality. By putting the emphasis largely on the mind instead of the body, the reverse split achieves no more productive result than looking for pathology only in tissues and organs. The tendency to specialize fragments a person's care. It may well be that fragmentation in the fabric of our society, or the structure of the patient's family or work situation, is precipitating the illness in the first place. The changing model of health care (see Chapter 1) requires that the body, mind, and spirit be integrated, since a demoralized patient can maintain neither physical nor mental health.

Thus, the major difference in the approach of the primary care physician, in contrast to that of the psychiatrist, is to help the patient make a more comfortable adaptation to the existing environment, without getting into the specific technicalities of the patient's personality structure, defense mechanisms, or even family dynamics, since these are difficult to change (except in a crisis). Instead, the physician focuses on the reaction that the person is experiencing to perceived stress from the environment. This reaction may be anxiety, depression, cr any number of physical complaints. By providing support and focusing the patient on constructive action, the physician helps enhance the patient's self-esteem and enables him or her to function at a more productive level.

THE PHYSICIAN'S VIEW OF THE PROBLEM

Perhaps the most important factor to keep in mind when doing psychotherapy in the fifteen minute framework is that the problem belongs to the patient. The process of medical education predisposes the physician to take on and solve problems. The first step in problem solving is to accurately define the problem. In this case, the problem must be defined as the patient's reaction. The physician cannot afford to get intimately involved in the details of the situation, understand the exact etiology, or even comprehend the specific effect of the circumstances on all the people involved. The physician does not have the responsibility to solve the patient's problem. Rather, the physician's responsibility is limited to supporting the patient so that he or she can identify the specific problem that may be underlying the experienced stress, making the patient aware that this problem is contributing to the feeling of illness that he or she is experiencing, and encouraging the patient to explore potential solutions for the problem.

Mrs. K., a 30-year-old Asian mother of a 3-month-old boy, is in the office for the third time in two weeks. She is complaining about feeling tired all the time, with headaches and some dizziness. She says that her body feels strange. On previous visits it has been determined that she is not anemic. Mrs. K. is delighted with her baby. She reports that her husband is very supportive and concerned and that her mother is living with them and helping to care for the child. As he leaves the room after an uneventful exam, the physician wonders what is really going on. He speculates whether having her mother there is making the patient feel competitive for the baby's attention. Perhaps the life-style change triggered by the birth is causing a conflict. Armed with specific theories, the doctor reenters the exam room. "Mrs. K., I really am sorry that you feel so bad. I found nothing on exam to cause me any concern. Still, there is something that is causing your symptoms. What do you think it might be?"

At first, the patient looks at him blankly and says nothing. The physician inquires, "What is going on in your life?" Hesitantly, the patient discloses that her mother is planning to return to Hong Kong and leave her to manage the baby alone. The physician asks how she feels about that. She admits that she is afraid to function independently. She does not want to be cut off from her mother and the outside world and feels inadequate to care for her son. The doctor explains how anxiety can produce physical symptoms. He then focuses on supporting the patient, accepting her feelings, and asking her to think about what skills she must learn while her mother is still there. Another appointment is made. The physician's plan is to enhance her sense of self-efficacy in an effort to convince her that she is capable of performing as a mother (see Chapter 4). He will motivate her by emphasizing how important this is to her and focusing on how she can gain the necessary skill and confidence. He will also continue to be there for her and provide support and advice.

When the physician communicates to the patient the expectation that the patient, having identified the problem, is expected to find some constructive resolution, a positive message is conveyed. The physician agrees to be part of the process and make suggestions for strategies that can be employed, but it is clear to both parties that the patient has the responsibility to deal with the problem (which, by definition, is expected to yield to resolution).

Focus on the Here and Now

Our approach, which focuses almost exclusively on the present, is very different from the usual psychiatric focus on the past. Patients are much less concerned about understanding the origins of their complaints than about getting relief in the present and having something positive to anticipate. Mrs. K. is not interested in exploring why she is so dependent on her mother. Rather, she needs to feel that she can manage her life and handle her child care responsibilities.

There have been several influential advocates for physicians engaging patients in psychotherapeutic relationships.[20,22] Most notable is Michael Balint, who taught physicians to look at themselves and their interactions with patients to determine the therapeutic or countertherapeutic effects, based on a psychoanalytic orientation. The seminal volume is Balint's *The Doctor, His Patient and the Illness*.[20] This text has helped many physicians understand some of the dynamics of the therapeutic encounter that interfere or promote the patient's response to treatment. This text and the subsequent volume, *Six Minutes for the Patient* (which was edited by E. Balint and J. S. Norell and which promotes making one really insightful comment in each medical interview), underscored the importance of understanding the psychodynamics of both the patients' and the physicians' personality structures from an analytical orientation.[28] Balint suggested that in order for physicians to deal effectively with patients' psychological problems, a change in their personality may be required.[20] We are far less ambitious, however. We suggest that physicians only need to engage in specific behaviors, since changing behavior (to include cognitive processes) is much more feasible than changing personality structures.

Castelnuovo-Tedesco, in *The Twenty Minute Hour*, also encouraged physicians to address patients' emotional difficulties as an integral part of the medical interview in order to enhance the value of treatment.[29] This author suggested that primary care physicians need to understand about psychotherapeutic treatment and do brief therapy with selected patients. Our approach is to integrate the emotional aspects routinely with all patients. Castelnuovo-Tedesco suggested that brief therapy needs to be planned in order to deal systematically with the interpersonal aspects of the patient's life. This implies a comprehensive and accurate analysis of the dynamics involved. Unfortunately, studies have not borne out the efficacy of this treatment approach by "general practitioners."[30] Many physicians may mistakenly cite the failure of this type of therapy in general medical practice as a justification for not engaging their patients psychotherapeutically. Our approach does not require detailed knowledge of a wide range of emotional disorders. It does not require an understanding of the etiology of the patient's discomfort. It does require the ability to recognize the symptoms and to provide psychological support for the patient's healthy functioning mechanisms.

Castelnuovo-Tedesco saw classical psychoanalytical treatment as ultimately the most effective psychotherapeutic modality.[29] Our approach integrates several newer techniques coming from the crisis intervention, stress management, cognitive, behavioral, and existential literature. Abreaction and insight have unfortunately not been shown to be more effective in combating psychological distress than have the direct approaches that we are promoting.[31]

The last point made by Castelnuovo-Tedesco is that when physicians do twenty minute therapy, patients do not develop transference because of the limited time involved.[29] It is our contention, quite to the contrary, that patients bring to the physician a highly developed and integrated transference relationship, consisting of expectations designed for benevolent authority figures. This power, which is ceded by the patient, can be used to enhance the therapeutic relationship.

Focus on the Patient's Strength

The essence of supportive therapy is to restore patients' faith in their own capacity to take charge of their lives in a productive and satisfying way. Every difficult situation is a variation on some previous situation. If patients had not survived these earlier traumas, they would not be presenting themselves at this time. It is the physician's job to remind the patient about having overcome past obstacles. This enhances the patient's sense of coherence.[32] Then, together they can factor out those techniques previously found successful. If patterns have consistently been destructive, then patients must be encouraged to make some small change in the way that they would normally react.

Each of us has a rather limited behavioral repertoire. In any situation, there is some way in which we naturally respond because that is what we have learned to do under those circumstances. We tell ourselves the story that this will work. When we do not get the expected or desired result, we often redouble our efforts and keep doing whatever we are doing, only longer and harder. We have what psychologists call a limited *response set*. The physician can suggest to the patient that a small change be made in the current behavioral pattern, with the expectation that there will then be a change in the resulting outcome. This change can be expected to be positive. Again, where the psychiatrist might focus on exploring why and how these behavioral patterns developed, we prefer to focus on what the patient gets by maintaining this behavior in the here and now. If this turns out to be nothing, or just pain, then we encourage him or her to change the behavioral repertoire. We specifically encourage the patient to act in some new and different ways, to develop a broader response set, and to monitor the result.

Involving the Patient's Family

The primary care physician, having a special relationship with the patient and the patients' family, is free to invite other family members to work with the patient in addressing whatever problem is most disturbing. Where the analyst is invested in helping the patient understand reactions to significant others, we focus on making their communication more open and direct, helping patients express feelings and ask for what they want.

We provide the knowledge that patients will not always get what they want but that by identifying their desires and stating them, the probability of getting gratification is enhanced. We encourage patients to explore options with their families and we teach strategies for conflict resolution and problem solving. It is important to make everyone aware that a problem that is experienced by one member of a family has an impact on all other family members. We charge them to discuss the matter, which also means listening to each other, and then to report back to us.

THERAPEUTIC APPROACH

The most important aspect of the therapeutic relationship is the physician's show of concern. This means concern for the patient both as a person and as a member of a family. The physician can show concern through the use of a variety of techniques.

Empathy

Carl Rogers suggested that in order for constructive personality change to take place, the following conditions need to be met and to continue over time.[33]

1. Two persons need to be in a psychological relationship, with one person specifically dedicated to helping the other. The physician, in this case, should experience "unconditional positive regard" for the patient.

2. The person in the therapeutic role experiences an empathic understanding of the patient's internal frame of reference and is able to communicate this understanding along with the positive regard to the patient, "at least to a minimum degree."

Physicians need to make a personal commitment to help patients cope with the emotional aspects of their lives. This commitment may entail an adjustment in the map of what it means to be a good physician. We have been told that we are redefining the job of primary care physician. That is probably true, and it is what the public is demanding. Making the choice to engage the patient concerning life issues establishes the psychological relationship that Carl Rogers specifies to be the first prerequisite for therapeutic change. It also demonstrates the positive regard that the physician has for the patient. This commitment becomes actualized by the physician inquiring how the patient is feeling about what is going on in his or her life, establishing the context of the visit, and redefining the limits of the physician's interest. Having determined how the patient feels and what he or she is most concerned about, the physician communicates an understanding of the patient's affective state through making an empathic response. Thus, Rogers's second condition has now been met.

If this process is repeated during every patient visit, the cumulative effect can be positive change in the patient's self-image and ability to cope constructively.

Exploration of Options

The second basic technique that physicians can incorporate into a brief office visit is to ask patients about their options. In many cases, people who are caught in a painful emotional situation are not aware that there are always options. Naturally, each potential choice has consequences, but awareness of the power to choose (even if it only affects our attitude) makes us feel less impotent and overwhelmed.

In the ealry 1970s, Stanley Milgram performed an experiment to determine people's response to authority.[34] An experimenter demanded that subjects behave in such a manner as to put another person at great risk. The experiment was disguised as a learning task, and the subjects were ordered to apply shock to a stooge, who pretended to be adversely affected by this treatment. Subjects routinely followed orders, though they appeared uncomfortable, especially after passing into a range of shock marked "danger." A movie was made in which the interactions between subject, experimenter, and stooge could be observed. Although most subjects performed as directed when they were simply told, "You must continue with the experiment," in those cases where the experimenter added, "You have no choice," subjects invariably stopped, thought, and then said something to the effect that of course they had a choice: They could walk out. Moreover, then they did walk out. It seemed that just having the word *choice* mentioned made people aware of the fact that there were options.

Most people, when looking back on what seem to be serious mistakes made during turning points in their lives, will say that it never occurred to them that there were other options. Of course, there are always options if we know to look for them. It is extremely helpful to remind patients that they always have choices, one of which is not to decide at that particular time; to choose not to choose, at least for the present. Having the physician suggest that there are options, that the patient go home and list them and then come back to discuss things further, is a powerful therapeutic technique.

Encouragement of New Behavior

Another powerful technique is to encourage patients to change certain behavioral patterns and engage in potentially more productive interactions with others. Although we discourage giving specific advice (the physician should not take responsibility for solving the patient's problem and thus give the patient the opportunity to sabotage), the options of taking time out, deciding not to decide, expressing feelings and asking for what is wanted, keeping a diary to document periods of heightened stress, noting eating or sleeping patterns, and starting a regular exercise program are all strategies that promote new behavior. Once patients become aware of their power to change their behavior and receive subsequent reinforcement from the environment, these positive changes will be sustained. The patient's verbal commitment to the physician that certain new ways of acting will be adopted in specific situations will give the patient a powerful push in new and constructive directions.

Providing Explanations

The physician's acceptance of the patient's difficulties in a particular situation can be a great source of relief. The physician makes what have been called ubiquity statements. These pronouncements point out that people who are undergoing situations similar to what the patient is experiencing will generally react by feeling overwhelmed and acting in potentially destructive ways. Stating that under these circumstances, anybody would feel very angry, or that it is common to want to walk out and let the other people cope with the mess makes the patient feel more competent and normal. When patients understand that under certain circumstances (e.g., unemployment, bereavement, birth of a child, separation, divorce, illness, promotion, moving, graduating, child launching, etc.), people are naturally more vulnerable and easily go on tilt, they will start to feel more comfortable with their own reactions. Once they feel more secure that their responses are within normal limits, it will be much easier for them to control their behavior. Sometimes, it may be necessary to explain to patients that children, spouses, or employers also have certain needs and that it is necessary for the patient to come to terms with unwanted changes in the interpersonal environment. It is important to reassure patients that it is not necessary to like these situations. It is only necessary to make adjustments and deal with them. Conversely, patients need to learn that sometimes they can have strong emotional reactions to people or events without having to *do anything* about them. This is very freeing.

Anticipatory Guidance

One of the most promising therapeutic opportunities available to the primary care physician concerns the ability to give anticipatory guidance. Anticipating problems allows people to devise strategies to cope with them before they arise. It also gives them time to readjust their attitudes, if necessary. When situations are expected rather than presenting as a shock, coping behavior will be more appropriate (meaning on a more mature level). Instead of saying, "Isn't this awful?" the patient will realize, "Goodness, I feel just like the doctor said I might. Isn't that interesting."

Since the physician sees the patient over time, anticipatory guidance about expected life-cycle crises or other situations can be incorporated into routine visits for school physicals, such as "Have you thought about how you're going to feel when Mary is in school all day?" or, "How do you suppose you're going to feel once Sam, Jr., goes off to college?" During prenatal visits, the physician can say: "You know, having a baby is going to change many aspects of your life. You and Henry need to carefully plan in order to assure private time for the two of you." During general physicals, the physician can comment: "This promotion is going to involve a lot of travel, as I hear it. Have you discussed with Debbie how this will affect your relationship?" "Now that you are going back to school, I would encourage you to plan to spend quality time with each of the children regularly. You do not need to feel guilty about spending less time, if you make sure that they each get some direct, positive attention daily." "Jane, now that you are going to be alone, you may find it very difficult at first. You may have trouble sleeping and not have much appetite. I expect that there will be times that you will be overcome by angry feelings for Charles. That is all normal, although right this instant that probably doesn't make you feel any better."

Making Contact at an Early Phase of the Problem

Perhaps the most significant difference between the approach of the primary care physician and that of the psychiatrist is that the physician sees the patient much earlier in the process of a developing problem, usually for medical symptoms. This can be of primary importance. In the case of recurrent depressions, for example, early interventions with a combination of pharmacotherapy and psychotherapy have been shown to shorten the overall length of the depressive episode by four to five months.[35] Panic attacks, whether in conjunction with or independent of depression, are also commonly treated pharmacologically with adjunctive "talk therapy." Although medication for this disorder is available, starting with behavioral therapy or other nonpharmacologic treatment is often recommended.[36]

Identifying problems in an early stage has other advantages. Attempts that we make to solve a problem often become more of a problem than the original difficulty.[37] Drinking to forget our troubles or to relieve anxiety, running away, making threats that are taken seriously, holding feelings in, setting unenforceable limits, and engaging in power struggles are only a few examples. The physician's intervention at a time when the situation is still fluid can often prevent dire consequences (primary prevention), reduce the severity of consequences (secondary prevention), or at least prevent further complications (tertiary prevention).

THE EFFECTS OF BRIEF SESSIONS

The most obvious difference between our type of therapy and the usual fifty minute therapeutic hour is the time limitation that we have imposed. Yes, it is beneficial to hold encounters with the patient to a quarter of an hour. When only a few minutes are spent during the regular medical interview to focus on the psychological aspect of the patient's situation, only one or two points can be made. Our experience has been that this has a very powerful positive effect. Since persons under stress have a limited capacity to concentrate and to process new information, dealing with only one or two issues has the beneficial effect of preventing informational overload. It also tends to make the problem seem less complex.

Setting Priorities

When patients become familiar with the physician's therapeutic style and expect the inquiry, another benefit is achieved. Patients learn to arrange issues in order of priority. This process of organization is helpful and therapeutic for them. It forces them to evaluate problems in terms of severity and urgency, choosing the particular issues to be brought up at each session. In looking forward to reporting about their experiences since the previous visit (while considering the limits of time), patients are forced to summarize and focus on the high points. It is always important for the physician to inquire about successes as well as failures and disappointments.

Homework Is Essential

Homework is an essential part of the therapeutic fifteen minute hour, since the brief time available must be used most efficiently. By giving the patient specific assignments, self-help and new behavior are encouraged, enhancing his or her self-esteem and sense of competence. For example, patients can be asked to make lists of options, resources, advantages, disadvantages, arguments, things that are bothersome, previous accomplishments, or goals to be achieved. Patients can also be asked to keep diaries documenting periods of being upset, diets, sleep patterns, examples of successful and unsuccessful coping, the best and worst thing that happened each day, ongoing problems, and potential solutions for these problems. Patients can be asked to do one new thing each day.

The effectiveness of homework assignments is enhanced by making contracts with patients certifying their agreement to carry out the assigned tasks. The joint expectation that the patient will return with the assignment successfully completed maintains the therapeutic connection to the physician between visits. The physician's interest and concern are clearly demonstrated, as is the physician's faith in the patient's resolve to tackle the assignment. Assignments need to be simple and feasible. In this way the physician supports the patient's two essential needs: personal competence and feeling connected to other human beings.

Promoting Independence

Brief sessions are also beneficial because they maximize the patients' own resources and minimize their dependence on the physician while providing a source of support. Patients feel more confident having a partner in their search for a resolution to their problems, especially when this partner is someone who cares enough to follow and encourage their progress.

MAKING REFERRALS

Once patients become aware of some of their inter- or intrapersonal difficulties in certain situations, they often feel that they would like to explore their psychological functioning to a greater depth. Perhaps the behavior of one family member makes the family aware that the dynamics that have become established are not constructive and that family therapy (restructuring) is indicated. Perhaps the physician feels that a particular patient would benefit from seeing a practitioner for lengthier sessions to work through some deep-seated conflicts. Perhaps an unresolved grief reaction needs an in-depth exploration of the elements of a complex relationship. In all these cases, the physician has the option of referring the patient after first reassuring him or her that the physician will continue to serve as the primary care provider and will continue to be concerned with what is happening to the patient.

Consultations with psychiatrists and other mental health providers can be extremely helpful for the physician, both in treating patients and in determining the need for referral. In one study of patients with somatization disorders undergoing ongoing management by physicians, one psychiatric consultation reduced the quarterly health care costs of the treatment group by over 53 percent.[38] However, T. C. Rosenthal and his colleagues have confirmed our experience that the most appropriate and fruitful referrals are made by those physicians who regularly incorporate counseling into their practice.[14] In their study, whether patients attended more than one therapy session was related to the number of visits to the primary care physician prior to the referral. In other words, if the patient had a solid relationship with the referring doctor, he or she was more likely to overcome the obstacles and the stress related to entering psychotherapy.[14]

We interpret these findings as confirming the importance of trust and continuity in the therapeutic encounter. When making referrals, the physician must adequately prepare the patient for the treatment, choose a practitioner known to be competent and sincere, and express positive expectations to the patient regarding the outcome of therapy. Then, if the physician and therapist establish ongoing communication, the prognosis is excellent.

In summary, the physician's commitment to the patient is always to provide the care that can be provided within the physician's expertise. The ability to provide pyschological support, as we have outlined it, is well within most physicians' expertise and can be expected to yield effective results. By refraining from analyzing or explaining the origin of behavior and by helping the patient focus on managing reactions to situations, the physician's approach is quite different from that of a traditional psychiatrist. However, it is highly effective.

SUMMARY

Differences between the therapeutic approaches of the primary care physician and the psychiatrist lie in the areas of patient expectations and reactions, the nature of the therapeutic relationship, and the physician's investment in the patient's problem.

Defining themselves as mental patients carries costs that patients do not incur when treated by their physician. Symptoms can be treated without psychiatric labels. Small doses of therapy at a time may prove quite effective. The patient does not feel rejected, and body and mind are not separated.

The relationship with the primary care physician has continuity, rapport is established nonjudgmentally, and knowledge of the family enhances the physician's effectiveness. The physician's support and interest are seen as a bonus. The primary care physician, in contrast to the psychiatrist, helps the patient make a more comfortable adaptation to the existing environment without getting into the specific technicalities of the patient's personality structure, specific defense mechanisms, or even family dynamics, since these are difficult to change.

The physician contracts to help the patient identify specific problems and expects that he or she will find some constructive resolution. This conveys a positive message. Attention is focused almost exclusively in the here and now, on the patient's strengths, and involves the family. The therapeutic approach consists of using empathy, exploring options, encouraging new behavior, providing explanations, and giving anticipatory guidance. Probably the most significant difference between the approach of the primary care physician and that of the psychiatrist is that the physician sees the patient much earlier in the process of a developing problem, usually for medical symptoms.

The time limit of the sessions helps the patient to set priorities, necessitates homework, and minimizes the patient's dependence on the physician. Referral remains an option and can be facilitated by the preparatory process.

REFERENCES

1. McHugh, P. R., & Slavney, P. R. *The perspectives of psychiatry.* Baltimore, Md.: Johns Hopkins University Press, 1983.

2. American Psychiatric Association. *Diagnostic and statistical manual of mental disorders, third edition, revised.* Washington, D.C.: American Psychiatric Association, 1987.

3. Behavioral Health Industries, Inc. cited by Buie, J. Psychiatry loses edge on market, new study shows. *APA Monitor*, July 1989, p. 30.

4. Carpenter, P. J., Morrow, G. R., Del Gaudio, A. C., & Ritzler, B. A. Who keeps the first outpatient appointment? *American Journal of Psychiatry*, 1981, *138*, 102–105.

5. Rosenberg, C., & Rayes, A. *Keeping patients in psychiatric treatment.* Cambridge, Mass.: Ballinger, 1976.

6. Olfson, M. Primary care patients who refuse specialized mental health services. *Archives of Internal Medicine*, 1991, *151*, 129–132.

7. Baekland, I., & Lundwall, L. Dropping out of treatment. A critical review. *Psychological Bulletin*, 1975, *82*, 738–783.

8. Koss, M. P. Length of psychotherapy for clients seen in private practice. *Journal of Consulting Clinical Psychology*, 1979, *47*, 210–212.

9. Rockwell, K.W.J., & Pinkerton, R. S. Single-session psychotherapy. *American Journal of Psychotherapy*, 1982, *36*, 32–40.

10. Bowden, C. L., Schoenfeld, L. S., & Adams, R. L. A correlation between dropout status and improvement in a psychiatric clinic. *Hospital and Community Psychiatry*, 1980, *31*, 192–195.

11. Szasz, T. S. The myth of mental illness. *American Psychologist*, 1960, *15*, 113–118.

12. Halleck, S. L. *The politics of therapy*. New York: Science House, 1971.

13. Gorenstein, E. E. Debating mental illness: Implications for science, medicine, and social policy. *American Psychologist*, 1984, *39*, 40–49.

14. Rosenthal, T. C., Shiffner, J. M., Lucas, C., & DeMaggio, M. Factors involved in successful psychotherapy referral in rural primary care. *Family Medicine*, 1991, *23*, 527–530.

15. Larson, D. L., Nguyen, T. D., Green, R. S., & Attkisson, C. C. Enhancing the utilization of outpatient mental health services. *Community Mental Health Journal*, 1983, *19*, 305–320.

16. Angyal, A. *Neurosis and treatment: A holistic theory*. New York: Wiley, 1965.

17. Bandler, R., & Grinder, J. *The structure of magic I: A book about language and therapy*. Palo Alto, Calif.: Science and Behavior Books, 1975.

18. Bateson, G. *Steps to an ecology of mind*. New York: Ballentine Books, 1972.

19. Lennard-Jones, J. E. Functional gastrointestinal disorders. *New England Journal of Medicine*, 1983, *308*, 431–435.

20. Balint, M. *The doctor, his patient and the illness*. New York: International Universities Press, 1957.

21. Adler, G. The physician and the hypochondriacal patient. *New England Journal of Medicine*, 1981, *304*, 1394–1396.

22. Harrington, J. A. Some principles of psychotherapy in general practice. *Lancet*, 1957, *1*, 799–801.

23. Hall, J. A., Roter, D. L., & Katz, N. R. Meta-analysis of correlates of provider behavior in medical encounters. *Medical Care*, 1988, *26*, 657–675.

24. Kaplan, S. H., Greenfield, S., & Ware, J. E., Jr. Assessing the effects of physician-patient interactions on the outcomes of chronic disease. *Medical Care*, 1989, *27*, S110–S127.

25. Bertakis, K. D., Roter, D., & Putman, S. M. The relationship of physician medical interview style to patient satisfaction. *Journal of Family Practice*, 1991, *32*, 175–181.

26. Gaylin, W. *Caring*. New York: Knopf, 1976.

27. Nemiah, J. C. *Foundations of psychopathology*. New York: Oxford University Press, 1961, p. 289.

28. Balint, E., & Norell, J. S. (Eds.). *Six minutes for the patient: Interactions in general practice consultation*. London: Tavistock, 1973.

29. Castelnuovo-Tedesco, P. *The twenty minute hour*. Boston: Little, Brown, 1965.

30. Brodaty, H., & Andrews, G. Brief psychotherapy in family practice: A controlled prospective intervention trial. *British Journal of Psychiatry*, 1983, *143*, 11–19.

31. Epstein, N. B., & Vlok, L. A. Research on the results of psychotherapy: A summary of evidence. *American Journal of Psychiatry*, 1981, *138*, 1027–1035.

32. Antonovsky, A. *Health, stress, and coping*. San Francisco: Jossey-Bass, 1979.

33. Rogers, C. R. The necessary and sufficient conditions of therapeutic personality change. *Journal of Consulting Psychology*, 1957, *21*, 95–103.

34. Milgrim, S. Behavioral study of obedience. *Journal of Abnormal and Social Psychology*, 1963, *67*, 371–378.

35. Kupfer, D. J., Frank, E., & Perel, J. M. The advantage of early treatment intervention in recurrent depression. *Archives of General Psychiatry*, 1989, *46*, 771–775.

36. Ferentz, K. Panic disorders and agoraphobia. *Postgraduate Medicine*, 1990, *88*, 185–190.

37. Watzlawick, P., Weakland, J., & Fisch, R. *Change: Principles of problem formation and problem resolution.* New York: Norton, 1974.

38. Smith, G. R., Jr., Monson, R. A., & Ray, D. C. Psychiatric consultation in somatization disorder: A randomized controlled study. *New England Journal of Medicine*, 1986, *314*, 1407–1413.

CHAPTER 6

The Structure of Therapy

Are we really suggesting that the patient's psychological needs should be addressed during *every* patient visit? Yes, we are. Just as there are recognized advantages to periodic health screening from an organic perspective, many benefits accrue from assessing a patient's emotional status as part of each visit. Moreover, by using our technique, the patient's psychological needs can be addressed in an efficient and effective manner.

Imagine a reasonably sensitive and specific screening test that takes about a minute, uses no supplies, is noninvasive, is generally acceptable to patients, has no harmful side effects, may pick up potentially serious problems in an early, treatable stage, and can be expected to yield *at least* 30 percent positive results.[1] Additionally, imagine that using the test might provide beneficial results for the patient, that is, might be therapeutic. Would you use such a test regularly? We think so.

DEFINING THE STRUCTURE OF THERAPY

Regardless of the unique opportunity inherent in the doctor-patient relationship, and the importance of the patient's emotional needs, these needs must be handled in a time-effective manner. The psychosocial aspect of patients' problems must be determined and the psychotherapeutic intervention must be organized into the regular fifteen minute medical visit. The therapeutic goal is to help patients reorganize some small aspect of their self-concept or behavior in a more comfortable, productive, or, at minimum, less destructive manner. The healing grows out of the physician-patient relationship, a personal relationship between the doctor and the patient that has already been established. As we discussed earlier, the physician has an inherent potential to influence the patient. Therefore, the physician is in an excellent position to apply psychotherapeutic principles.

The specific treatment attempts to modify patients' images of themselves, their problems, and their options by adjusting some aspect of their *assumptive worldview*, the story they tell themselves about the way things are. Good interviewing techniques, a caring manner, and genuine interest demonstrated by paying serious attention and concentrating on the patient's problems pave the way toward establishing a psychologically therapeutic milieu. In the process, patients feel supported and less stressed, and are able to raise their level of self-esteem as well as reengage their healthier coping styles.[2] The physician not only gains a healthier and more reasonable patient, but by applying this technique, with its small investment of time, on the occasion of each patient visit, the physician may save a tremendous amount of time in some future encounter. If a patient's unaddressed psychological needs are allowed to compound over time, they can become overwhelming. The patient's expressed needs at that time may overextend the physician's resources to deal with a monumental problem.

DETERMINING THE CONTEXT OF THE VISIT

Optimally, every physical complaint or office visit should be seen in the context of the patient's total life situation. This means that in addition to descriptions of presenting symptoms, which may well represent a response to family or situational stress, the physician must determine what is going on in the patient's life as part of the history of present illness.

Nowadays, most primary care physicians organize their charts around the problem-oriented medical record.[3] Problems are listed and notes are arranged in SOAP fashion. We are all familiar with this system, which classifies progress notes into subjective, objective, assessment, and plan elements.

In order to understand patients' problems in the context of their total life situation, primary care physicians need a larger concept of SOAP.[4] The total package of patient assessment requires the determination of the background situation, the patient's affect, what is troubling the patient, and how the patient is handling the stress, and is followed by an empathic response.[5]

BATHE

The acronym BATHE connotes the protocol to determine the context of the visit.

B Stands for Background. A simple question, "What is going on in your life? will elicit the context of the patient's visit.

A Stands for Affect (the feeling state). Questions such as "How do you feel about that?" or "What's your mood?" allows the patient to report the current feeling state.

T Stands for Trouble. The question, "What about the situation troubles you the most?" helps both the physician and the patient focus on the situation's subjective meaning.

H Stands for Handling. The answer to, "How are you handling that?" gives an assessment of functioning.

E Stands for Empathy. The statement, "That must be very difficult for you," legitimizes the patient's reaction.

Following the information gathering, the empathic response reassures the patient that the physician has understood the situation and that the patient's response is reasonable, given the circumstances. This is all that is minimally required to make the patient feel supported.

By BATHEing the patient early in the visit, an effective and efficient psychotherapeutic intervention is structured into every patient encounter. The context of the visit has been incorporated into the session, and there is closure. A basic screening for anxiety or depressive disorders has also been accomplished. The physician then proceeds with a further medical history and the appropriate physical examination. If necessary, additional support and provision for follow-up is structured into the later part of the visit.

A 34-year-old woman, who had been a patient at the family practice center for about a year, presented in the office complaining about a vaginal discharge. She appeared to be quite agitated. The physician inquired about what was going on in her life, and the patient started to cry.

"I just found out that my husband has been having an affair with my oldest sister for the past year and a half."

"How do you feel about that?" (The physician felt a little foolish. It seemed like an inane question to ask under the circumstances—but he really did not know what else to ask.)

"I feel angry. I have mood swings. I go up and down. I also feel depressed."

The physician then asked what about the situation troubled the patient the most. She replied, "I have two children. They are two and five, and I really don't want to be a single parent."

(The physician was surprised. He would have expected her to be most troubled because of the familial involvement or the time frame.)

"How are you handling it?" was his final question.

The patient felt that she was handling things very badly. She was angry and did a lot of shouting at her husband. She also added that she was afraid that the children were starting to be affected and that she did not want that to happen.

The physician was taken aback by this history. Still, he managed to respond, "That sounds like a horrendous situation."

"Yes, it is," said the patient, who visibly relaxed.

"Why don't we examine you now and find out what we can do about your vaginal discomfort," said the physician, "and then we'll talk some more."

SUPPORTING THE PATIENT

In Chapter 2 we defined social support as a psychological mechanism that provides positive information to the individual about his or her interaction with other people. Social support has been shown to be critical in mitigating the effects of various stressors.[6] Social support can be seen as encompassing one or more of the following: (1) an expression of positive affect; (2) an endorsement of the person's behavior, perception or expressed views; (3) giving symbolic or material aid; and (4) giving the opportunity to express feelings in an accepting atmosphere.

Gerald Caplan has described social support as the outgrowth of an enduring relationship.[7] The significant elements of social support stressed by Caplan include (1) helping the individual to mobilize his or her own resources, (2) helping in sharing tasks, (3) helping by providing information or guidance to facilitate handling of the situation, and (4) providing material supplies or skills to affect the situation.

It is clear that by BATHEing the patient at every visit, many of the above criteria will be satisfied. Interest and positive affect have been expressed, and feelings have been accepted. Information is gathered that helps both patient and physician understand the patient's reaction, and the diagnosis becomes a large part of the cure. Clearly defining the problem helps focus the patient and the physician on the resources necessary to reach resolution.

Dealing with Multiple Problems

Often the physician encounters multiple problems in the course of interviewing a patient. Here, again, having a practical structure for dealing with the problems is helpful in keeping the physician focused and meeting the patient's needs. If an unexpected emotional response occurs during the interview, the physician finds out what is going on, explores the issue using three questions, and effects closure with an empathic statement. In this way, a simple technique, sequentially applied, can effectively be used to handle complex situations. The following case, reported by one of our senior residents, is illustrative of the principles we are promoting.

A new patient, a 38-year-old woman, presented with multiple concerns, including contraception, vaginal itching, dyspareunia, and frequent headaches. On further questioning, she was found to be a working mother of three teenage children, who was widowed six years previously and had remarried one year ago. Family history was positive for hypertension and diabetes in the grandparents, and for multiple sclerosis in her mother. The mother was currently 56 and had been in a nursing home for twelve years. At this point in the interview, the patient appeared tearful but attempted to suppress the tears. I asked her what was going on, and then used the rest of the BATHE technique. The patient started to cry, saying that she had not cried for years about her mother. I asked her what her mother had been like. She stated that she had always admired her mother's energy and unselfishness, which was why she felt so guilty about having her in the nursing home. I empathized, and we went on. Subsequently, I found out that her mother's diagnosis had been made at the age of 38. I asked her what she thought might be causing her headaches. She said I shouldn't think she was crazy, but she had considered whether it might not be multiple sclerosis (MS). I supported her by telling her that this was a natural concern under the circumstances and that I would do a thorough evaluation in that regard.

At this point, about ten minutes into the interview, I pointed out that she had come with quite a few concerns, and asked her which one she wanted most to deal with in this visit. She stated that she was most concerned about her vaginal itch. After some routine questions regarding the genitourinary (GU) system, I asked how this condition was affecting her sexuality, to which she replied that she and her husband had not slept together in six months. She stated that she suspected him of having an affair. Six months ago also corresponded to the anniversary of her first husband's death. I asked a background question about the circumstances of her marriage, and again finished the BATHE sequence. I then asked her to prepare for the physical examination and assured her that I would check for venereal disease. She appeared relieved and revealed that she herself had had a "fling" just prior to the onset of the itching.

During the physical exam, I did enough of a review of systems to assure myself that her headaches were not of an immediately serious nature, and I reassured her regarding her pelvic exam. I supported her by stating that she seemed to be handling things well under such stressful circumstances. I asked her to make an appointment for evaluation of her headaches and further discussion of her other concerns, including contraception. I asked her if she had any questions and she said no, but that she was very relieved after talking with me.

The entire session lasted twenty-five minutes.

In this case, the physician sequentially dealt with a variety of problems, related to both present circumstances and unresolved grief from the past. By repeatedly using the BATHE structure, she dealt with these problems in a timely and sensitive manner.

The Resistant Patient

There certainly are patients who are highly invested in separating their bodily symptoms from the emotional states. These patients may be taken aback when questioned by their physicians about what is going on in their lives, and may respond with "nothing." The practitioner has several choices when this happens. First, the subject can be dropped. We do not recommend this because it reinforces somatization and wastes an opportunity to help the patient learn to connect physical conditions to emotional states. The second option, to repeat the word "nothing" with a questioning inflection, often results in the patient hesitantly revealing some current problem. The rest of the BATHE sequence is then followed. The third option is simply to continue with the BATHE protocol, asking how the patient feels about the fact that nothing is going on. Physicians tell us that they get some fascinating responses. "Just dreadful. I'm bored to tears," or "Awful. I was expecting to be promoted, and nothing has happened," are common examples. Regardless of the patient's reaction, BATHE usually provides important insights for the patient, as the following case illustrates.

A 29-year-old woman came to the Family Practice Center complaining of having had a headache for four days. Her past history included headaches which started twelve years previously and reoccurred intermittently around the time of her period. After getting a complete description of her symptoms and the history of the present illness, the resident, who was not the patient's regular doctor, asked her what was going on in her life. She replied, "Nothing." "How do you feel about that?" he continued, as taught. "How am I supposed to feel with nothing going on?" He tried one more time: "What about it troubles you the most?" She seemed exasperated, "What is supposed to trouble me when there is nothing going on in my life?" The resident dropped the subject and proceeded with his exam.

Discussion of the case with the preceptor led to the conclusion that this was most likely a muscle tension headache, probably precipitated by stress or conflict. A decision was made to treat.

When the resident went back into the room and gave the patient the prescription for the analgesic, he gently posited, "There is something going on in your life, isn't there? You just don't want to talk with me about it."

The patient looked at him with admiration and smiled slightly. He suggested that she might want to come back and talk with her regular doctor. The resident felt terrific. There had been a moment of real communication, and he was sure that the patient had felt it also.

WHEN THE PATIENT COMES BACK TO TALK

In subsequent chapters we will be providing many specific suggestions and techniques for use in a fifteen minute visit. At this point, let us look briefly at how Alan Buchanan, a psychiatrist at the University of British Columbia, has used the BATHE protocol to teach primary care physicians to structure a ten minute "counseling session."[8]

The Ten Minute "Counseling Session"

B Stands for Background. The opening two minutes belong to the patient. You open with, "Tell me what's been going on since our last visit." The underlying message is, I'm here to listen to you and there is no need to rush.

A Stands for Affect (the Feeling State). Summarize the feelings. The underlying message is, "I have been listening." Buchanan suggests that since many patients cannot label feelings on their own, this can be very helpful to them.

T Stands for Trouble. "What is the worst thing about this situation?" The underlying message is a combination of "We can talk about anything here," and "Our time is short so we must focus."

H Stands for Handling. "And how did you handle this?" sends the message that "You can handle this situation." What is important here is to manage this crisis, not to get stuck in overwhelming feelings.

E Stands for Empathy. Normalize the patient's reaction to the crisis. "It sounds awful, and I agree with what you have done so far—anybody would have had problems with this situation."

In the final few minutes, the physician asks, "What is the best thing that has happened lately?" Buchanan comments that this sometimes injects humor or initiates the process of seeing the crisis as an opportunity for change. Then the physician states, "For the next time I'd like you to . . ." (The request may be to write the problem out in detail, list some available options, or reach out to some specific sources of support). The underlying message is, You *can* handle this situation.

The physician ends the interview with a closing statement such as, "I'm glad we had a chance to talk about this," "I feel like I know you better," or just, "Sorry, but our time is up for today." More will be said in Chapter 8 about how to structure visits when the patient comes back to talk.

THE USE OF MEDICATION

We have talked very little about the role of medication since this is a book about how to do psychotherapy. The individual physician must determine how and when to prescribe pharmacological treatment to ease the patient's symptoms. In general, if patients' acute distress is so severe as to seriously interfere with their functioning, we recommend treatment with short-acting anxiolytics to help patients sleep and restore some measure of equilibrium. In treating depression, the physician has the option of prescribing psycho-tropic medication along with providing supportive therapy. Although comparative outcome studies continue to challenge researchers, according to the literature, the combination of medical and psychological treatment is generally more effective than either modality by itself.[9–11]

While medication can be extremely useful in managing acute problems, treating symptoms without addressing the underlying causes in a chronic condition perpetuates the patient's sense of powerlessness and hopelessness. A prescription for Xanax does nothing to fix a bad marriage in which communications have broken down. Patients need to be mobilized in order to change their behavior. If the patient is requesting medication, however, an ongoing negotiation may be required to titrate the medication over time.

DIFFERENTIATING APPROACHES FOR CHRONIC AND ACUTE PROBLEMS

In contemplating verbal means to help people cope with the stressors, losses, and other pain in their lives, it is useful to look at those operational theories that assign responsibility for causing problems and for resolving them. People create internally coherent models in their heads that establish culpability for the creation of a problem and designate responsibility for who is to fix it.[12] This is another example of stories that must be understood before they can be adapted.

In order to make effective therapeutic interventions, it is important to distinguish between two models: the familiar medical model and the less familiar compensatory model. The medical model lends itself particularly well to acute situations or very dependent patients, while the compensatory model is more useful with chronic problems because it promotes independent functioning.

The Medical Model Is for Acute Problems

Physicians are trained to operate in the medical model. The story that supports this model relates that the patient is not to blame for creating the problem, since he or she is sick, and cannot be held responsible for fixing the problem, since he or she is not capable of doing so. All that is required of the patient is to accept treatment by an expert.

As the expert, the physician is called in to take responsibility for finding a solution for the problem: to diagnose, counsel, suggest, prescribe, and give orders that must be followed. When patients are facing acute stress or living through acute problems that diminish their functioning, the medical model is very useful. First of all, it establishes that the patient is not to blame for having created the problem, thus relieving guilt. Then, the physician takes responsibility for helping the patient solve the problem through medication, counseling, or specific assignments that make the patient feel supported.

Traditional medical training has prepared the physician to take care of the patient in this way. For example, with a presenting complaint of recent-onset rather than recurrent headaches, a determination may be made that these headaches are caused by a sinus infection and a specific medical therapy directed at eliminating the cause of the infection would be the most efficacious. In the absence of an infection (for example, if, instead, the patient is reacting to a family crisis), the physician can prescribe relaxation training or biofeedback techniques (behavioral medicines) and expect compliance. This is also an application of the medical model. The physician takes responsibility for determining the therapeutic fix and allows the patient to be dependent. Other options open to the physician include prescribing medication, making a family intervention, and involving community agencies.

The more acute the problem, the more important for the physician to take charge, at least temporarily. In an emergency situation (and emergency for the patient is a subjective state), authoritarian behavior relieves anxiety. Ultimately, however, the responsibility and control need to be returned to the patient, and that requires a different operational model.

The Compensatory Model Is for Chronic Problems

The story that supports the compensatory model relates that people are not held responsible for creating problems since they have been handicapped, uninformed, or deprived. Placing blame is not important. Perhaps it was circumstance, karma, some unavoidable breakdown, lack of experience, or just bad judgment. Regardless, this story says that the patient is responsible for effecting solutions by asking for and accepting the help that is available, coping constructively with the problem, and using it as a learning opportunity. In dealing with patients who are having chronic problems, this is a very useful approach. The removal of blame for creating the problem is therapeutic. It relieves guilt and raises the patient's level of self-esteem. No blame is placed for developing chronic conditions or for being in a position where chronic problems exist. However, the physician implies that the patient is responsible for and capable of dealing with these problems constructively and finding solutions. The physician expects to help, to be a sounding board, and to lead the cheering section, but the patient retains responsibility for managing the problem. This affects the patient's sense of self-efficacy. The physician's positive expectation regarding the patient's ability to resolve the problem—the infusion of hope—is a powerful therapeutic tool.

Actually, the physician may think that the patient is responsible for creating the problem, as in the case of the 38-year-old woman who had had a "fling"; however, pointing this out is rarely therapeutic since it underscores the patient's sense of hopelessness and self-deprecation. Relieving patients of blame allows them to direct their energies outward, to work on trying to solve their problems or transform their environments without wasting energy berating themselves for their role in creating these problems or permitting others to create them.[12]

For example, consider the commonly encountered problem of a patient who presents with recurrent headaches, which, after appropriate study, are determined to be tension headaches. The tension, and consequently the pain, can be assumed to be triggered by his or her reaction to the current life situation. Applying the inherently nonjudgmental compensatory model becomes part of the therapeutic strategy. Patients must be convinced that resolving whatever conflicts are causing the symptoms is more clinically efficacious than medicating the symptomatology. The pain in their heads is related to the pain in their lives. They are encouraged to identify the sources of their stress, even though, it is understood, they have not been personally responsible for creating them. They will be expected to label the situation as a problem and then devise strategies for managing the problem and exploring potential solutions. In addition, they will be encouraged to make those changes in behavior that are necessary to effect the most constructive outcome. This includes learning effective stress management techniques and practicing them regularly. Naturally, this will not be accomplished in one or two visits, but over time, with consistent encouragement and support, people are capable of making momentous adjustments.

As we have seen, determining whether a problem is chronic, requiring application of the compensatory model, or acute, calling for the medical model, allows the physician to choose the more effective therapeutic strategy. In either case, the focus is on dealing with the problem. In general, the compensatory model fosters higher self-esteem in the patient, whereas the medical model satisfies dependency needs. The application of either helps the patient feel and function better. Both models combat the pessimistic explanatory style characterized by the story that the situation is caused by internal, stable, and global factors and can never be fixed, since the focus is on helping the patient change the outcome.

Aiming for Small Wins

In previous chapters we have pointed out that it is the feeling of powerlessness, or demoralization, that brings the patient to a therapist.[13] It is feeling helpless in the face of threat that is devastating, both physically and mentally.[14–16] In many cases, the overwhelming scope of problems faced by individuals, and for that matter, by society as a whole, predisposes people to feeling helpless, since there appears to be little that can be done to effect any kind of meaningful solution. K. E. Weick suggested that very often when we try to tackle overwhelming societal problems such as crime, traffic congestion, and pollution, the attempted large-scale solutions create new problems such as increased law enforcement, removing needed funds from other services; multilane highways, drawing more people away from mass transit; and the cost of pollution control, raising taxes.[17] The most detrimental aspect of the problem, however, is that peoples' level of arousal gets raised without their having access to responses that will effectively impact on the situation. This is stress. People go on overload (or tilt) because they perceive the severity and intensity of a problem while feeling helpless to do anything about it.

The corrective strategy proposed by Weick is to focus on minor leverage points that enable people to engage in productive problem solving. In other words, people can act to make other people aware of the problem, organize rallies, write letters, wear red, white, and blue ribbons, and get attention from the newspapers, and in that way they can feel they are accomplishing something. They are not just standing idly by, watching the world go to ruin.

Achieving small wins has the effect of reversing both overarousal and apathy, which result from feeling demoralized. When working with patients, focusing on small wins provides practical, immediate, and surprisingly effective results. Anything that can be construed to lower the patients' levels of psychological distress, that is, get them off "tilt," is a therapeutic milestone. Getting patients to focus on some small change that they can personally effect in their own behavior—changing a schedule slightly, carving out time for themselves, organizing a list, clearly asking for something they want, learning to express feelings without attacking or blaming, writing a letter or perhaps only a post card—can result in a small win. Sucessfully doing one little task can provide a sense of having some power. There is less risk for patients when they tackle a problem in stages, since less is riding on each particular behavior. Not only is the outcome more likely to be successful, but it will be less traumatic if it fails. The main idea is to make patients aware that what they do can make a difference. Weick explained:

Brief therapy is most successful when the client is persuaded to do just one thing differently that interdicts the pattern of attempted solutions up to that point. Extremely easy or extremely difficult goals are less compelling than are goals set closer to perceived capabilities. Learning tends to occur in small increments rather than in an all-or-none fashion. (p. 45)[17]

Small wins increase the chance of success, foster optimism, help people refocus their energy productively, and restore belief in personal control. When belief is positive, firm actions are more likely to occur than when belief is negative or doubtful. The effectiveness of the therapy grows out of the physician's faith in the patient's ability to make small, meaningful changes.

Engaging the Patient in a Psychotherapeutic Contract

After the physical examination is done and medical management decisions have been made, the physician returns to the psychosocial aspects. Determining the nature of the problem and giving an empathic response constitutes a psychotherapeutic intervention. As has been stated, it focuses the patient and legitimizes his or her feelings. The physician now suggests that regardless of the origin of the problem, little is gained by placing blame. Rather, it is important to determine what can be done to manage the situation so as to evaluate the available options. The physician becomes the patient's ally in dealing with the problem. One approach is to advise the patient to take some time to think about it and return the following week. If a patient is feeling overwhelmed and the problems are numerous and complex, a contract, specifically a verbal understanding, is made for follow-up. It is helpful to specify that the physician will meet with the patient for a particular number of sessions.

In Chapter 9 we discuss specific considerations that must be applied to patients presenting with certain problems, or, perhaps we should say certain problem patients: those who are hypochondriacal, depressed or suicidal, or grieving. All these individuals lend themselves to therapeutic intervention by the primary care physician, provided that the contract is made clear. The physician's role, commitment, and limitations must be clearly spelled out. The patient's responsibilities must also be stated, acknowledged, and documented in the chart. Any time that the physician feels overwhelmed by the extent of the patient's problems, a psychiatric consult or referral is indicated. Patients to be referred include psychotic, addicted, or violent patients, or any patients whose condition makes the physician feel uncomfortable. When referring an individual, there is an understanding that the physician will continue to be involved with the patient and to provide ongoing medical care.

Example: The Suicidal Patient

Suicidal patients should be seen as experiencing excruciating psychological pain. They are able to see only one potential for turning off the pain, that is, turning themselves off. After acknowledging their suffering, the doctor imparts confidence that there are less drastic measures for relief than permanently destroying one's self. Suicide is a permanent solution to what may turn out to be a temporary problem. The doctor elicits a promise that the patient will discuss options and postpone making any decisions or doing anything that cannot be changed. A specific appointment is made for follow-up, and the patient is expected to honor this commitment. Hope is thus rekindled. Respect and caring are also communicated. A note in the chart documents the interaction and the patient's acceptance of the specifics of the contract. Patients can be asked to verify their commitment to refrain from self-destructive behavior and to come in for follow-up by signing the chart.

Please note that is is important to ascertain whether the patient has made actual plans for suicide. If there is a realistic danger of a suicidal gesture or attempt, the patient has to be hospitalized, although this may be avoided if there is a support person available to stay with the patient through the acute phase of despondency. More will be said about this later.

DETERMINING THE NUMBER OF SESSIONS

We know from crisis theory, as described by Gerald Caplan, that a situational crisis is usually resolved in six to eight weeks.[6] As discussed in Chapter 2, crisis is a time of great stress, meaning that people are having to adapt to a particular acute or anticipated change. During a period of crisis, people function less efficiently than when they feel secure and have a sense of well-being. People under stress regress to more primitive modes of behavior; they have a narrower view, resulting in a harder time with problem solving and an inability to see possible options.[17] The physician's role in providing support engages the person's sense of well-being and provides an ally in dealing with the problem. In making a contract for follow-up, the physician commits to following the patient through the time of greatest stress. From crisis theory, it is obvious that six or eight weeks provide a reasonable expectation of problem resolution. The physician arranges to see the patient regularly during that time. Once a week is appropriate if the problem is serious, while once every other week is sufficient if the patient is less overwhelmed. If the patient is feeling totally overwhelmed, a twice-a-week contact may be necessary during the acute phase of the crisis. By agreeing to see the patient regularly, and briefly, for a specified number of sessions, a message is conveyed that the problem is solvable and that the physician expects resolution to occur within a reasonable period of time. Conveying this message is part of the therapeutic intervention. Hope is engaged since patients recognize that the physician is seeing factors that mitigate against their feelings of despair and feel that perhaps the problem is manageable after all. Patients regain a sense of worth that is conveyed by the physician's offer to engage with them in the resolution of this situation. It is a consistent message. The physician is not only saying that the patient is worthy and deserving, but he or she is also making a commitment to work with the patient. The fact that the physician places no blame but rather suggests that the problem needs to be resolved is practical. Contracting to help the patient resolve the problem is one of the most affirming and therapeutic messages that can be conveyed. The patient gains a partner and will feel less overwhelmed by the problem and less isolated. Often, the patient will feel so much better that the number of sessions can be reduced.

Example: The Grieving Patient

Grief work can usually be accomplished in six or eight sessions. When working with a bereaved patient or discovering a situation of unresolved grief during a routine inquiry, the physician should explain the need for working through the feelings related to significant relationships that have been terminated through death or other circumstances. The process of mourning requires that patients come to terms with both the positive and negative feelings related to the person who is gone. This can be a painful process. The physician may contract with the patient for a brief period of therapy to do grief work or can refer him or her to a mental health practitioner or an ongoing support group. In any case, therapy must focus on reviewing the significant aspects of the terminated relationship, accepting the pain and finality of the loss, coming to terms with the good and bad aspects, and finally letting go.

THE EFFICACY OF TIME

Using the framework of *The Fifteen Minute Hour*, the physician provides a special time and environment for the patient to tell and assess some aspect of his or her story. The patient has a chance to reexamine responses to situations, look at options, chart new goals, and get a more positive sense of self-efficacy. The doctor helps the patient to focus on one particular problem and suggests that the process can then be replicated by the patient.

The time constraint is useful because it prevents overloading the patient and adding to the confusion. The doctor conveys optimism that problems can be resolved one at a time and indicates that he or she is there to help the patient work through the problems. By returning to patients the sense of having some potential for affecting the course of their lives by making their own decisions and choices, the physician is acting in a most effective psychotherapeutic manner. In addition, when the physician routinely incorporates this approach into every patient encounter, he or she builds efficiency into the practice. A little energy invested in this process on each visit fosters the image of the physician as an empathic and involved figure. As a result, the physician is able to handle patient problems in an effective and timely fashion, often before they assume overwhelming proportions.

SUMMARY

It is essential to include the psychotherapeutic intervention into a fifteen minute office visit. The therapy grows out of the physician-patient relationship. The letters BATHE connote memory jogs for handling the context of the visit. *B* stands for background: "What is going on?" *A* stands for affect: "How do you feel about it?" *T* stands for trouble: "What about it bothers you most?" *H* stands for handling: "How are you dealing with that?" *E* stands for empathy: "That must be very difficult for you."

By BATHEing the patient early in the visit, an effective and efficient psychotherapeutic intervention is structured into every patient encounter. Multiple problems can be handled by sequentially applying the simple technique. BATHE can also be used to structure a return visit. Medication is available as an adjunct to psychotherapy.

While the medical model is supportive in acute situations, the compensatory model, which holds patients responsible for managing their own solutions, is better for chronic problems. Small wins, which help the patient experience success, are effective in promoting change through establishing confidence. Thus, they combat the sense of being overwhelmed.

The physician engages the patient in therapy by establishing a contract to follow the psychosocial context of the patient's life. Suicidal patients may be treated if they can be made to understand that they are considering a permanent solution for a temporary problem. When they are encouraged to leave their options open, hope can be rekindled.

Crises can generally be resolved within six or eight weeks, which is also a good estimate for accomplishing grief work. The time constraint inherent in the brief session is useful because it mitigates against overloading the patient. The physician's optimism and focus on one problem at a time are effective.

REFERENCES

1. Barsky, A. J. Hidden reasons some patients visit doctors. *Annals of Internal Medicine*, 1981, *94*, 492–498.

2. Vaillant, G. E. *Adaptation to life*. Boston: Little, Brown, 1977.

3. Weed, L. L. *Medical records, medical education, and patient care*. Cleveland, Ohio: Press of Case Western Reserve, 1969.

4. Kallman, H., & Stuart, M. R. *BATH—A simple mnemonic to integrate psychosocial data into a soaped chart*. Unpublished manuscript, 1980.

5. Tallia, A. F. Verbal communication. Sept. 1983. (While team teaching a seminar for fourth-year medical students, Dr. Stuart presented the BATH protocol as a way to solicit psychosocial data. Dr. Tallia then suggested adding "E for Empathy" to the acronym BATH, creating the acronym BATHE.)

6. House, J. S., Landis, K. R., & Umberson, D. Social relationships and health. *Science*, 1988, *241*, 540–545.

7. Caplan, G. *Principles of preventive psychiatry*. New York: Basic Books, 1964.

8. Buchanan, A. Counseling tips for family physicians. In A. Sehon, & A. Buchanan (Eds.), *Syllabus from psychiatric update conferences for physicians 1991–92*, p. 82. Vancouver, B.C.: Sehon-Buchanan Medical Media.

9. Weissman, M. M. The psychological treatment of depression: Evidence for the efficacy of psychotherapy alone in comparison with and in combination with pharmacotherapy. *Archives of General Psychiatry*, 1979, *36*, 1261–1269.

10. Power, K. G., Simpson, R. J., Swanson, V., & Wallace, L. A. Controlled comparison of pharmacological and psychological treatment of generalized anxiety disorder in primary care. *British Journal of General Practice*, 1990, *40*, 289–294.

11. Kendall, P. C., & Lipman, A. J. Psychological and pharmacological therapy: Methods and modes for comparative outcome research. *Journal of Consulting and Clinical Psychology*, 1991, *59*, 78–87.

12. Brickman, P., Rabinowitz, V. C., Karuza, J., Jr., Coates, D., Cohn, E., & Kidder, L. Models of helping and coping. *American Psychologist*, 1982, *37*, 368–384.

13. Frank, J. D. Psychotherapy: The restoration of morale. *American Journal of Psychiatry*, 1974, *131*, 271–274.

14. Spilken, A. Z., & Jacobs, M. A. Prediction of illness behaviors from measures of life crisis, manifest distress and maladaptive coping. *Psychosomatic Medicine*, 1971, *33*, 251–264.

15. Cox, T., & MacKay, C. Psychosocial factors and psychophysiological mechanisms in the aetiology and development of cancer. *Social Science and Medicine*, 1982, *16*, 381–396.

16. Levy, S. M., Herberman, R. B., Malvish, A. M., Schlien, B., & Lippman, M. Prognostic risk assessment in primary breast cancer by behavioral and immunological parameters. *Health Psychology*, 1985, *4*, 99–113.

17. Weick, K. E. Small wins: Redefining the scale of social problems. *American Psychologist*, 1984, *39*, 40–49.

CHAPTER 7

Rationale and Techniques for Fifteen Minute Therapy

Patients generally assume that their physicians are technically competent to diagnose and treat disease. The physician's interest in the patient as an individual and his or her demonstrated warmth and support, particularly in the presence of debilitating, painful, or frightening symptoms, are an added bonus.

McWhinney has pointed out that physicians are much more adept at applying the biological and physical sciences to the practice of medicine than they are in utilizing knowledge from the behavioral sciences. Every patient with an organic illness also "exhibits some form of behavior" (p. 384).[1] It is important for the physician to pay attention to this behavior, as well as to the social context of the patient's symptoms. Even where psychiatric symptoms are the chief complaint, McWhinney feels that most of the emotional disorders in general medical practice fall into the category of "problems of living," that is, the natural anxiety of people who are responding to perceived threats to their health or well-being. Although a patient's response to illness is determined by many factors, including genetic makeup, early history, previous experience with illness, current life situation, and aspirations for the future, McWhinney emphasized that of all these factors, the current life situation is the most amenable to alteration by the physician. For this reason, it is critical that the physician routinely ask all patients about what is going on in their lives.

ROUTINE INQUIRIES ABOUT THE CURRENT LIFE SITUATION

The situational context of the patient's life helps the physician understand the significance of the patient's symptomatology.

Sickness Is Often Triggered by Psychological or Social Stress

The list of psychological factors that may precipitate illness is extensive. McWhinney has devised a taxonomy that identifies seven general areas:

1. Loss: either personal, such as bereavement or divorce, or the loss of something valued, such as a home, position, or object;
2. Conflict: interpersonal or intrapersonal, having to do with conflicting internal demands;
3. Change: either triggered by life-cycle events or a geographical change;
4. Maladjustment: interpersonal problems not having to do with acute conflicts; failure to adjust to occupational or home demands;
5. Other stresses, whether acute or chronic;
6. General isolation; and
7. Failure or frustrated expectations.

We would add to this list:

8. Any anniversary of a significant loss or traumatic event.[2,3]

These are the types of situations that impact on patient health. They are also the situations that lower the patient's threshold of tolerance for the discomfort of symptoms or the threshold for anxiety about symptoms. Since patients are often not aware of this relationship, they are very relieved when the physician helps them make this connection.

Stress Often Exacerbates Chronic Conditions

A diabetic may have been well controlled for years yet suddenly presents in the office because routine dipstick testing revealed spilling of sugar. Perhaps the most important question that the physician can ask is, "What is going on in your life?" It may turn out that the patient is afraid of getting fired, his wife is threatening to leave him, a teenage daughter has an older boyfriend who is making sexual demands on her, or perhaps that there are financial problems related to college costs for children. These or any other situational stresses can easily precipitate an exacerbation of the diabetic symptomatology and can best be managed with a psychological rather than chemical intervention.

The Physician's Interest Is Supportive

The physician's interest in the patient as a person is demonstrated by the inquiry about the social context of his or her problem. In this way, the physician demonstrates warmth and caring and affirms the patient's individuality and importance. The patient has to make sense out of the physician's show of interest. One explanation is that the physician is a warm and caring person. This makes the patient feel safe and secure. Another explanation is that the patient is a worthwhile person who has some significance for the physician. This also makes the patient feel good. In either case, the patient will feel supported and hence be able to tolerate symptoms better.[4]

When physicians routinely inquire into the circumstances of a patient's life, the patient becomes aware of the physical-psychological interaction. Understanding the effects of stress on the physical responses of the body help make the patient feel more in control and, therefore, less anxious. Becoming aware of the effects of stress is a prerequisite for learning to manage it.

One of our faculty members relates the case of a 36-year-old social worker who is presently divorced but living with a significant other. F. L. presented with severe stomach cramps and wondered if she had ovarian cancer. A quick BATHE revealed high stress at work which may also have accounted for a slightly low white blood cell count and an elevated cholesterol reading. During the follow-up phone call to discuss the test results, the patient suddenly volunteered that she only gets the stomach cramps when there is high stress at work.

If we are not aware that we are becoming tense, then there is no behavioral cue for applying relaxation techniques, be they physical or cognitive. Precipitants of stress are not always connected to the current situation. Understanding the significance of an anniversary, its potential for precipitating illness, and the high correlation of anniversaries with accidents can keep patients from overreacting, turning acute events into chronic conditions, and setting unrealistic expectations for themselves.[2,3]

A patient will almost sheepishly present with chest pain on the anniversary of his father's heart attack, saying, "I know it's probably psychosomatic, Doc, but check it out anyway and relieve my anxiety. Every year at this time, I seem to develop these symptoms." After ruling out the acute condition, it would be appropriate to encourage the patient to reassess his relationship with his father. If he has not completely dealt with his grief, it is important for him to focus on both the good and bad memories of his youth and come to terms with the remaining ambivalent feelings.

DEALING WITH PATIENT REACTIONS

Once the physician has determined the context of the visit in terms of what is going on in the patient's life, it is important to inquire about the patient's emotional reaction. "How do you feel about that?" is the most efficient question to ask, not, "Why do you think this is happening?" or, "What does your wife think about it?" The point is to get the patient to make an affective response. "How do you feel about it?" usually elicits a response that starts with "I feel." If the patient starts to offer other information, it is important for the physician to interrupt and to persist: "Yes, I understand, but how does it make you *feel*?" We would caution practitioners not to get caught up in the details of the patient's situation. Finding out who said what to whom has no therapeutic significance. We are interested in having the patient label and express feelings so that we can empathize and then attempt to focus the patient on the problem-solving strategy. Often, patients may admit to feeling anxious or depressed. Just having the patient acknowledge, "I am angry," or "I am sad," or, "I feel rejected," "scared," "powerless," "overwhelmed," or, "totally confused," are all useful. Most people react automatically or semi-automatically to most of the events in their lives, without much conscious awareness or thought about what they are feeling. When we focus their attention on their current affective experience, we break the pattern. If feelings are experienced, accepted, and acknowledged, they do not become transformed into psychosomatic symptoms.

When the physician inquires about how the patient is feeling about a specific situation, he or she changes the focus from what is happening to how the patient is reacting. This puts the emphasis on the patient and demonstrates the physician's concern. The doctor is extending an invitation to get at the root of what is actually troubling the patient. Some patients have extreme difficulty identifying or labeling their feelings. Their stories will focus on what happened and what they did in response. In this case, the physician can use active listening as a way to focus on the affective domain: "Sounds like you were surprised and hurt when your request was denied." Then, it is important to follow up by asking, "What about it troubled you the most?"

By inquiring about the significance of the event, the physician in a subtle way implies that the interpretation about what is troubling the patient is not necessarily obvious. This simple device may prepare the patient to see the situation as less catastrophic or at least to recognize the need to develop potential solutions. The physician assumes no meaning or judgment. The same situation has different significance for different people. The nonjudgmental nature of the physician's response makes the patient feel accepted and creates the necessary conditions to promote psychological change.[5]

As part of the initial inquiry, the physician now has a choice. One option is to ask the patient how the situation is being handled and then respond empathically. The other choice is first to acknowledge that the situation must be difficult and then to ask how the patient might handle it.

Many physicians schedule patients with emotional problems for the end of the day in order to leave time to explore the situation fully. We strongly recommend against this practice, since it involves too much of an investment of valuable time on the part of the physician, creates unrealistic expectations on the part of the patient, and may not necessarily result in increased therapeutic benefits. Since it has generally been established that, given a positive doctor-patient relationship, little difference can be found in outcome among psychotherapeutic techniques, we strongly urge primary care physicians to practice and overlearn the techniques we are describing (do them so often that they become automatic), since they are effective and efficient, taking little of the physician's time.[6-8]

Ordinarily, when a physician invites a patient to talk without structuring the interview, it is possible that the patient will gain many benefits, but the process is quite random. Our experience is that patients will complain incessantly and repeatedly about the behavior of other people and circumstances that cannot be changed, thereby reinforcing their limited interpretation of reality. Allowing patients to go on indefinitely about these matters is countertherapeutic, tries the patience of the physician, and sets up unreasonable expectations on the part of the patient regarding the amount of time the physician has available. Not only that, we often find that the longer the patient talks, the more upset he or she gets. By giving the patient valuable time and listening attentively to unchanging complaints, the physician supports the patient's distorted perceptions and the story remains unchanged. Ultimately, the physician may decide that it is not worth trying to treat the psychological aspects of a patient's problems.

Perhaps over time the patient's self-esteem may be enhanced by the attention of the accepting physician. This is the assumption behind Rogers's client-centered therapy.[5] However, we have found that it is much more economical in terms of time and emotional energy to make one or two interventions that challenge and potentially change patients' behavior or assumptive worldviews, rather than just letting them retell their stories.

A 55-year-old woman comes to the office complaining of fatigue. She says that she has been tired for weeks. She has had no physical exam for years and there is no significant medical history. When asked about what is going on in her life, she says that both she and her husband work full time, she is also a homemaker and takes care of her 17-year-old son, who is legally blind but has just been accepted into college. She looks frightened, depressed, and essentially closed. When asked how she feels about what is going on, she only volunteers that she is tired. The physical exam is unremarkable; blood and urine tests and a pelvic exam are all normal. The physician thinks that perhaps the patient is depressed. He asks, "Do you have any idea what you might be depressed about?" The patient replies: "Depressed? I don't know if I'm depressed. I know I'm tired. I work a 40-hour week. Keep my own house. Cook dinner every night. I have a nice husband who would be happy with a bologna sandwich, but wouldn't make it for himself." She pauses, and then adds: "Oh yes, my sister cares for our 90-year-old father. I go over there every Saturday to help out. I really wish she'd put him in a nursing home, but I feel guilty when I think that, and my sister won't hear of it."

The physician responds that he thinks that this is a perfectly reasonable way to feel. The patient sighs. She looks relieved and volunteers that she has done nothing for herself in recent times. The physician suggests that she make just one small change. The patient smiles, saying: "I can do that. Thank you so much, Doctor, I feel so much better."

As we have said previously, psychological intervention consists of interrupting fixed patterns of behavior by focusing attention either on the behavior or away from it (by distracting the person or focusing on other options). By BATHEing the patient, we are focusing on his or her feelings and behavior and setting the stage for change.

Often, the initial sequence is all that is required in the way of psychological support. It is only with those patients whose situational stress is currently unmanageable that the physician should engage in a specific therapeutic contract.

Dealing with Unexpected Reactions during the Interview

Often as part of taking a history, a routine question about previous hospitalizations, family illness, or previous geographical moves may elicit a strong emotional reaction in a patient, that is, may trigger painful memories. The physician may be at a loss whether to ignore, soothe, or deeply explore the reaction. BATHEing provides a constructive alternative.

A young woman presented in the office complaining of a sore throat. Initial inquiry was unremarkable. However, when asked if there was any family history of rheumatic fever, she suddenly started to cry and recalled that while she was in high school, she had been put to bed for several months because of rheumatic fever. The physician was first taken aback and hesitant to get into an old, painful experience. However, since something had to be done, the physician decided to apply the BATHE technique. The physician inquired about the *background*: "You were in high school, about what grade?"

"I was just starting my senior year."

Going right to *affect*, the physician inquired, "And they put you on complete bed rest, how did you feel about that?"

The patient replied, "I felt so isolated and out of it."

The physician did not allow herself to explore these feelings further but inquired directly about *trouble*: "What about the situation troubled you the most?"

"I was afraid that I would not graduate with my class."

"How did you handle that?" was the final question.

"Well, there wasn't much I could do. I had to go to summer school. It was awful."

The empathic response followed. "I can see that that was a very difficult time for you. Tell me, any other serious illnesses?"

The patient answered, "No." Then, after a pause, she reflected: "You know, at this point it really doesn't make any difference. As a matter of fact, now that I think of it, I think I did better in college because I worked for a year first."

The physician responded. "I'm glad. Now I'd like to examine you and make sure that everything else is OK."

FOCUSING ON OPTIONS

In dealing with a patient's situational stress, it is crucial that the physician not take responsibility for solving the patient's problems. In S. Shem's *The House of God*, a biting satire about medical education, one of the primary truths, Rule Four, clearly states, "The patient is the one with the disease."[9] If the patient is the one with the disease (or the problem), the patient also has a right to decide what, if anything, should be done about it. The physician has the opportunity to intervene in the process simply by making the patient aware of the options and encouraging him or her to make an informed choice about what will be done. There are three strategies that the physician may choose to present to the patient: looking at the consequences, applying tincture of time, and choosing not to choose.

Looking at Consequences

The physician can encourage the patient to think about or list several possible courses of behavior and to sort out the consequences inherent in these choices. A good structure is to ask the patient to specify what the best and worst possible outcomes might be. Patients who are very angry often talk about wanting to kill the offending party. Rather than responding, "You don't mean that!" (yes, they do, at least for the moment), or "You can't do that!" (yes, they can; it may not be a good idea, but it is possible), the effective reply is: "I can understand that you would feel that way, but that does not sound like a very practical option when you consider the consequences. Let's talk again next week, and see what you might do that's more constructive."

The implication here is that the feeling is legitimate (it is), but that once the patient thinks about it, other behavioral choices will appear and the decision about what to do can be deferred at least until the following week.

Applying Tincture of Time

It is often true that the more important a decision is, the less information we have to base it on and the less time we take to make it. We put a deposit on a desirable house after one or two brief visits because if we do not act immediately, someone else is likely to snap it up. Then we spend hours choosing among shades of paint or wallpaper patterns.

Often a patient who is reacting emotionally to an event may feel impelled to make a decision. Having learned of her husband's unfaithfulness, a wife may feel that either she must leave him immediately or that she should have an affair herself. The physician encourages the patient to take time to sort out the feelings. Reacting to an acute loss involves an increased intensity of pain. The physician offers support and schedules an appointment to talk again. The implication is that tincture of time will provide relief.

Choosing Not to Choose

In a case in which all apparent choices are unacceptable and the patient does not want to choose the lesser of the evils, the physician can also instruct him or her that for the moment at least, the best course of action may be to do nothing. Sometimes, all the important information is not available to make an intelligent choice. The physician should ask, "What is the worst thing that can happen if you don't make a decision about this?" To choose not to choose is an option that many people never consider. Psychological pain is something that must be felt but does not necessarily require a behavioral response. Often there is no need to act, especially if the pain is induced by the actions of another person over whom we have no control. In many cases, breaking patterns by not acting in response to provocation by another person shifts the balance of power.

THE EFFECTS OF SYMBOLISM

One of the more fascinating aspects of practicing primary care medicine is the opportunity to interact meaningfully with a variety of people. The specialist who treats limited organ systems is only excited by unusual manifestations of disease and opportunities to diagnose rare cases, whereas the primary care physician can be endlessly impressed by the different reactions that individuals experience to the same circumstances. The particular meaning that each of us attributes to an event determines our reaction, and not the event proper. In every case where a person appears to be overreacting to a particular situation, we can assume that a symbolic meaning to that circumstance is triggering the reaction.

Mr. Harris, a 28-year-old white male, presented in the emergency room with chest pain and difficulty breathing of sudden onset. He had no risk factors for heart disease, and examination, electrocardiogram, and enzyme studies were totally normal. The physician was aware that Mrs. Harris was due to deliver the couple's first child momentarily and that the couple was extremely happy about the prospect of becoming parents. Arrangements were complete, and Mr. Harris had planned to stay with his wife during the delivery.

After reassuring the patient about the condition of his heart, the doctor inquired about what was currently happening. She was informed that the obstetrician had just told the couple that the baby was in breech position and that he had decided to do a cesarean section. At this point the patient started to cry. He revealed that he himself had been a breech delivery and that his mother had died in childbirth. He was sure that his wife would not survive. Moreover, he had very much wanted to be present at the birth but now could not face the prospect.

The physician was able to reassure him about the improvement in obstetrical procedures over the past twenty-eight years and the relatively low risk associated with breech presentation when delivered by cesarean section. However, the physician did point out that it was perfectly all right to be concerned and scared. The patient was then able to connect his severe reaction to his own tragic birth circumstances rather than the current situation. The physician suggested that perhaps the patient needed to bring to the hospital a support person for himself. The following week, a proud father, gowned and masked, held his wife's hand in the operating room and watched his son take his first breath.

When helping the patient tie particular reactions to their historical roots, the physician implies that the patient now can break the pattern of response and reassess the significance of particular situations in the here and now. You may have a particular intolerance to people's loud arguing because when you were a child, your parents fought bitterly. Listening to them, you felt helpless and frightened because your security was threatened. Whenever you hear people arguing, you feel helpless and frightened, just as you did then. If a physician were to ask you gently: "Are you really helpless now? As an adult, is your security threatened?" you would become aware of the change in your circumstances and learn to monitor your reaction to loud arguments, thereby, affecting a change.

The physician's brief inquiry about the historical roots of an event can have a profound effect on a patient's self-esteem, sense of control, feelings of acceptability, and assumptive worldview. It is not necessary to explore the circumstances, distortions, or details in depth. Simply point out to the patient that there appears to be an inconsistency in the severity of the reaction in relation to the apparent face value of the event. Patients can be asked to write an autobiography, keep a journal of current reactions, or compare memories with various living relatives in order to sort out the origins of some of their stories and troubling interpersonal reactions. Often, this will promote constructive dialogue between the patient and the significant persons in his or her life. The important factor here is that the patient is the one who must understand and, ultimately, change the reaction. The physician's understanding of the situation by and of itself accomplishes absolutely nothing. If, as Shem said, "The patient is the one with the disease," then it is the patient who must make the connections and change the responses.[9]

FOCUSING THE PATIENT IN THE PRESENT

Although all reactions to current life stress are significantly affected by past experience, when engaging a patient in a brief therapy session, it is crucial for the physician to stress that regardless of the problem's origin or historical significance (fascinating as that may be), the past is past, and all we have to deal with is the here and now. Dwelling on past hurts is not useful: "Do you still resent your brother now, because your mother always favored him when you were kids? Really?" "Gee, I guess I do." "My guess is that your mother did the very best that she could. What would it take for you to forgive her?" The reality is that when we hold on to grudges or nurse our resentments, or bodies pay a price.[10] We make ourselves miserable and do not actually affect the people that we are angry with.

Just as there is no benefit to obsessing about past hurts, assumptions that are made about the future are usually wrong and destructive. When a patient generalizes from a current unfavorable situation to speculate about a bleak outlook, the physician needs to challenge this distortion by saying, for example: "I understand that your husband has left you, and that you feel very hurt. However, it is not legitimate to assume that no one will *ever* love you again." "Yes, it is very painful to have your article rejected by the *AAI Journal*. You worked very hard on it and were sure it would be accepted. However, that does not mean that *no one* will ever publish it." "You are feeling very unhappy right now, that does not mean that you will *never* be happy again." When a patient says, "I *know* that such and such will happen because it always has," it is important to correct him or her by restating: "You *assume* that such and such will happen. What is it that you could possibly do to change that?"

It is important to encourage the patient to take one day at a time. If the patient is in extreme pain, it may be necessary to suggest taking it only five minutes at a time. Then, the patient should acknowledge that accomplishment to him- or herself. Patients must also be cautioned that wallowing in their pain is not constructive. If occasionally they really feel the need to wallow, they may be given permission to do so, providing they limit themselves to five minute wallowing sessions. Patients respond quite well to these kinds of instructions. It puts their pain into context and gives them a sense of control.

These edicts, stated with the authority of the physician and with the attributed social power inherent in the role, help the patient reassess the resources that are available for dealing with current problems. The physician's encouragement to appraise reality in the here and now rather than dwelling on the past, which cannot be changed, or the future, which cannot be predicted accurately, is very productive. Patients are generally depressed about the past and anxious about the future. When we focus them in the present and engage them in constructive problem solving rather than fight-or-flight behavior, they respond amazingly well.

THREE-STEP PROBLEM SOLVING

In this volume we have promoted several "cookbook" approaches to therapy because they provide a simple structure through which to trigger the physician's efforts to help his or her patients. In Chapter 4 we introduced the PLISSIT structure to determine levels of intervention from simple permission giving to limited information, specific suggestions, and finally, a contract for intensive therapy. In Chapter 6, and in this chapter as well, we have repeatedly preached about the benefits of BATHEing the patient to determine and manage the situational context of the patient visit. Now we propose a three-step sequence of questions to apply to any disturbing situation. These questions are:

1. What am I feeling?
2. What do I want?
3. What can I do about it?

This is often a useful framework for physicians to apply to their own reactions, as will be discussed in Chapter 10. For the present, let us focus back on the patient. The series of questions now becomes:

1. What are you feeling? (Label the actual feeling.)
2. What do you want? (Specifically state your goal.)
3. What can you do about it? (Focus on what you can control.)

For example, a patient may be complaining about how his daughter's attitude disturbs him. The physician asks, "What are you feeling?" The patient may try to continue ranting about his daughter's behavior and give examples to illustrate that she is not acting the way she should. He says they fight all the time and he screams at her. The physician persists, "What do you feel in that situation?" or, "How do you *feel* about that?"

It may turn out that the patient feels angry, hurt, frightened, discounted, disappointed, devalued, disgusted, or some other unpleasant sensation, depending on the meaning of his daughter's attitude to him.

At this point, the physician acknowledges that feeling and asks, "What do you want?" At first, the patient will respond that he does not want to be in this situation and does not want his daughter to treat him in this way. The physician persists, "What *do* you want?"

"I want her to change her behavior." (Sometimes, patients say they do not really know, in which case the physician can encourage them to think about it and come back to talk again.)

The final question is: "What can you do about that? I understand that fighting with her has not been helpful." The patient may decide that he can reward appropriate behavior, make a contract, discuss it quietly, present the situation to his daughter as a problem to be solved, and let his daughter know that he truly loves and accepts her. On the other hand, sometimes nothing can be done. In this case, what the patient feels about the situation changes to sadness, which is appropriate. It is hard to accept the fact that we cannot control other people's attitudes and behavior.

In any case, this three-step process labels feelings, clarifies what the patient wants, and points to a direction for achieving these goals. It is economical in time and direct in therapeutic value, since it encourages new ways of thinking and behaving and discourages the passive role. It also involves teaching the patient a strategy that can be applied to any number of situations.

PHYSICIAN SUPPORT PUTS THE PATIENT IN CONTROL

We have said that the feeling of being overwhelmed is generally the trigger for patients' help-seeking behavior. When the physician engages the patient in problem solving, patients become aware that they have some control over the circumstances of their lives. Since the relationship with the physician is an ongoing one, patients sense that they have a partner, and therefore feel less isolated. Someone cares and wants to follow their progress. If feelings of abandonment helped to trigger unpleasant reactions, now there is an assurance of ongoing support that will continue to be available over time.

The second important factor concerns the patient's reaction to the physician's expectation that he or she is capable of handling the situation. The physician indicates that the patient has choices, that his or her reactions are legitimate, and that there are actions available to the patient that will improve the current situation. If the patient is able to hear and accept these messages, they will change how the patient feels about the particular circumstances. Certainly, the patient is no longer helpless and will no longer feel hopeless. This may even make the situation appear less difficult, and ultimately improve it.

A constructive attitude toward the physician's intervention will engage a positive cycle. Since the patient will feel less overwhelmed, the patient will resume normal (more effective) functioning. Mature coping mechanisms will again become available. The patient's view of the situation will broaden, and novel stimuli will be experienced and processed. This can be expected to lead to more effective problem solving and more of a sense of being in control. As a result, the patient will be able to communicate more clearly and directly to let others know what is needed. This improved functioning will then be reinforced by more success in achieving desired outcomes.

Focus on Strengths

Every person or situation has both good and bad potential. It is definitely more therapeutic to focus on positive aspects of a situation and the positive qualities of a person. A glass that is half full is to be preferred over one that is half empty. There is strong evidence to support the need to be optimistic and to speak in positive terms. A recent study showed that patients react much more favorably to being told there is a 68 percent survival rate than when hearing that there is a 32 percent mortality rate.[11] We can speculate that in the first instance, a patient focuses on the word *survival*, while in the second, only *mortality* is heard. The numbers are strongly discounted.

In every case, we are seeing patients who have clearly demonstrated their ability to survive; had they not, we would not be seeing them in our office at this time. One way or another, patients have surmounted the many challenges that are part of living in our rapidly changing society. Once focused on their healthy resources, they will manage their problems and their lives in remarkably competent ways.

The Patient Is Responsible

Although the physician's help and support can be asked for, and received, the problem still belongs to the patient. The patient is therefore held responsible for applying particular strategies that have been discussed and for investigating various options. This is in accordance with the compensatory model. The message here is that there is no blame for finding oneself in the current position, but it is up to the patient to gather the resources necessary to arrive at a positive outcome.

The patient is encouraged to stay in the here and now and to take things one day at a time. There is an understanding that the situation will be discussed further at the next visit, as the physician is interested in following all the developments. The time interval is clearly specified: "I want to see you next week and we will talk more."

The New Scoring System

We would like to add a final word about evaluating the patient's response. We have invented an innovative scoring system for keeping track of new behavior. In the best behavioral tradition, it is designed to focus only on positive changes and ignore lapses.

Since we know that under stress, people regress and find themselves unable to apply their most recently learned behavior, patients are instructed to keep track of every time they engage in new behavior.[12] We are not interested in their recording failures (too many patients are stuck in their failure image), but only instances of success. They are to give themselves credit (two points) when they become aware of reacting, thinking, behaving, planning, or doing anything in a new way; that is, changing old patterns.

Since it is hard to act in new ways or apply new behavioral techniques, the act of doing so and recognizing the fact deserves two points. It is essential to caution patients not to become angry or abusive with themselves when they become aware that they are reacting in old ways. On the contrary, they get credit just for the recognition. It is normal, and to be expected, that under stress, patients will react in automatic old ways. That is how they have done it for years: It has been overlearned and has become a habit. Breaking habits is very difficult. The first step to changing habitual behavior is to become aware of the behavior as it is occurring. That is the reason why we suggest that patients give themselves credit (one point) every time they catch themselves doing something in the old way.

Becoming conscious of behavior as it is occurring (starting to self-monitor) is a prerequisite for making lasting changes. By suggesting that the patient is doing something good (recognizing the behavior as it is happening), even when acting in the usual old way, we can change the patient's story. In this way, we help patients break the destructive cycle of feeling helpless and then abusing themselves for feeling that way. Instead, by changing the story even before the target behavior has changed, we put patients back in control, enhance their sense of self-efficacy, and induce positive changes.

In the next chapter we will look at the content of the fifteen minute therapy session and introduce some further strategies and suggestions.

SUMMARY

Since illness or accidents exacerbate chronic conditions, and since sickness is often triggered by psychosocial stress, the physician should routinely ask all patients what is going on in their lives. The physician's interest indicates care for the whole person. By making the inquiry routine, patients are educated to become aware of the interaction between their physical and psychological well-being.

If a patient is upset about his or her present situation, the physician extends an invitation to talk. The physician tries to establish the significance of the event for the patient and accepts the patient's feelings. When a patient unexpectedly reacts emotionally during the course of an interview, the physician briefly explores the issue with the BATHE technique. In difficult situations, the physician suggests that there may be options, invites the patient to consider consequences related to different choices, and suggests that applying tincture of time (deciding not to decide) are viable options.

The physician makes the patient aware that events have a symbolic significance (which is different for all people), that certain feelings are triggered by old memories, and that self-esteem, the sense of control, and the sense of being lovable are all affected by the patient's interpretation of certain historical events. The physician then points out that these old interpretations can affect current relationships.

The patient thus is focused in the present. The physician stresses that the past is past; all we have to deal with is the "here and now." Dwelling on past hurts is not useful, while assumptions made about the future are usually wrong. It is important not to generalize and instead to take life one day at a time. Under extreme circumstances, taking life only five minutes at a time may be better. Patients generally feel guilty about the past and anxious about the future; consequently, focusing in the present and engaging in active problem solving are therapeutic.

A three-step approach to problem solving involves asking what the patient is feeling, what he or she wants, and what he or she can do to succeed. The physician's support makes the patient feel more in control because the patient now has a partner. The physician indicates confidence in the patient's ability to handle things. The patient feels less overwhelmed and resumes functioning in a healthier mode.

The physician focuses on the patient's strength, acknowledges that the latter has survived similar situations, explains that support is available and can be asked for, and indicates that the situation will be discussed further at the next visit. A scoring system that only records successes is instigated in order to reinforce new and more productive behavior.

REFERENCES

1. McWhinney, I. R. Beyond diagnosis: An approach to the integration of behavioral science and clinical medicine. *New England Journal of Medicine*, 1972, *287*, 384–387.

2. Bornstein, P. E., & Clayton, P. J. The anniversary reaction. *Diseases of the Nervous System*, 1972, *33*, 470–472.

3. Cavenar, J. O., Jr., Nash, J. I., & Maltbie, A. A. Anniversary reactions presenting as physical complaints. *The Journal of Clinical Psychiatry*, 1978, *39*, 369–374.

4. Cassel, J. Psychosocial processes and "stress": Theoretical formulation. *International Journal of Health Services*, 1974, *4*, 471–482.

5. Rogers, C. R. The necessary and sufficient conditions of therapeutic personality change. *Journal of Consulting Psychology*, 1957, *21*, 95–103.

6. Frank, J. D. Therapeutic components in all psychotherapies. In J. M. Myers (Ed.), *Cures by psychotherapy: What effects change?*, p. 15–27. New York: Praeger, 1984.

7. Stiles, W. B., Shapiro, D. A., & Elliot, R. Are all psychotherapies equivalent? *American Psychologist*, 1986, *41*, 165–180.

8. Crits-Christoph, P. The efficacy of brief dynamic psychotherapy: A meta-analysis. *American Journal of Psychiatry*, 1992, *149*, 151–158.

9. Shem, S. *The house of God*. New York: Dell Publishing, 1979, p. 72.

10. Smith, T. W. Hostility and health: Current status of a psychosomatic hypothesis. *Health Psychology*, 1992, *11*, 139–150.

11. McNeil, B. J., Pauker, S. G., Sox, H. C., & Tversky, A. On the elicitation of preferences for alternative therapies. *New England Journal of Medicine*, 1982, *306*, 1259–1262.

12. Cohen, S. Aftereffects of stress on human performance and social behavior: A review of research and theory. *Psychological Bulletin*, 1980, *88*, 82–108.

Contents of the Fifteen Minute Therapy Session

We have now reached the point at which to address the interaction between the physician and the patient in sessions that are devoted primarily to counseling or psychotherapy (whichever term is preferred). Our bias is to use the term *psychotherapy*, because the physician is actively trying to promote change in the patient's behavior, emotional, or cognitive reactions. From an interpersonal point of view, *psychotherapy* has been defined simply as "the systematic use of a human relationship for therapeutic purposes."[1] From our point of view, this means that a therapeutic interaction with a physician is intended to affect the story that patients tell themselves about the way things are.

In contrast, *counseling* suggests a process of giving advice related to a particular situation. It fosters dependency and implies that the physician has more insight into the situation than does the patient. We would like to propose a compromise: that the physician be *aware* of doing therapy but refer to it as counseling. Jay Fidler, a renowned psychiatrist and teacher, once remarked that the primary difference between play therapy and just playing with a child is what goes on in the therapist's head.[2]

As long as the physician recognizes that what transpires in the fifteen minutes with the patient is psychotherapy, it can be presented to the patient as counseling, which may make both parties more comfortable. Thus, the patient is scheduled for a brief counseling session. In this way, everyone can be satisfied. We do urge the physician to interact with the patient with the awareness that the psychotherapeutic process implies facilitating change in the patient's assumptions about the world and how the world can be accessed to provide more generously for his or her needs. The physician's words and actions must be geared to promote the patient's sense of personal competence and connection to other people. The physician also intentionally supports strategies that help foster the patient's sense that the world is a reasonably reliable place. This is designed to impact the patient's sense of coherence, which is the factor cited as most significant in promoting health.[3]

Basically, the physician uses a variety of techniques to help the patient adapt to the environment in ways that will promote mental and physical health. Let us look at how all this can be effectively incorporated into a fifteen minute therapy session.

OPENING INQUIRY

It is important to start every session with an open question and let the patient talk about whatever the patient has been planning to say, has been thinking about, or finds most important to discuss at this time.

"What has been happening since I saw you?" "Tell me how you've been doing?" "What sort of things have you been thinking about since last week?" "Tell me how you've been feeling, and what's been going on." These statements are all good for openers. Then, it is important to let the patient talk without interruption for about two or three minutes. This gives him or her the opportunity to reflect on what currently seems to be most important. After about three minutes, it is critical to summarize what the patient has said in order to let him or her know that the physician has been really listening.

If the patient has not focused on events that have occurred since the previous visit, it is necessary to focus on the current situation and shortcut any elaborate background material. One helpful question is, "What's the most significant thing that has happened since I saw you last?"

Next, the physician may assess the patient's affect and inquire by reflecting, "You look less tense; how do you feel about what's been going on?" or, "How have you been feeling since I saw you last?" In cases where patients are out of touch with their feelings or have a hard time expressing them, it is useful to summarize the emotions that appear to underlie the story: "Sounds like you are disappointed [discouraged, frustrated, annoyed]; are you?" "I hear you blaming yourself and taking all the responsibility—do you feel guilty?"

Next, it is constructive to ask, "What is the worst thing that has happened since last time?" What has bothered the patient the most? It may be useful to explore what about the situation made it bothersome. It is the symbolic meaning of the event for the patient that is important. Finally, the physician asks how the patient feels about the way in which things were handled. The physician can interject an empathic response whenever it seems appropriate.

It is also a good thing to focus on a success: "Tell me about one thing that you handled well, or that you feel good about," or, "What is the best thing that has happened since I saw you?" The small wins, and the sense of mastery that grows with effecting them, are very important.

The sequence of these questions is deliberate. If it sounds familiar, it should: It is the BATHE sequence. It focuses the patient in the present and helps him or her identify and express feelings. It looks at what was most troubling (cognitive assessment) and the way in which things were handled (behavioral assessment). It helps the patient develop an awareness that both good and bad things happen during each time period and that the patient makes choices in responding to them. These techniques are generic to the process of therapy. We are promoting them because they are useful and easy to remember—and they work. They are certainly not the only way to do therapy, but they fit well into a brief session framework, and maximize the potential for positive outcome.

Having gone through the opening inquiry, it is now important to make an empathic statement based on an understanding of the patient's experience during the intervening time since the last visit. If there is something positive on which to focus, the physician might say, "I would think that you could feel very proud about having handled things in a new way."

If the patient has not been successful, a useful intervention could be: "It must be really discouraging and painful when you are trying so hard to make a change, that things don't seem any different. Still, you do get points for having made some changes. What could you modify further?"

REPORTING ON HOMEWORK ASSIGNMENTS

After the opening inquiry, the focus shifts to the homework assignment: "Do you have the list of options that are available to you?" "Did you talk to your wife and let her know exactly what is troubling you?" "Did you keep a log of all the times that you got very upset?" "What sources of support were you able to come up with?" If the assignment has been done, the physician takes this as a positive sign that the patient is exhibiting responsible behavior and taking control. The session can then center on what has been learned from the assignment or on one thing about which the patient is most concerned.

If the assignment has not been completed, the physician must accept the fact. It is imperative that the physician not scold or try to induce guilt in the patient. The process of therapy is designed to provide new responses to old patterns. The physician communicates to the patient that for some reason, he or she chose not to do the assignment at this time, adding that it might be useful to identify what obstacles were allowed to get in the way of doing the assignment and to recognize that there is always another opportunity.

"Mary, I can understand that you did not take the time to list the activities that really make you feel good. I wonder what makes it so hard for you to focus on things that make you feel good? Do you want to do it for next week, or would you rather talk about it now?"

This approach communicates three important messages:

1. It is all right to be where you are. I accept you.
2. You are making choices that have some meaning for you.
3. However, there may be more constructive choices that you can make.

Starting Where the Patient Is

The most important generic principle in doing psychotherapy is that we have to start where the patient is (on his or her map). This is true in any type of teaching situation. If we are to promote learning of any type, we first have to assess the level of the student's knowledge. If we were to present something that the student already knows, no learning would take place, since the student already has access to that information.[4] If we were to start at a level far more advanced than the student's background preparation, there would also be no learning because the new information could not be understood or incorporated.

If we are to be effective, we must start where the learner is at this time. That means that we must accept our patients at their current levels of functioning, recognizing that as we do this without implied criticism, it facilitates patients' abilities to make small but positive changes.

Attentive Listening

Whenever the patient is speaking, the physician should communicate interest and attention. This can be done by concentrating, maintaining eye contact, leaning toward the patient, and nodding approvingly whenever anything positive is related. It is valuable to notice the patient's affect as positive and negative material are being related. If there is a discrepancy between the affect (facial expression and body language) and the content of the patient's story, this can be gently pointed out: "I notice that as you are telling me about all the terrible things that are happening, you are smiling." This is important information for the patient to access. Perhaps he or she is just nervous, or perhaps this incongruent affect is a long-time problem and one of the reasons why the patient has difficulty with personal relationships.

Summarizing and reflecting back to the patient what has been heard and seen is critical, as it demonstrates that the physician has been paying attention and has understood. Consequently, it allows the patient to move on and to make changes.

Probing for Feelings

Probably the most efficient psychotherapeutic strategy is the two-step process of asking patients to identify feelings and then to accept these feelings as appropriate, given their subjective experience.

When the patient relates what has been happening, whether good or bad, the physician inquires, "How did you feel about that?" It is interesting to observe the reactions. Patients often stop, look surprised at the question, and have to think for a moment before labeling the feeling. Many people are out of touch with their emotions, and are astonished when an authority figure expresses interest in their feelings. Often, patients do not respond with a label for a feeling, but instead tell you what they thought or what someone else did. Let us look at an example:

Mr. Graham is relating how he asked his wife to make some changes in her schedule to accommodate him and adds that she agreed without giving him any argument.

Physician: "[breaking in] How did you feel about that?"
Patient: "I thought she would just refuse to go along with me."
Physician: "I understand that, but how did it make you feel."
Patient: "I was surprised and pleased."
Physician: "You really felt good."

In active listening, it is useful to reflect understanding and acceptance by paraphrasing.

A patient has just related that he tried hard to get his wife to listen to how he felt about having to go to her mother's for dinner every Saturday night. Instead of responding, she simply gave him "one of her looks" and went out of the room.

Doctor: "So when Ethel walked away, how did you feel? Angry?"
Patient: (Nods.)
Doctor: "I understand that. You must have felt awful."

Giving patients permission to feel the feelings that have been aroused requires a minimal investment of time, energy, and understanding. A patient is overheard saying to her friend in the waiting room, "My doctor told me that my feelings are legitimate, even if other people see things differently or feel some other way." Her affect would have been appropriate for announcing that she had just won the lottery.

Having accepted the patient's feelings, if the physician thinks that it would be useful for the patient to become aware how his or her behavior helped to bring about the situation, the next question might be: "Tell me more about that? Then what did you do?"

When asking for details or an elaboration of events, we encourage focusing on the patient's behavior—what he or she thought and did, and not on stories about the thoughts and actions of other people. The underlying message is that patients have choices. Indeed, they have power. Perhaps until now, the patient has not been aware of this.

Incorporating Medical Treatment

After the opening inquiry has been completed, the physician may wish to follow up on any physical complaints. If there is an opportunity to "lay on hands," this may be useful in helping the patient to connect physical and psychological symptoms. At this time, the physician may also discuss any changes in medications, if they are part of the treatment. Medication is always an option to be used along with psychotherapy (as discussed in Chapter 6). In the case of panic disorder,[5] generalized anxiety disorders,[6] depression,[7] and bulimia,[8] medication as an adjunct to cognitive types of psychotherapy has generally been shown to improve outcome. The written prescription should not, however, be seen as part of the ritual offering that the physician presents to the patient (see Chapter 1). After a brief inquiry into the physical aspects, the physician refocuses on the psychosocial area: "All right, now let's talk about what you are going to do for next week."

Collateral Visits with Family Members

As discussed in Chapter 3, one of the strong advantages that the primary care physician brings to the therapeutic encounter is an established relationship with both the patient and the patient's family. A colleague who is in solo private practice and has been trained in our method reported the following case:

Gail, age 35, moved from Mississippi to New Jersey because of the demands of her husband's job. She is the daughter of alcoholic parents and has been suffering from an anxiety-depression syndrome for years. She has been treated with a variety of tranquilizers and anti-depressants and is now struggling to adjust to life in a new community.

Because of our inability to find a counselor with whom she felt comfortable, I, as her family physician, agreed to see her for some regular, brief sessions. Some of her problems focused on the unresponsiveness of her husband, Jim. She felt that he would not want to come in, but agreed to ask him. I had seen him several times in the office, with the children and for problems of his own, and was confident I had sufficient rapport to enable us to talk freely.

I began the interview by saying that I understood that it was his wife who had asked for help, but that I felt it was important at this time to elicit his support. During the introductory comments, Jim assured me that he felt he had a good relationship with his wife, even though they did not communicate much. It took very little to make him happy. Knowing that his wife and children were provided for and having some peace and quiet for himself were all he really needed. He realized that his wife needed more, such as a lovely home and an active social life. She also liked to be touched and caressed, but he was not "into" these things.

"How do you feel about these differences and the obvious lack of communication?" I asked.

He replied that he felt they should improve their communication, and after some prompting, agreed that it was also probably important to their relationship to pay more attention to each other's interests. He added that he "just hadn't thought much about it."

"For example," I asked, "what do you say when your wife says she wants to redecorate the dining room?"

"I tell her we don't have the money," he replied.

"Is that all?" I asked.

"Yes," he replied, "and the subject is dropped."

"Is there no way you could be more creative about this in order to satisfy your mutual interests?" I queried.

"Like what?" he wanted to know.

"For example, you might get a second job," I said.

"Or she might get a job," he replied quickly. This was something that Gail had been wanting to do but was afraid her husband would not support. We agreed that this might solve several problems.

Moving on, I asked, "Do you remember your wife on Mother's Day?" (I knew that he had remembered this year.)

"Not usually," he said.

"How about birthdays?"

"Not usually. My family never made much of these things."

"How does she feel when you do remember her?" I asked.

"Oh, she loves it."

"Doesn't that give you pleasure also?" I wondered.

"Sure, but I just don't usually think about it."

"And in relation to sex, which you say you like, and touching, which you are not into, are you aware of some common differences between men and women in these areas?"

"Not really."

Here I mentioned some typical needs of women (often not understood by spouses) that were similar to those expressed by his wife. He seemed quite interested.

As we ended the interview (after fifteen minutes, exactly), he brightened up and said that this session had given him new ideas and much to think about, and that he might be glad to talk with me again after he had had time to do some homework.

In this case, the physician, by virtue of her established relationship with the family, was able in one visit to sensitize the husband to some very real problems experienced by his wife, which under normal circumstances he would completely exclude from his map. The intervention proved to be extremely effective, and Gail's self-esteem increased dramatically as she experienced herself functioning well in her new job and having her husband act more attentive to her needs.

FOCUSING THE PATIENT IN THE PRESENT

Since, by definition, we can only act in the here and now, we recommend that the patient generally be focused in the present. The only major exception to this rule is a person working on a grief reaction, who will need to review the history and sort out various feelings about the person, relationship, object, or position that has been, or is about to be, lost. (We will say more about this in the next chapter.)

If a patient complains about how his mother treated him as a child, the physician can respond with some sympathy but then wonder whether that is really relevant to the way in which the patient presently treats his wife. What can the patient do to get more satisfaction out of his marriage? Moreover, what does the patient want from his mother now?

Dealing with the Run-On Patient

Often patients will find it difficult to stay within the structure prescribed by the physician. They will elaborate endlessly or repeat themselves. When this occurs, it is essential that the physician interrupt and summarize by saying: "Yes, you told me about _____. I guess that is really important to you. Tell me how it makes you *feel*." When patients talk about past events that cannot be changed, the physician should respond: "I hear how upset you are that things didn't work out. How does it make you feel *now* and what might you do differently the next time?"

Getting patients to express guilt, anger, rage, or sadness helps them to accept their feelings and subsequently let them go. Then, they can examine the options for dealing with matters now. They will become unstuck. Having escaped from the internal, stable, global explanatory style box (see Chapter 4), they will feel less helpless.

Behavioral Options

In general, it is good to focus on options for behavior. In Chapter 7, we introduced the sequence:

1. What are you feeling?
2. What do you want?
3. What can you do about it?

At this point, we are helping patients focus on novel approaches to getting their needs met. Encouraging patients to respond to situations in a different way promotes new behavior. Breaking old destructive patterns is useful even if not successful at first. It demonstrates that there are alternative ways of behaving. If a wife cannot stop her husband from excess drinking, she can decide that since there is nothing she can do to affect his behavior, she can change her own. She will stop arguing and fighting with him, stop aggravating herself about it, and instead engage in some activity that she enjoys. She may also decide to go to Al-Anon and get some support for herself. In this case, the patient has chosen an alternate way of responding to a situation. The situation has not changed, but her perception of it—and her response—have changed. As a result, she feels less overwhelmed. Moreover, since she has disturbed the homeostasis of the conflict in their relationship, the husband's behavior may ultimately also change.

Alternate Interpretations of the Situation

Another useful approach is to encourage patients to find new ways to interpret a situation. Every difficult task can be viewed as an opportunity to gain skill and experience, to learn something of value, or to become stronger or more flexible. Seen in this light, the situation can prove more valuable and rewarding than had things worked out as originally desired or planned.

Patients need to learn that there are four healthy options for handling a bad situation:

1. Leaving it;
2. Changing it;
3. Accepting it as it is (and getting support elsewhere); or
4. Reframing it (interpreting the situation differently).

Option 1. When considering leaving a situation, be it a relationship, job, or other intolerable circumstance, patients should be encouraged to assess what the best and worst possible outcomes might be should they leave. They can then be encouraged to weigh the likelihood of these occurrences. Having a specific strategy to employ will give these patients a sense of competence and power in making the decision. If they decide to leave, they can be encouraged to plan the timing, obtain needed resources and other support, and practice what they want to say when informing the various affected parties. It is important that they consider contingency plans and explore all the relevant details. For instance, a patient with a chronic medical condition should think carefully about leaving a job and losing health insurance coverage without being certain that a new position will provide adequate benefits. This type of behavioral rehearsal fosters a high order of adaptive coping. These behavioral preparations, or potential scripts, constitute useful homework assignments, which should be brought back to the physician for discussion.

Option 2. In considering whether a situation can be changed, patients need to look at what resources are available and what strategies might be employed. Has the patient communicated clearly with the powers-that-be regarding the level of dissatisfaction? Can the patient clearly define the problem and make suggestions for a positive resolution? Behavioral change on the part of the patient may ultimately change the responses of significant other people, thereby changing the situation. Sometimes, outside pressure can be brought to bear on the situation, and often, time alone will effect a change. In this case, it may be appropriate to accept the situation as it is, for the moment.

Option 3. Accepting a situation as it is and not aggravating oneself by thinking about the fact that it should be different is a very constructive option. If a situation is tedious, interesting and satisfying outside activities can be encouraged. Support groups, close friends, and exercise programs are all means of relieving stress. Taking pride in the quality of one's work and interactions with other people can also help make acceptance of the situation more pleasant. Recognizing that time will probably bring a change suggests making oneself comfortable while waiting for something to occur. It always does, although usually in unexpected ways.

Option 4. Changing the interpretation of a situation (that is, reframing or looking at it in a new way) is the most creative and satisfying way of dealing with difficult circumstances. When patients use novel ways of reinterpreting situations, they are adapting in a growth-producing fashion, and thus enhancing their mental and physical health.[9] It is the meaning that we attribute to a situation that determines how we feel about it.

Barbara D. was a patient with multiple problems, including severe back pain that was generally unresponsive to treatment. She was moderately depressed and very concerned about her demanding husband, and also about her mother-in-law, in whose home they lived. Barbara's treatment included 50 milligrams of Elavil at bedtime, referral to a bio-feedback practitioner, and some assertiveness training. When Barbara complained that her husband "should not be so demanding," the physician suggested that this could be reframed to provide Barbara with the opportunity to practice her assertiveness skills. The change in Barbara's attitude proved remarkable. She simply glowed the following week while reporting how she had handled several situations that previously would have left her feeling only an impotent rage. Not only that, but her back pain had almost entirely resolved.

THE PHYSICIAN'S ACCEPTANCE IS PART OF THE TREATMENT

In discussing stressful elements of the patient's life, the physician's attention and calm acceptance of the circumstances will have a beneficial effect on the patient.

Accepting the Patient

The patient will feel accepted as a person. The physician's interest is seen as supportive. The patient feels valued, understood, and connected. Moreover, the absence of criticism helps to counteract discouragement and self-doubt.

Accepting the Situation

By calmly accepting the situation, the physician provides a model for the patient. Together they look at a set of circumstances that, however unfortunate and difficult, must first be accepted, and then handled. Just labeling the situation as a problem will change it. Problems lend themselves to a variety of solutions, some of which are better than others. There is now a direction for thinking constructively.

Accepting the Patient's Reaction

The physician's acceptance of the patient's reaction to the situation is therapeutic. The statement, "This must be very difficult for you!" communicates to the patient that anyone would be stressed in similar circumstances. Usually, it focuses the patient back on his or her strength: "Actually, I'm doing OK, all things considered."

Assuming That There Are Options

Probably the most empowering aspect of the physician's approach is his or her assumption that options exist. We have talked a great deal in previous chapters about patients' assumptive worldview, which is the story that they tell themselves about how the world operates. None of us experiences the world directly. Rather, we experience subjective representations of circumstances that we filter through our visual, auditory, tactile, or other senses and then interpret, based on our previous experience. We delete cues that do not fit into our previous frame of reference as though there were no such territory on our map. The resulting model of the world, or the story that we create, determines what choices and limitations we think we have or that we impose on ourselves. When we mistake our limited representation of the world for the real world, we limit our options.

When the physician assumes that there are more options than patients are seeing (and it is not even necessary for the physician to be able to generate them), patients begin to expand their models of the world and their stories may allow for new interpretations. Patients start to include more options and reexamine their limitations. The whole idea of therapy is to help them be more open to possibilities; to look at their world, including themselves, in a new way and become aware of having choices.

Enhancing the Patient's Self-Esteem

Being open to possibilities is probably the hallmark of mental health. There is an impressive amount of data to show that positive illusions, rather than accurate contact with reality, lead to a sense of well-being and mental health that is characterized by the ability to care for others and do creative work.[10] As discussed previously, the attitudes involved in having a positive view of the self, an exaggerated belief in one's ability to control the environment, and an optimistic view of the future are protective of mental and physical health. It is the physician's job to help patients focus on positive aspects of themselves and their lives. When the patient expresses doubt about the ability to overcome some obstacle, the physician's confidence can be expressed by saying something like, "You may have had problems with this in the past, but I see no reason why you cannot accomplish this now."

GIVING ADVICE

Physicians are notorious for giving advice, and patients generally ask to be advised. They feel dependent, look up to the physician, and often want to be told what to do because they are afraid to make decisions or rely on their own abilities. Since they feel inadequate, they also feel out of control of their own destinies. Giving specific advice is always less effective than focusing patients back on their own resources, with appropriate instructions for developing alternatives. When the physician gives advice, the implication is that he or she has a better understanding of the patient's problems and options, than the patient has. This does not empower patients. On the other hand, making them aware of their own abilities and encouraging them to exercise their options is both therapeutic and practical. There are, however, certain suggestions that the physician can make. These focus primarily on the process of problem solving.

Behavioral Management of Children

Raising responsible children and enjoying the process requires that parents develop specific skills. In response to particular behavioral problems that parents relate, and also as part of well-child or routine visits, we encourage physicians to support the following principles: rewarding good behavior and ignoring the bad, setting strict limits on unacceptable behavior without making threats, using time-out to achieve control in bad situations, allowing children to express feelings of all kinds but not allowing destructive behavior, and giving them choices whenever possible.

Rewarding Good Behavior. When patients complain about their children's behavior, they can be instructed to apply behavioral principles. Primarily, this means reinforcing (rewarding) good behavior and extinguishing (ignoring) inappropriate behavior. Parents are instructed to try to catch their children "doing something right" and then to reward them.[11] Patients must understand that attention is a reward, so acknowledging good behavior consistently, instead of focusing attention on bad behavior, promotes rapid improvement.

Setting Limits. Parents must learn to set strict limits on completely unacceptable or dangerous behavior. They must be instructed to be firm without making threats so that their children understand that the parents really mean what they say. When a parent says, "If you do such and such again, I will spank you." That implies that the child has an option. The child has to decide whether doing the forbidden thing is worth the spanking, provided that the parent actually follows through with the threat. If, on the other hand, a clear statement is made, such as, "I don't want you to do that," there will be no argument. Limits must be set reasonably and enforced consistently. If necessary, parents can be instructed to remove a child from a situation physically(firmly but gently), and to instigate a time-out, or respite in a boring place, as an effective form of discipline.

Using Time-Out. Anytime a child is out of control, failing to behave according to set standards, or failing to respect another person's rights, time-out becomes a way to allow him or her to contain emotions without damaging the self or others. The child is escorted to a predetermined area (many psychologists recommend the bathroom) with a door that can be closed. The child is told that once he or she is quiet, back in control, and willing to cooperate, time-out will be suspended. Depending on the age of the child, three to fifteen minutes is usually sufficient to have him or her calm down.

Expressing Feelings. It is essential that parents encourage children to express feelings but not to engage in destructive behavior such as physical violence. Negative feelings must be allowed as well as positive ones. Children need to learn that getting frustrated, angry, sad, confused, or cranky are all part of the normal human experience. When children make statements such as, "I hate you," this needs to be interpreted by the parent as, "Right this instant, you are very angry with me." This can be followed with, "I'm sorry that you feel this way but you may not . . ." Children must learn that conflict is part of life but cannot be allowed to become physical.

Giving Children Choices. Parents must be encouraged to give children choices whenever possible. The opportunity to practice, from an early age, making decisions that impact on one's life helps establish a positive sense of self-esteem and self-efficacy. For example, after a long day of shopping, one of our patients had a hard time getting a tired and cranky 3-year-old to wash his hands before dinner until she asked him whether he would rather wash his hands in the sink or in the bath tub. He laughed, chose the tub, and immediately complied.

Dealing with Teenagers. Parents should be encouraged to discuss limits with their adolescent children and to jointly agree on acceptable rules. Teenagers must be allowed to take part in the decision-making process and then be held responsible for living up to their commitments. When a teenager fails to follow through, this must be addressed as a problem and renegotiated. In this way, self-esteem and self-control are taught and the parent can relinquish the role of police officer.

Parents must be cautioned not to get into power struggles with their adolescent children. In a power struggle, both parent and child lose, since when the parent wins the battle, the child's sense of control and self-esteem are compromised, generally leading to more destructive behavior. It is more constructive to jointly discuss options and give the teenager an opportunity to decide between several acceptable alternatives. When parents treat teenagers as responsible individuals, express trust in their judgment, and respect their privacy, this information becomes part of the adolescents' sense of self, and they can be expected to act accordingly.

There are many popular books available to help parents learn these techniques. *P. E. T.: Parent Effectiveness Training* by T. Gordon and *How to Talk So Kids Will Listen and How to Listen So Kids Will Talk* by A. Faber and E. Mazlich are practical and effective.[12,13] *Peoplemaking*, by Virginia Satir is a very readable and useful guide for managing children.[14] All of these are available in paperback. Parents can be encouraged to go to their libraries and browse or to look for paperbacks in their local stores. The psychology/self-help sections of most book stores have an incredible array of helpful, inexpensive manuals directed at very specific problems. Relevant books can be read and discussed in subsequent sessions. The physician can save much time when patients get information from books and then come back to discuss their reactions. This is called *bibliotherapy*. Appendix B describes a list of helpful books that can be recommended to patients for this purpose.

Regardless of the recommendations made, it is important that the physician not forget to give the usual support: "It must be very difficult to manage a teenager (3-year-old, two active children, or whatever) when you have all these other things going on in your life. Let's talk more about that, next time."

Assertiveness Training

Behavioral therapists have found that people can be effectively trained to be more assertive. Patients should be encouraged to ask for what they want. In dealing with other people, patients are encouraged to see themselves and their desires as neither more nor less important than the desires of other people. Patients are encouraged to send "I" messages, learn to state their feelings, ask for what they want, and give their reaction to other people's behavior, as in these examples: "When you ignore me as I walk into the room, I feel discounted," or, "When I make dinner, and you don't come when I call you, I feel very angry." Saying "I don't like it when you don't do what you say you are going to do," is much more effective in getting another person to follow through on a promise than saying, "You never do anything you say you are going to do!"

Patients must be encouraged to persevere and repeatedly insist that their rights be respected. Again, there are several books that the physician can recommend: *Your Perfect Right*, by R. E. Alberti and M. Emmons, and *When I Say No, I Feel Guilty*, by Manuel Smith, are two examples.[15,16] As before, encouragement and interest coming from the physician are more important than reading self-help books. However, the support of the physician in conjunction with the outside reading is probably the most effective strategy.

Taking Care of Oneself

One prescription that we encourage the physician to give patients is the instruction to be kind to and take care of themselves. When patients are experiencing periods of high stress, they must be told to modify the demands they make on themselves. They cannot expect to function at optimal levels, and they will feel much better if they lower their expectations. Moreover, they should give themselves credit for dealing with a difficult situation.

Patients should be encouraged to give themselves treats, to take breaks, and to plan desirable activities on a regular basis so that they always have something to look forward to. It is important that they work on maintaining supportive relationships with people they enjoy and make the time to visit or at least keep in touch by phone. The message here is: "You are important. Your happiness and sense of well-being are also important and must be a priority for you."

Patients should be encouraged to learn stress management techniques such as controlled breathing, progressive relaxation, and meditation. They need to be encouraged to exercise regularly, choosing a modality they enjoy, and also need to learn to monitor and change their thinking patterns.

Distinguishing between Thoughts, Feelings, and Behavior

Patients must be advised to distinguish between thoughts, feelings, and behavior. Thoughts are constant internal messages that often go unnoticed, but they are powerful enough to create our most intense emotions. We are constantly describing the world to ourselves and comparing these descriptions of the way things are to the way we want them to be. Based on these judgments, we decide whether things are good or bad, painful, dangerous, or just not as they should be.[17,18] Our thoughts then influence the way that we feel about a situation, another person, or ourselves.

Feelings constitute an automatic emotional response based on our judgments and interpretations. Feelings must be accepted, as they cannot be controlled directly. Given our interpretation of a situation (based on our personal description), we feel as we do. Cognitive therapy consists of challenging the underlying value judgments and assumptions that determine what we think. When we learn to modify our thought processes, moderate our expectations, and change our judgments, our feelings will change.

Behavior is voluntary. We choose how we will act. When we are in touch with our feelings, we can learn to control our behavior. Our behavior is probably the only thing in life that we really can control, and it should be aimed at getting us what we want and enabling us to present ourselves to the world as we wish to be seen. A physician can be very angry with a patient but keep the feeling hidden by choosing his or her words carefully in order not to intimidate the patient and to maximize the patient's cooperation.

In a brief counseling session, the physician can help the patient to make distinctions between thoughts, feelings, and behavior; challenge irrational thoughts (absolutes, unrealistic expectations, generalizations, and unfounded prognostications); accept feelings; and focus on behavior that can be changed.

Taking Responsibility for Our Feelings

The last bit of specific advice we suggest that physicians offer patients is that it is useful to take responsibility for our own feelings. Few people realize that no one can actually make us feel anything. We feel the way we do as an automatic response to our interpretation of a given situation. A change in interpretation changes the feeling. For example, if we presume that all physicians reading this book will agree with our approach to therapy, we will feel very badly if some reviewers object to parts of the text or do not like it. On the other hand, if we hope simply that a few people will find this book helpful and use the techniques that we are proposing, we will be delighted when some individuals let us know that they are finding it useful.

Our current level of self-esteem, expectations for the future, and general outlook determine how we feel far more than what actually happens to us. It is the physician's task to make the patient aware that we make ourselves feel hurt, angry, frustrated, and rejected by the stories we tell ourselves about what has happened or is going to happen. The feelings we generate are bad and painful. If we are going to turn off the pain, we must first become aware of what we are feeling, and then learn to modify those feelings through a reinterpretation (revised story) of our circumstances.

ENDING THE SESSION

Ending the session on time is important for both the physician and the patient. It is an affirmation of the patient's ability to cope and to apply the strategies discussed in the session, and it ensures that the contract is valid and that the physician intends to follow through. Thus, it secures the sense of connection.

At the end of the allotted time, the physician should make an honest comment focusing on some positive aspect of how the patient is dealing with the situation. It is helpful for the physician to express the feeling that it would be nice if there was more time (it lets the patient know that the physician values the contact) but that the discussion will be continued at the next scheduled session. The importance here is keeping the connection. The patient is instructed to call if something serious changes in the meantime.

HOMEWORK

The specific homework task for the intervening time is jointly determined. The patient makes a contract with the physician, agreeing to keep a journal, prioritize problems, find a specific book, or in general monitor changes in behavior and the resultant consequences.

It is important that the time spent with the physician be devoted to building skills that the patient can use to change interactions with the significant others in his or her life. The visit with the physician provides direction and helps make the patient aware of options and his or her personal power to put them into effect. All this is part of the homework that will be examined at the next session. Knowing that the physician will be expecting a report helps motivate the patient to follow through on the assignment.

Carol G., a 22-year-old white female, mother of two children, ages 3 and 5, who is currently living with a boyfriend, came to the office complaining of two weeks of dizziness. She seemed totally overwhelmed by the multiple problems in her life. For a homework assignment, the physician suggested that Carol keep a diary and record all instances of dizziness and the particular circumstances under which they occurred. Returning the following week, Carol was able to recognize that her dizziness occurred primarily when she felt most out of control, such as when dealing with her estranged husband, her in-laws, her child's teacher, and her mother. For the following week, she was given the assignment to "do one nice thing for yourself." The resulting change was dramatic. Carol had decided to have lunch with a friend, leaving her mother to babysit. She and her friend talked over her problems, and she finally contacted a lawyer to start divorce proceedings.

TIME ALLOCATION

In general, the patient should be allowed to talk for about twelve minutes out of the fifteen. Brief comments from the physician should keep the patient focused on one or two tasks that can be used as preparation for the next session. By only dealing with one or two issues during a particular session, the patient does not become confused or overloaded. Thus, the physician is both teaching a process and treating a person.

In the next chapter we will look at some specific approaches to difficult situations. We will give some suggestions for treating patients who are hypochondriacal, grieving, anxious or depressed, or suicidal, and for treating the patient who must be referred because the physician feels uncomfortable. We will also discuss how these techniques can be applied to children.

Now let us look at a case that was handled by a young physician under our supervision and is typical of the effective outcome that can be expected over time.

Daniel G., a 16-year-old white male, presented at the Family Practice Center on a Tuesday afternoon in late November complaining of dizzy spells. The previous Sunday he had felt light-headed and dizzy, and had actually passed out. The patient said there had been two or three previous episodes but denied recent fever, palpitations, or chest pain.

Daniel and his mother had recently moved into the area to live with his grandmother. He related that he had no friends and was mostly interested in his baseball card collection. He admitted that he felt badly about the fact that he had no father and that his mother was handicapped and confined to a wheelchair. The patient revealed that he wanted to become a carpenter.

A physical examination, including a complete neurological exam, was normal, allowing the physician, for the moment, to rule out an impending catastrophic medical event. His impression was vasovagal syncopal episodes. For completeness, routine labs were ordered, but the physician was more concerned that this patient needed emotional support. Daniel G. was a shy, sensitive individual with many emotional problems and no one to talk to. This made him feel very depressed. The physician made a contract for follow-up in one week with the expressed intention of seeing the patient for counseling.

In the course of having blood drawn, the patient became dizzy and his blood pressure dropped to 60/40, reinforcing the contention that this patient's symptoms were manifestations of vagal activity. In a half hour, his blood pressure had returned to normal and the patient was released.

The patient returned the following week. There had been no further episodes of dizziness. He then started to talk about his home situation. There was a horrendous history of abuse on the part of a man living with the mother, and constant moves. The physician gave support and focused the patient on the present situation. Daniel had made a new friend in school and felt good about that, but he expressed a desire to transfer to vocational school. The physician said he would look into the possibility.

A contract was made to see Daniel regularly once a week for fifteen minute sessions. The third week, he appeared nervous and depressed. His affect was rather flat, and he seemed to have nothing much to say. He wondered aloud why the physician was interested in seeing him. The physician said that he enjoyed talking with Daniel and would help him learn to make more friends and focus on planning his life.

By the fourth week, the patient was much more cooperative. He was happy about a project in school and spontaneously started to share some of his interests. During Christmas week, the patient canceled his appointment. He arrived early in January complaining of a head cold but feeling much happier. It was during this session that the patient revealed a history of sexual abuse occurring several years previously and expressed how happy he was to be receiving counseling. The physician assured

Daniel that it was not his fault that he had been abused and acknowledged that the experience must have been awful for him. This seemed to relieve the boy. The subject was brought up again several weeks later, but seemed to have lost its impact.

Daniel was seen regularly for counseling every other week. Over time, he became involved with the golf club at school and made one close friend. He was treated for a sore throat and some nose bleeds, and developed a very relaxed and trusting relationship with his doctor. After about a year, his afternoon job prevented him from attending their sessions regularly. A sports physical clearing him for team participation is the last item in the chart. When Daniel moved away at 17½ years of age, he appeared to be a rather confident and reasonably well-adjusted young man who was clear about his goals and directed toward achieving them.

SUMMARY

When starting a therapy session, the opening inquiry should focus on the present situation, with a report on the homework assignment and on the best and worst things to have happened in the interim since the previous visit. The physician always starts with the patient's experience and communicates interest through attentive listening. Questions should generally probe for feelings and for information about what the patient personally did in response to circumstances. Medication and laying on of hands through examinations, as well as collateral visits with family members, constitute other options that can be exercised.

In general, the patient should be focused in the present. Four healthy options for handling a painful situation are leaving it, changing it, accepting it with additional support, and reframing or reinterpreting it in a positive manner.

Physicians must gently set limits on the amount of detail or repetition that a patient presents. The physician is supportive of the patient, and this acceptance is therapeutic. The physician accepts the patient, the situation, and the patient's reaction to the situation, but assumes that there are options.

In giving advice, the physician focuses on the process of dealing with problems rather than on their content. Advice may be given regarding behavioral strategies for managing children, for becoming assertive, and for taking care of the self. The physician points out the difference between thoughts, feelings, and behavior, and explains how thoughts (judgments) may be modified, with resulting emotional changes. Patients are held responsible for their own feelings. At the end of the session, the physician extends the contract through the assignment of homework and the expectation that the patient will return to report on the accomplishment of a particular task. During the session, the patient should speak for about twelve minutes, with brief comments from the physician focusing on constructive elements.

REFERENCES

1. Anchin, J. C., & Kiesler, D. J. *Handbook of interpersonal psychotherapy.* New York: Pergamon, 1982. Cited in S. F. Butler and H. H. Strupp, Specific and nonspecific factors in psychotherapy: A problematic paradigm for psychotherapy research, *Psychotherapy*, 1986, *23*, 36.

2. Fidler, J. Personal communication. Rutgers Community Mental Health Center Group Psychotherapy Training Program, October, 1974.

3. Antonovsky, A. *Health, stress, and coping.* San Francisco: Jossey-Bass, 1979.

4. Whitman, N. A., & Schwenk, T. L. *Preceptors as teachers; A guide to clinical teaching.* Salt Lake City: University of Utah School of Medicine Press, 1984.

5. Sheehan, D. V., & Soto, S. Diagnosis and treatment of pathological anxiety. *Stress Medicine*, 1987, *3*, 21–32.

6. Power, K. G., Simpson, R. J., Swanson, V., & Wallace, L. A. Controlled comparison of pharmacological and psychological treatment of generalized anxiety disorder in primary care. *British Journal of General Practice*, 1990, *40*, 289–294.

7. Silver, F. W., & Ruckle, J. L. Depression: Management techniques in primary care. *Postgraduate Medicine*, 1989, *85*, 359–366.

8. Agras, W. W., Rossiter, E. M., Arnow, B., Schneider, J. A., Telch, C. F., Raeburn, S. D., Bruce, B., Perl, M., & Koran, L. M. Pharmacologic and cognitive-behavioral treatment for bulimia nervosa: A controlled comparison. *American Journal of Psychiatry*, 1992, *149*, 82–87.

9. Vaillant, G. E. Natural history of male psychologic health: Effects of mental health on physical health. *New England Journal of Medicine*, 1979, *301*, 1249–1254.

10. Taylor, S. E., & Brown, J. D. Illusion and well-being: A social psychological perspective on mental health. *Psychological Bulletin*, 1988, *103*, 193–210.

11. Blanchard, K., & Johnson, S. *The one minute manager.* New York: Morrow, 1982.

12. Gordon, T. *P. E. T.: Parent effectiveness training.* New York: Penguin Books, 1975.

13. Faber, A., & Mazlich, E. *How to talk so kids will listen, how to listen so kids will talk.* New York: Avon Books, 1980.

14. Satir, V. *Peoplemaking.* Palo Alto, Calif.: Science and Behavior Books, 1972.

15. Alberti, R. E., & Emmons, M. *Your perfect right,* rev. ed. San Luis Obispo, Calif.: Impact Press, 1974.

16. Smith, M. J. *When I say no, I feel guilty.* New York: Dial Press, 1975.

17. Beck, A. T. *Cognitive therapy and emotional disorders.* New York: New American Library, 1979.

18. Ellis, A. *A new guide to rational living.* North Hollywood, Calif.: Wilshire Books, 1975.

CHAPTER 9

Handling Special Patients

There are patients who are hard to treat because they are hard to be with. How can we relate to them? There are suicidal patients who pose a danger to themselves, addicted patients, hostile patients, and anxious and depressed patients, to mention only a few types. What do we do with patients suffering from the current "disease of the month," whether it be chronic fatigue syndrome or some other form of somatization disorder? Can we help them? Most important, can we help them without feeling totally put upon—without feeling burned out and unable to relate with sufficient empathy to other patients?

Also, what, if anything, can we do to treat children and adolescents who are reacting to the circumstances of their lives? First of all, how do we get them to talk? Then, what do we do with the information?

A word of caution is in order: The techniques outlined in this chapter build on previous material. The physician must have acquired a thorough understanding and reasonable comfort level using our supportive techniques in routine patient care before applying these specific approaches to the care of the most difficult patients. Providing supportive psychotherapy is a skill that must be practiced consistently and applied broadly to all patients.

DEALING WITH DIFFICULT PATIENTS

J. E. Groves wrote an article provocatively entitled, "Taking Care of the Hateful Patient," in which he developed four stereotypes of particularly difficult patient personalities and behavioral categories.[1] The four stereotypes are dependent clingers, manipulative help-rejecters, entitled demanders, and self-destructive deniers. Physicians are sorely tried by contact with these types of patients. Such individuals precipitate negative feelings on the part of physicians, who feel depleted by the need to provide endless emotional supplies when no objective positive outcome seems to result. After describing symptom differences and similarities, Groves developed specific approaches for dealing with each of these patient types. Our approach is simpler: We start by believing that each patient is behaving in the best possible way, for this person, at this time. That does not mean that it will always be so, but it is that way now. People make fundamental changes when properly motivated, either in response to catastrophe or by a series of small steps. We recommend the small steps.

Except in situations posing an immediate threat to life or limb, we suggest that physicians limit contact with patients who arouse negative emotions to no more than fifteen minutes, regardless of the complexity of the problems or lists of complaints. During that time, the physician is encouraged to integrate medical and psychosocial concerns, treating the patient in the context of the total life situation. If there are too many problems for one visit, the patient can be brought back the following week. This has the additional payoff of demonstrating the physician's interest. It addresses the patient's needs in a supportive manner. The patient, in turn, will feel less rejected (and these patients are highly skilled at getting doctors and others to reject them) by having frequent, brief sessions. Ultimately, this will result in much better utilization of time, since there will be no lengthy and frustrating sessions of miscommunication. It has been our experience that patients learn to organize the details of their stories to fit into the time available. The physician may have to take charge quite directly by saying something like: "I can hear that you have several things that really bother you. You have some abdominal pains that come and go, you feel all shaky inside, and there is very little cooperation at home. However, I need to understand what, specifically, you would like me to do for you today."

One of the techniques that we can apply is to learn to reframe the situations that give us the most problems and instead to look at them as providing us with the opportunity to practice the skills we have been promoting in this book. Thus, rather than thinking, "Oh, good grief, it's Mrs. Brown. I hate to see her since she has numerous problems, doesn't take her medicine, and never feels grateful, gets better, or stops complaining," we can think, "Oh, it's Mrs. Brown. I feel sorry that she is so needy. Seeing her will give me an opportunity to try out some of these new techniques I'm learning. I will let her talk for about two minutes. I will paraphrase what she has said so she will know I listened. Then, after I find out what is going on in her life and acknowledge her suffering, I will ask her to concentrate on one specific problem and try to get her to identify one small change that she can make to make herself feel better. If I can make the time with her more productive, I will feel good. I will aim for one small win and limit the time with her to no more than fifteen minutes."

If the physician learns to reframe the situation and take satisfaction from dealing with difficult patients in a smooth and effective manner, the practice of medicine may well become more gratifying. Seeing people relax and become less anxious, hostile, or demanding is a rewarding experience. As we change our approach, we may find that unreasonable patients may actually become more reasonable.

Patients are sometimes unpleasant, critical, or hostile. Many times, patients are frustrated, tired of not feeling or functioning well, and discouraged by their dependency on doctors who are often not able to help them. Therefore, they become hostile. They are so sure that they will not get their needs met that their attitude and behavior guarantees the completion of the self-fulfilling prophesy. However, there is a way to break this pattern. By acknowledging the patient's frustration instead of demanding that it be held in check, the situation will be immediately changed. Let us look at some practical examples.

The Hypochondriacal Patient

Perhaps the most difficult patients to deal with, over time, are hypochondriacal individuals, whose preoccupation with real or imagined illnesses generally will try the patience of the most dedicated physician.[2,3] A recent study found hypochondriacal patients to be dissatisfied with their physicians, the physicians to be frustrated by the patients, and the use of the term *hypochondriasis* to impair "the physicians' accuracy in assessing the levels of the patient's anxiety and depression."[4] Hypochondriacs really do suffer from anxiety and depression. These patients focus much of their time and attention on their physical symptoms and seem determined to suffer loudly while being unsuccessful in finding anyone to cure them. Hypochondriacs need to be scheduled for regular visits at predetermined intervals (every two weeks, to begin with, is often tolerable for both patient and physician), whether or not they are complaining about acute symptoms.

Letting these patients know that they will get regular care whether or not they are feeling acutely bad is the first positive step in managing hypochondriasis. After acknowledging their concerns about their current symptoms and emphasizing that it must be awful not to ever feel well, it is essential to follow the BATHE protocol during every visit. It is also very important to record important psychosocial data so that inquiries can be made about outcomes of situations in the patient's life. This communicates the fact that the physician is interested in the patient as a whole person and not just a collection of disease symptoms. The patient does not have to be sick to get attention or a response.

It is important to acknowledge patients' physical suffering and to allow them a reasonable amount of time to discuss it, but it is always equally important to put things back into the context of the patient's life: "How does that affect your ability to spend time with your grandchildren?" "What can you do to maximize enjoyment of the times when you feel good?"

Over time, this approach may offer these patients the opportunity to focus on other aspects of life besides physical complaints. Their previous life experience may have led them to believe that care and attention could only be obtained through illness-related behavior. Now, however, there are alternatives. By structuring therapy regularly and including broader aspects of the patient's experience, the physician can treat the hypochondriac quite successfully. We again caution physicians not to let the length of the session exceed their own tolerance for contact with this type of patient. Perhaps it will be necessary to limit the time to seven or eight minutes. If so, the session would start with the physician making this clear: "Mary, we have about eight minutes. Tell me what you are most concerned about this week?" Since there are regularly scheduled visits, each session can focus on one or two problems. Our experience has been that patients respond very well to this type of treatment. After a while, they will tolerate longer periods between visits, but they will usually need to be seen at least once every six weeks or else they will regress. However, because the focus on physical ailments is so central to a hypochondriac's self-image, it is important to allow these patients to keep at least one or two symptoms. Watzlawick has pointed out the critical importance of allowing patients to keep the unresolved remnant.[5]

The Chronic Complainer

There is a subtle difference between hypochondriacs who are truly anxious regarding the state of their health (sometimes referred to as the "worried well") and the chronic complainers,[6] a group of troublesome patients who have multiple complaints, feel the need to be seen frequently, and fit into the group of entitled demanders so aptly described by Groves.[1] These patients rarely get well and never seem to appreciate the efforts the physician makes on their behalf. It would appear that these patients need their disease in order to function at all.

Mary S. has been seeing Dr. L. for almost eight months on a regular basis. She is a 47-year-old divorced, obese, white female, with moderately well-controlled hypertension, who also complains of insomnia and a variety of aches and pains. Mary had been laid off from her job as a factory worker and been put on temporary disability payments. She is very angry because her benefits are about to expire; she also has problems paying her rent, argues constantly with her 21-year-old son, who lives with her, and feels that her married daughter and son-in-law treat her badly. Mary talks loudly and fast. It is as though she wants to get twenty minutes of conversation into a ten minute session. Dr. L. usually feels as though he has been assaulted, or perhaps run over by a lawn mower, after spending any amount of time with her. Routine lab work and careful examination has convinced Dr. L. that Mary's problems are primarily stress-induced, and that she herself generates the stress, for both herself and others. He has developed a clinical style that allows his patient the first minutes of the interview in which to complain about whatever is bothering her the most, after which he takes control and examines one problem in detail. After monitoring medications and laying on hands, Dr. L. wonders aloud what Mary could do differently in a specific interaction with her son. He sees her regularly, every two weeks. Her improvement is obvious and she is starting to become aware that she has power to make things happen, and not just by being demanding. There are even indications that, since she feels accepted, she is learning to listen a little.

There is a growing body of contemporary literature focusing on various somatization disorders.[7-14] The basics of psychosomatic medicine were proposed in a 1943 article by Franz Alexander, in which he explained that some patients experiencing certain emotions, such as anger, fear, frustration, neediness, or sorrow, which they are not free to express because of internal conflicts, developed the physical symptoms that were concomitants of the emotion.[15] Psychiatrists contend that once these emotions can be expressed directly, the need to somatize will decrease.[16] Recent studies evaluating the utilization of outpatient medical services have documented their high use by patients who somatize and experience psychological as physical distress.[17,18]

The stress response (the stress can be self-induced, as it is with the chronic complainer) will activate physiological reactions that are acutely felt and can become chronic, ultimately precipitating organic problems. Patients experience physiological symptoms that result from sympathetic arousal that does not get discharged productively. Many patients do not know how to get any kind of care or attention without complaining. When their complaints are not effective, they persevere and complain louder and longer. This further increases their stress.

Life stress has been shown to be predictive of increased medical care utilization for all patients, but particularly for somatizers.[19] J. Miranda and colleagues suggested that outpatient medical services need to focus on stress reduction as a way to manage this problem. The effectiveness of cognitive stress-management interventions that help people reinterpret situations, thereby changing their actual emotional reaction, becomes obvious. Until patients become aware of the mechanisms involved and their power to ameliorate their reactions, they are trapped. Anyone who is trapped or pushed into a corner is not nice to deal with. Anything that the physician can do to empower patients and to slowly, over time, convince them that they can affect their health, improve the course of their lives, and get their needs met through other means than complaining about physical symptoms is highly therapeutic.

When a chronic complainer bemoans the fact that his wife offers him no sympathy, the physician can respond: "I can see that that is very difficult for you. What is it, specifically, that you want from your wife?"

Patient: "I want her to pay attention to me."

Doctor: "That makes sense. Does she pay attention when you tell her about your pain?"

Patient: "No, she ignores me. Then she starts complaining about her headaches."

Doctor: "I see. Is there anything that you can do to change the situation?"

If the patient responds negatively, it is important not to argue. Power struggles are not constructive. When we convince patients that they are wrong, we lose because we damage their self-esteem. In Chapter 3, we pointed out the enormous power that is attributed to physicians and how that power can be used therapeutically to great advantage. However, it can also be used detrimentally, to diminish the patient.

It is useful to get the patient to commit to doing one small task that has a positive and realistic potential. When a patient says that his wife complains about her headaches, perhaps the patient could give her the kind of sympathetic response that he himself desires. It would certainly get her attention.

One of the great challenges of out-patient medicine is that the physician has no control over what patients actually do after they leave the office. Therefore, it is important to find ways to motivate patients to do what is necessary. If they are not willing, they will sabotage the physician's best efforts. Patients must be convinced that changing a behavior is important, that change is possible, and that there is a payoff for trying. Assignments must be broken down into modest, feasible tasks; then, small wins will accumulate and make big differences.

Therapy for Patients with Anxiety

"Anxiety is the enemy of health."[20] It is a signal that the body sends to warn of danger. The signal is real and its manifestations are frightening, but the danger is often nonexistent or self-induced. There are many effective treatments, both pharmacological and behavioral, for anxiety. It is imperative for the physician to assure the patient that all the varied symptoms are real, and that although frightening, they can be managed. When patients learn to control their symptoms through learning relaxation strategies and cognitive restructuring, practicing meditation, establishing hierarchies of feared situations, or engaging in regular exercise programs, they will feel much better.[21] Patients can be taught progressive muscle relaxation techniques and asked to practice them twice a day for fifteen minutes. The physician can also encourage patients to become aware of their thoughts, to monitor them for distortions (generalizing, "awfulizing," and catastrophizing), and to substitute more positive or functional thoughts. Once the patient becomes aware that negative and frightening ideas, and not the actual situation, are precipitating the anxiety, the physician can teach him or her to challenge these thoughts by reflecting on one or more of the following questions presented in the work of A. T. Beck and G. Emery: (1) What is the evidence? (2) What is another way to look at the situation? and (3) So what if that does happen?[22] This is another area where bibliotherapy, using suggestions from Appendix B, can be very helpful. When patients learn techniques that make them feel they can control their symptoms, they will feel safer. There will appear to be less danger. Sometimes it will be necessary for patients to make major life changes in order to escape from situations that are truly destructive. Having the physician as a sounding board can be very supportive.

For symptomatic relief, while the patient is learning skills or preparing to make life changes to reduce the source of the anxiety, Beck and Emery suggest using the AWARE technique to help patients accept anxiety.[22] The elements of AWARE are as follows:

A: Accept the anxiety.

W: Watch your anxiety. Rate it on a scale from 0 to 10 and watch it change.

A: Act with the anxiety. Act as if you are not anxious. Breathe normally and slowly.

R: Repeat the steps until the anxiety goes down to a comfortable level.

E: Expect the best.

Having a structure for dealing with the symptoms puts the patient back in control. This strategy is also useful for physicians dealing with anxious patients.

The Substance Abuser

It is no accident that the literature on physician referrals to psychiatrists shows the highest rate of referrals for patients with various substance abuse or addictive disorders.[23,24] The alcohol or narcotics abuser is difficult to treat because, by definition, these patients do not exercise control or take responsibility for their behavior.

If a physician wishes to become involved with this type of patient, the abuser must be held responsible for having created the situation—because of trying to run away from, rather than deal with, problems. The patient must agree to accept help and follow the instructions of the physician. Substance abusers are not generally capable of mustering the resources for solving the situation alone. The first constructive step in overcoming a substance abuse problem is for the patient to admit his or her helplessness to control the addiction and accept help from an outside source.[25] A firm contract must be made, with the patient committing to abstinence from the drug of choice (or other nonprescribed chemicals), following the physician's orders explicitly, and most of all, reporting any infringement of these conditions. Firm limits must be set, and the contract depends on the patient's compliance. If the patient becomes involved in a twelve-step support group, the odds of success will increase dramatically.

The Depressed Patient

It can be very depressing to have to spend time with depressed patients. It is even more depressing to read that long-term follow-up studies show that depression that is not diagnosed or treated by primary care physicians is highly associated with long-lasting symptomatology, decreased quality of life, and suicide.[26] Not all depressions are major ones, but even mild-to-moderate depressions will negatively affect peoples' lives. Depression can be treated very effectively using brief sessions. Since there is something contagious in the negativity, heaviness, hopelessness, and neediness expressed by these unhappy people, it is important to set realistic expectations for both the patients and ourselves. The patient can be expected to suffer, but he or she can also be encouraged to make some small changes, minute ones if necessary. D. C. Klein and E. P. Seligman have demonstrated conclusively that getting people to successfully accomplish small tasks can reverse learned helplessness (the story based on experience that there is nothing to be done to escape a bad situation), which is the correlate of depression.[27] Therefore, in treating a depressed patient, we first give the patient permission to be depressed. We do not suggset that these patients should feel any differently than they do. If they could, they would. We do not focus these patients on the positive features of their lives. That only sets up resistance and guilt. We do *not* point out that other people also have horrible problems. Depressed people do not care about the experience of others. We do tell the family to stop trying to cheer the patient up. Patients who are depressed and are told to look on the bright side of things or to count their blessings often feel misunderstood, wrong, ungrateful, unworthy, or any number of unpleasant feelings, which simply exacerbates their underlying depression. Instead, we agree that it seems as though right now things are really bad and state that we can understand that the patient would feel awful. Sometimes, if we are lucky, the patient will actually respond with something positive. Perversity is an endemic human quality.

Certainly, if necessary, the physician can prescribe an antidepressant. However, while waiting for the medication to take effect, and subsequently, along with the medical treatment, behavioral suggestions and cognitive therapy are very effective. Behavioral treatment might start by suggesting one activity that will give the patient a subjective sense of control: "I want you to get some exercise, take a brisk walk, perhaps ten minutes, twice a day. It is not required that you enjoy it, you just have to do it." "Do one small thing for yourself each day." "Make a list of all the tasks you have to do, and feel that you can't. Then do just one—the one that takes the least time." "Forget about mornings, you probably will feel rotten, but plan to do one constructive thing every afternoon." If there has been a previous history of depressive episodes, it is useful to ask; "What sort of things did you do previously that helped you to feel better?"

Cognitive therapy consists of challenging some of the negative assumptions and generalities that the patient makes. The physician will agree that right now, things look very bad, but will add that there is no evidence to show that they will always be that way. It is effective to focus on the fact that the patient has an illness which will resolve. Whenever the patient makes a negative statement, the physician can edit the statement by inserting the word *yet*: "Yes, I understand that you have not been able to motivate yourself to exercise, yet." "No, your appetite has not improved, yet." The implication that things will change—that the patient is not stuck in the internal, stable, global explanatory box—is very powerful. The physician's confidence stirs hope in the patient. Hope is the antidote for depression.

The physician must not expect to change the patient's situation, but he or she should see the patient regularly, be supportive (reinforce the patient's strength), prescribe and monitor medications (if appropriate), and set reasonable limits on the patient's allowable wallowing time. Labeling wallowing for what it is and setting a five minute limit on this activity at any given time is very effective.

The Grieving Patient

In Chapter 6 we pointed out that grief work can usually be accomplished in six to eight sessions. Whenever a patient appears to be overreacting to a current loss, an unresolved grief reaction may well be contributing to the severity of the response. The physician needs to probe in order to ascertain if this is true. He or she then explains the significance of completing the mourning process and how difficult this can be sometimes. First of all, it is painful. Moreover, although all people feel some ambivalence toward the significant others in their lives, they are uncomfortable with the anger that is generated when they feel abandoned through death or other circumstances. Conversely, when a troubled relationship ends in divorce or separation, patients may be uncomfortable experiencing the sense of loss of the positive aspects. It is important for patients to talk about these feelings as well as reviewing the significant aspects of the lost relationship.

The six or eight sessions do not necessarily have to occur weekly. In a resistant patient, the physician can simply bring up the subject briefly every time that the patient is seen for any medical problem. However, ideally the patient will be cooperative and willing to work. Because grief work does require a thorough airing of the issues, reminiscing about important details and homework in the form of writing about the person or the details of the loss can be very helpful.[28] Talking to relatives or friends, reviewing photographs, and visiting significant places can be very beneficial. The fifteen minute session with the physician is then used to highlight important understandings. As stated previously, the grieving process involves reviewing the significant aspects of the loss, coming to terms with the good and bad aspects, feeling the pain, accepting the finality, and finally letting go.

Anniversary reactions are extremely common, and patients benefit from being told to expect a variety of somatic symptoms and mood shifts around the anniversary date of a loss or other significant event.[29] Patients primarily need to be given encouragement to feel their pain rather than try to shut it off. There is little that is required of the physician except to be there.

The Suicidal Patient

When working with depressed or grieving patients, suicide is always a potential risk. These patients are experiencing such a high degree of subjective pain that the need to escape it may make the option of killing themselves appear quite attractive. In general, serious consideration of suicide corresponds with strong feelings of poor self-esteem, lack of social support, and lack of hope. People who talk about suicide will kill themselves if their attempts to get help fail.

In our experience, primary care physicians can treat potentially suicidal patients very effectively. Once these individuals feel that someone is really concerned about them, they readjust their notions that there is no one in the world who cares and that everyone would be better off if they were dead. The physician acknowledges that suicide is always an option, which may seem desirable at a given time, but that once exercised, suicide excludes all other choices. Since it is always better to keep one's options open, the physician might say: "I hate to see you use a permanent solution, for what may turn out to be a temporary problem. Let's keep your options open. There may be a way to turn off the pain without turning yourself off. Why don't we see how you feel in a few weeks. Let's take it one day at a time and see if together, we can't find a better way to deal with this situation."

It is imperative to check whether the patient has a plan. If so, the patient must either commit to postponing such action or will require hospitalization for his or her safety. Even with a potential plan, the therapeutic connection with the physician can be powerful enough to overcome the feelings of hopelessness and demoralization that lead to thoughts of suicide.

The doctor who chooses to treat a potentially suicidal patient must be available for him or her should he or she need to feel connected. If the doctor is going to be away and someone else will be on call, the covering physician must be informed about the seriousness of the situation and the support that must be given. Hopefully, family and friends will also be mobilized. As an assignment, the patient will be told to ask for support from significant others. It is important to have him or her verify a commitment to call at a certain time or to come in for an appointment in two days, or whatever time period is mutually agreeable. The patient must be given clear instructions to call at a time when the physician will be personally available to talk. A patient's promise to call or come in at a specific future time can be safely interpreted as a statement that he or she expects to be alive at that time. A note to that effect must be put into the chart: "Patient promises to call tomorrow to check in. Will be seen on Wednesday for follow-up. Will take no action before discussing further. Patient instructed to go to the Emergency Room if the situation worsens." The patient can then be asked to sign the note.

Treating Children

When we say that every patient should be BATHEd, we are including children. A wonderful rapport can be established by asking children what is happening in their lives, how they feel about it, what troubles them the most, and how they are handling it, and then giving them empathy. It is often fascinating to compare what a child tells us about what is going on to the story that we get from the adults in the family. Often, the discrepancy can be used to make an effective intervention. Sometimes, we can help the child to interpret the situation differently, while at others, we can intervene with the parent, using the principles outlined in Chapter 8.

Young children or children who are reluctant to talk can be asked to draw a picture. Since children usually draw what is important to them, asking them to tell a story about the picture provides an easy way to get useful information and connect with the child.[30] Asking a child to "Draw-a-Person"[31] or

"Draw-a-Family" is a lovely way to keep a youngster occupied while examining a parent and can be used to screen for developmental or situational problems. (First devised as a "culture-fair" intelligence test, the drawing also provides valid information about a child's sense of self.)[31] A blank piece of paper and a pencil are all that is required. The physician first asks the child to "tell me about this person." Then the physician can pose specific questions about the various people in the family drawing. How do they feel about each other? What makes them happy? What makes them sad? What do they do when they get mad at each other? The physician can ask the child, "If you could change one thing in this family, what would it be?" Except in unusual circumstances, interventions focused on changing the parents' behavior toward the child (see Chapter 8) are more efficient and effective than trying to engage the child in a psychotherapeutic relationship. When a case is difficult, referral to a family therapist is an option to consider.

Treating the Adolescent

Parents of young teenagers should be informed that the physician needs to establish a separate relationship with the adolescent. Every visit must include time without the parent in the exam room. Establishing confidential relationships with teenagers is paramount in gaining their trust and respect. Continuity in the relationship also helps. Teenagers can be BATHEd around issues of home, school, their ambitions, sex, and drugs.

It is important to support adolescents' self-esteem and to acknowledge the difficulty of sorting out the many choices that are available. The physician can either act as a trusted advisor or encourage the adolescent to find another adult (not the parent) to fulfill that role. If teenagers are angry with their parents, they must be cautioned not to "self-destruct" (engage in risky behavior) just go get back at their parents. When teenagers do not get positive support at home they often choose and emulate a peer group that will confirm their parents' worst fears. In general, parents should be told to stop nagging (since it does no good) and stop criticizing (since it causes harm). Teenagers and young adults respond equally well to our techniques. Indeed, physicians in college health services have reported exceptionally good results using our methods.

Dr. A. assumed that Ken was pretty healthy because this was his first visit to the office since his college health physical and he was now a member of the junior class. His presenting request that "I would like to have my blood pressure checked" was a bit unusual, particularly when, as a matter of routine, the college nurse had checked his vital signs and found them to be textbook normal. After dispensing with the usual amenities, Dr. A. got to the issue of Ken's concern about his blood pressure and quickly ascertained that his problem was fatigue, which he interpreted as a sign of "low blood pressure." Further questioning about the duration and nature of his fatigue, his work and sleep habits, and related symptomatology was less productive except that Dr. A. got the sense that something was disturbing Ken. He struck gold when he used the BATHE technique.

Dr. A.: "Ken, what is going on in your life?"

Ken: "Well Doc, my roommate and his girlfriend are using our room to do their thing, it's gotten to the point that I can't even get in there to get a good night's sleep."

Dr. A.: "How do you feel about that?"

Ken: "It makes me really angry; I am paying for that room and I can't even use it."

Dr. A.: "What troubles you the most about that?"

Ken: "Well he claims he is not keeping me out; both he and his girlfriend suggested that my new girlfriend and I join them, but we're just not ready to take that step in our relationship."

Dr. A.: "How are you handling that?"

Ken: "Not well. I mean, I am not getting very much sleep and I'm getting more and more irritated. It's beginning to affect my grades as well as my relationship with my girlfriend."

Dr. A.: "That must be very difficult for you."

When Ken acknowledged that indeed it was difficult, Dr. A. suggested that he think about his other options. Ken returned the following week to report that he had had a long talk with his roommate and that they had come to an agreement with which Ken was comfortable. Ken was feeling very good about himself and how he had handled the situation. He thanked Dr. A. for his support and said he could not have done it without him.

Just supporting Ken and making him aware that he had other options empowered him to do what he had to do to solve his own problem (this is generally the case). In the next chapter we will look at how to reconcile the needs of the patient with those of other family members.

SUMMARY

In taking care of hateful patients, awareness that these patients are attempting to solve problems in the best way they can is helpful. Setting limits regarding time spent and number of problems discussed, as well as reframing the situation as a learning opportunity, will help the physician cope.

Hypochondriacal patients can be helped by giving them regular appointments and exploring the context of their lives along with their symptomatology. Their suffering is thus acknowledged, and they are allowed to retain one or two symptoms. Chronic complainers are recognized as needing their disease but encouraged to make small changes that will help them feel more in control of their lives.

To successfully treat substance abusers, strict limits must be set. Depressed patients must be given permission to be depressed, while also being encouraged to make small changes in the circumstances of their lives. Grieving patients are instructed to examine the significant aspects of their terminated relationships and to actively mourn their losses. They need to be encouraged to feel their pain rather than trying to shut if off.

Serious consideration of suicide generally corresponds with feelings of poor self-esteem, lack of social support, and lack of hope. The physician counters these by a show concern and a commitment to help. A contract is made, and the patient's promise to call or come in at a specific time is elicited. Clear documentation and backup are required.

Children and teenagers can be BATHEd during a regular office visit. Children's drawings help facilitate communication with the physician. When dealing with teenagers, their confidentiality must be respected.

REFERENCES

1. Groves, J. E. Taking care of the hateful patient. *New England Journal of Medicine*, 1978, *298*, 883–887.

2. Adler, G. The physician and the hypochondriacal patient. *New England Journal of Medicine*, 1981, *304*, 1394–1396.

3. Barsky, A. J., & Klerman, G. L. Overview: Hypochondriasis, bodily complaints, and somatic styles. *American Journal of Psychiatry*, 1983, *140*, 273–283.

4. Barsky, A. J., Wyshak, G., Latham, K. S., & Klerman, G. L. Hypochondriacal patients, their physicians, and their medical care. *Journal of General Internal Medicine*, 1991, *6*, p. 413.

5. Watzlawick, P. *The language of change: Elements of therapeutic communication.* New York: Basic Books, 1978, p. 73.

6. Rittelmeyer, L. F., Jr. Coping with the chronic complainer. *American Family Physician*, 1985, *31*, 211–215.

7. Lipkin, M. Functional or organic? A pointless question. *Annals of Internal Medicine*, 1969, *71*, 1013–1017.

8. Pierloot, R. A. The treatment of psychosomatic disorders by the general practitioner. *International Journal of Psychiatry in Medicine*, 1977–1978, *8*, 43–51.

9. Cavenar, J. O., Jr., Nash, J. L., & Maltbie, A. A. Anniversary reactions presenting as physical complaints. *Journal of Clinical Psychiatry*, 1978, *39*, 369–374.

10. Barsky, A. J., III. Patients who amplify bodily sensations. *Annals of Internal Medicine*, 1979, *91*, 63–70.

11. Escobar, J. I., Burnam, M. A., Karno, M., Forsythe, A., & Golding, H. M. Somatization in the community. *Archives of General Psychiatry*, 1987, *44*, 713–718.

12. Monson, R. A., & Smith, G. R. Somatization disorder in primary care. *New England Journal of Medicine*, 1983, *308*, 1464–1465.

13. Smith, C. W. The irritable bowel syndrome. *The Female Patient*, 1985, *10*, 81–90.

14. Lesser, I. M. Alexithymia. *New England Journal of Medicine*, 1985, *312*, 690–692.

15. Alexander, F. Fundamental concepts of psychosomatic research: Psychogenesis, conversion, specificity. *Psychosomatic Medicine*, 1943, *5*, 205–210.

16. Fenichel, O. *The psychoanalytic theory of neurosis*. New York: Norton, 1945.

17. Barsky, A. M., Wychak, G., & Klerman, G. L. Medical and psychiatric determinants of outpatient medical utilization. *Medical Care*, 1986, *24*, 548–560.

18. Escobar, J. I., Golding, J. M., Hough, R. L., Karno, M., Burnam, M. A., & Wells, K. B. Somatization in the community: Relationship of disability and use of services. *American Journal of Public Health*, 1987, *77*, 837–840.

19. Miranda, J., Perez-Stable, E. J., Munoz, R. F., Hargreaves, W., & Henke, C. J. Somatization, psychiatric disorder, and stress in utilization of ambulatory medical services. *Health Psychology*, 1991, *10*, 46–51.

20. Gabriel Smilkstein. Caveat: Patient centered care. Theme-Day Presentation, Society of Teachers of Family Medicine, 25th Annual Spring Conference, St. Louis, Mo., April 25, 1992.

21. Barlow, D. H. *Anxiety and its disorders: The nature and treatment of anxiety and panic*. New York: Guilford Press, 1988.

22. Beck, A. T., & Emery, G. *Anxiety disorders and phobias: A cognitive perspective*. New York: Basic Books, 1985.

23. Robertson, N. C. Variations in referral pattern to the psychiatric services by general practitioners. *Psychological Medicine*, 1979, *9*, 355–364.

24. Hull, J. The use of psychiatric referrals by non-psychiatric physicians. *Medical Care*, 1979, *17*, 718–726.

25. Brickman, P., Rabinowitz, V. C., Karuza, J., Jr., Coates, D., Cohn, E., & Kidder, L. Models of helping and coping. *American Psychologist*, 1982, *37*, 368–384.

26. Murphy, J. M., Olivier, D. C., Sobol, A. M., Monson, R. R., & Leighton, A. H. Diagnosis and outcome: Depression and anxiety in a general popoulation. *Psychological Medicine*, 1986, *16*, 117–126.

27. Klein, D. C., & Seligman, M.E.P. Reversal of performance deficits and perceptual deficits in learned helplessness and depression. *Journal of Abnormal Psychology*, 1976, *85*, 11–26.

28. Pennebaker, J. W., Kiecolt-Glaser, J. K., & Glaser, R. Disclosure of traumas and immune function: Health implications for psychotherapy. *Journal of Consulting and Clinical Psychology*, 1988, *56*, 239–245.

29. Bornstein, P. E., & Clayton, P. J. The anniversary reaction. *Diseases of the Nervous System*, 1972, *33*, 470–472.

30. Gardner, R. A. *Psychotherapeutic approaches to the resistant child*. New York: Jason Aronson, 1975.

31. Goodenough, F. L. *Measurement of intelligence by drawing*. New York: World Book Co., 1926.

CHAPTER 10

Applied Psychotherapy for Special Situations, Staff, and Physicians

Having looked at ways to treat specific problem patients, we should now ask: What about the myriad of other problems related to dealing with family members, especially when they present a divided or a self-righteous front? Is there a way to handle these situations smoothly? We think so. In this chapter, we also discuss constructive approaches that can be taught to nurses, receptionists, and other staff to cut down on patient frustration and anxiety. Then, we will address the application of psychotherapeutic (cognitive) principles for the personal benefit of the physician. In other words, since this is a book on applied psychotherapy, we will actualize the principle, "Physician heal thyself."[1]

HANDLING DIFFICULT FAMILY MEMBERS

Dealing with the patient's family can be one of the most rewarding, or most frustrating, aspects of practicing medicine. Often, family members will call and provide unsolicited information about a patient or make suggestions about the treatment. Physicians can clearly see the confidentiality issue in this situation and will not share patient information, but they may feel stressed by the lack of clarity regarding their relationship to the family members. In general, it is important for physicians to avoid power struggles and confrontations. Although family members can be assumed to have their own agendas, the physician is not responsible for figuring out their issues or making judgments as to their merit.

Avoiding power struggles or offense to family members are important considerations. We recommend that the physician learn to practice "verbal aikido." Aikido is a Japanese martial art, which is sometimes referred to as "the dance." When a person who is skilled in aikido is attacked, the automatic response is to turn quickly, join with the attacker, and go along in the direction of the attack. Then, after a few seconds, the practitioner gently turns both him- or herself and the attacker around, so that they are both going in the opposite direction. After this, he or she can gracefully disengage or knock the attacker out.

Verbally, this translates into always acknowledging the legitimacy of others' requests or positions. It catches them off guard and leaves them open to hearing what the physician has to say. By first showing respect for the family member's position and anxiety, the physician defuses any potential defensiveness. Therefore, when making treatment or discharge plans or when discussing anything with a family member, including the behavior of a teenager, we suggest that the physician automatically start with the phrase; "I can hear how concerned you are, but . . ." and then state your case. If it is more comfortable, you may prefer to say, "I know you care a great deal about your mother [father, husband, son, aunt, niece, etc.], but . . ."

It is irrelevant whether you actually subscribe to the above statement. Making the statement is an effective strategy that earns you the other person's attention and positive receptivity. The same thing can be accomplished by starting with the phrase, "I agree with you that . . . ," and then find some part of their suggestion that you can accept.

People hear better when you start by agreeing with them. The critical issue here is that the more difficult and demanding family members may be (regardless of whether you see any merit in their suggestions or even feel that they have a legitimate stake in the outcome), there is nothing to be gained by direct antagonism. This explains the effectiveness of this technique.

You may say to yourself: "That drunken bum hasn't given two hoots about his mother in the last five years. Why should he tell me how to treat her now?" You may be absolutely right, but it will be more difficult to deal with the son if you confront him with that now. Instead, saying: "I can see how concerned you are. This must be very difficult for you. I am really glad you are letting me know what you would like me to do, but my impression [clinical judgment, good medical practice] demands that I do such and such. I will keep you informed," deprives the other person of ammunition. In a later section, "Confronting the Patient," we will discuss the technique for direct confrontation, which should be done only if absolutely necessary.

Another important consideration to keep in mind when dealing with families is that often there are large elements of guilt. When the son from

Chicago suddenly calls you and demands that absolutely everything be done for his father, whom he has neglected for years, it is a clear sign that an attempt is being made to resolve the guilt. We recommend that physicians absolve family members of guilt whenever possible. Very often it stems from projected resentment. In any case, however, guilt is such an unpleasant emotion that a concomitant hostility is generated toward the person who "makes us" feel guilty. Actually, guilt and hostility are opposite sides of the same coin. It is always therapeutic to say, "I feel confident that you did as much as you could." That is always true. It may not have been enough for the other person, but if the guilty individual could have done more (given his or her map), he or she would have done so. Do not say, "You have no reason to feel guilty." The person is likely to argue. Just say: "I'm sure that you've expressed your love as best you could. No one can expect more than that."

All these interventions are designed to facilitate communications while also allowing us to practice according to our best judgment. As in aikido, instead of meeting the opponent head-on and absorbing the impact of the forward movement, we come from the side, join in the other's movement, and then effectively spin the opponent around. Sometimes this can be fun. Reframing can also help. Instead of thinking, "Why do I have to deal with all these impossible people?" (and it is clear that some people *are* more impossible than others), we think, "Here is an opportunity to practice my new skills and see how I do." To the upset husband, we say: "I know you have Jane's interest at heart, *but* at this time, I must do what she wants. In the long run, it will be very beneficial for her, which I know is what you want."

DEALING WITH CONFLICT BETWEEN FAMILY MEMBERS

In dealing with family members who disagree over goals and strategies, it is most important to acknowledge the legitimacy of each person's position and reaction. Remember, they all have different maps. They have all had different experiences of their family and tell different stories. In trying to achieve some sort of consensus, it is important that they focus on a superordinate goal: the welfare of the patient. If they cannot agree, then perhaps the physician's best judgment of the patient's needs will have to prevail. If the physician has been supportive of the family and the patient, it is likely they will agree on this. The physician takes responsibility because he or she has control of the treatment. Trying to modify the family dynamics is an important challenge and lends itself to creative interventions by the physician (which are beyond the scope of this book).[2]

CONFRONTING THE PATIENT

There are times when a person's behavior goes beyond acceptable limits or causes a problem, making confrontation necessary. Under these circumstances, it is important to point out to the individual in what way the behavior is a problem, that is, how it affects the physician, the staff, or the practice, and to suggest a specific correction. Sometimes this is enough, and the person will apologize and make the correction. More often, however, the person will become defensive and abusive, and will refuse to discuss the issue. The way in which people react to being confronted with negative information about themselves that they do not wish to acknowledge (it is on their map, but they pretend it is not) or change, is usually stereotypical.[3] People will react as though they had been zapped. We can expect one of three potential behaviors in response to a "zap": counterattack, retreat, or diffusion. The three responses work as follows:

Counterattack: "Really doctor, I have not been pleased with the way that you treated my mother. I think I will ask someone else to take over her care."

Retreat: "I'm sorry, Doctor, I don't have time to discuss it now [or ever]. I'm late for an appointment."

Diffusion: "You think that I'm hard to deal with. My son has been giving me so much trouble lately. What do you think is wrong with the current generation?"

Any of these reactions are typical for persons being zapped: that is, being confronted and having to deal with an issue they have been trying to avoid. When a counterattack is launched by the "zappee," it is important for the physician not to get caught in feeling defensive but to switch to active listening and verbal aikido, and then to repeat the original message. When the negative reaction is expected, the physician can be prepared to handle it smoothly: "Yes, I agree, that sometimes you have not been pleased with the treatment choices, *but* you must cease bringing alcohol into the hospital." "Mr. Jones: I know you are in a hurry, *but* I want you to get that blood test done today." "Yes, I can see how frustrated you are with your son, *but* I must have your signed consent for this procedure now." "Mrs. Smith, I understand how angry you are when I sometimes don't call you right back, how your boss makes unreasonable demands on you at work, and how unreliable your babysitter is, *but* I cannot continue to treat your diabetes if you will not take your medicine as prescribed."

Anytime we confront another with something they really do not want to hear, it can be considered a zap. Zaps, by definition, are subjective experiences of the receiver, who will react (or rather, overreact) in typical fashion. Recognizing this as normal, being prepared for it, and not reacting to the counterattack as though it were a zap are useful tactics. Retreats or diversions can also be expected (and must be accepted) before a reiteration of the initial problem can be productive. Sometimes it is necessary to go through several rounds before finally being heard. This insight is helpful in all interpersonal situations involving conflict that must be addressed, and particularly in dealing with difficult patients or their families.

TRAINING THE OFFICE STAFF

The office staff represents an important element of the environment that the patient experiences when coming to the physician for treatment. In fact, when calling to make an appointment or wanting to speak to the physician on the phone, the staff acts as the ultimate gatekeeper.

It is important that receptionists and nursing personnel become aware of the effects of stress on patients, as outlined in Chapter 2, and learn a few simple and effective interventions for managing their patient interactions. For example, our receptionist complained that some patients are very difficult and demanding on the phone and that it is they who should learn to be more cooperative. However, people who are upset are often unreasonable. It is not useful to focus on the fact that they should not act that way; the reality is that they do. Instead, the question becomes: "What can be done to make the person feel sufficiently supported that healthier responses can be expected? How can we deal with unreasonable patients without contributing to our own stress?"

Fielding Phone Calls

Sometimes when a physician has not returned a patient's call, for whatever reason, patients will become frustrated and abusive of the staff. While we certainly do not condone this type of behavior, it is not useful for the receptionist to get upset and respond angrily to the patient. Instead, the receptionist should make a supportive statement; such as: "It must be difficult to have to stay home and wait for the doctor to call back, when you have so much to do [you are feeling so bad]." "It must be hard when you are worried about Nancy's fever to be unable to reach the doctor right away. Time passes slowly when you're anxious, doesn't it?" This type of understanding response makes the patient feel supported and connected to another human being who acknowledges the reaction to the stress as reasonable—which it is.

The second function that the staff must be encouraged to assume is helping the patient set realistic expectations. It is of little value to get the patient off the phone by saying, "Yes, I'll tell the doctor to call you right away," when the doctor is at lunch, solidly booked with patients all afternoon, and scheduled to make hospital rounds after 5:00 P.M., before going to an out-of-town medical society dinner at 7:30. Instead, it is better to say that the doctor will probably not be available to speak to the patient and ask if there is a specific question that needs to be answered or if it can wait until morning.

It is important to specify when to expect the doctor's call. The implication is that the patient's time is also valuable and that he or she has other things to do besides just sitting by the phone waiting for the physician to call back. If it becomes impossible for the physician to contact the patient within the agreed-on time period, someone else should call and inform the patient *when* the physician can be expected to be free.

We like to compare the experience of the patient to our own, when we are phoning someone whose line is busy and we are put on hold. It is very reassuring to have the operator periodically break in and report that the line is still busy. The wait is no less interminable, but we know that we have not been forgotten. There is a sense of being acknowledged and remaining connected. We need to be sure that patients do not feel forgotten or disconnected. If these procedures are adopted, there will be a minimum of angry repeat calls from frustrated patients.

Patients in the Office

There are also potential problems connected with patients in the office. Because of their particular personalities, certain patients are extremely difficult for the staff to deal with. We know that these patients' personalities are not going to change, but often their behavior can be managed more effectively. Objectively, these patients' problems may not be serious, but subjectively, their problems are disturbing their precarious equilibrium or they would not be coming to the doctor for help. The staff needs to understand that under stress patients will not be at their best behavior. They may become demanding, unreasonable, angry, unhappy, or impatient with the staff, though they often behave in a passive or ingratiating manner with the physician, on whom they feel dependent.

The staff needs to learn to set reasonable limits, always acknowledging patients' rights to feel as they do but asserting the need to control their behavior. The receptionist must inform patients who are reciting a laundry list of troubles, insults, and concerns that: "I understand that it must be very difficult for you." "I can see how upset you are." "I can hear how angry and frustrated you feel, but . . . ." Direct acknowledgment of their suffering saves patients from continued efforts to convince someone of their plight. Once they have successfully communicated that they are unhappy, they will be more apt to hear what others want.

The staff also needs to help patients set realistic expectations for the visit. It is better to say that there will be at least a half hour wait when the doctor is running behind schedule than to say nothing, or, worse yet, to say "The doctor will be right with you" when this is untrue. When patients feel as though their concerns are receiving serious consideration, it is more likely that they will be able to respond appropriately to others' concerns.

Care for the Caring

The physician has a responsibility to support the staff while encouraging concern for patient well-being. We would remind the physician that the staff needs to feel competent and connected as well. It is important that the physician frequently acknowledge the contribution the staff is making to the supportive environment of the office: "I really appreciate the way you've handled Mrs. Brown. She must be very difficult for you to deal with." "You must really get tired of having to field all these phone calls, when I sometimes have trouble getting back to these people."

RULES FOR PHYSICIAN SURVIVAL

We have been doing a great deal of preaching in this book regarding the need of taking care of patients' psychological, as well as physical, needs. We are aware that in order for physicians to follow through on these practices, their own psychological needs must be met. Since we try hard to be consistent, we will now provide a set of rules that the physician can apply to assure personal psychological well-being. These rules were developed out of our teaching experience with residents. Here are the dozen that we have found to be the most helpful in practice.

Rule 1: Do Not Take Responsibility for Things You Cannot Control

The implication of this rule is that if we did not have control of the circumstances that helped create a situation, we do not have to take responsibility for the effect of the situation on others. The practical application of this rule is that when a person complains about a situation over which we have no control and that we did not create, we are able to empathize with their frustration, pain, or other discomfort, without becoming defensive. Since it is clearly not our fault, we can sympathize with patients about the inflexibility of rules made by hospitals, HMOs, or the government, without feeling as though we have to do anything about them. It is a situation over which we have no control. We are not responsible for creating the patient's disease. However, we may (or may not) be able to treat it effectively.

The corollary of Rule 1 is that we must take responsibility for what we can control: our own behavior. It is a given that in order to control our behavior, we must first be aware of it. We must also recognize our limits.

Rule 2: Take Care of Yourself or You Cannot Take Care of Anyone Else

It is really important that physicians become aware of their own limits and tolerance for certain situations. When we find that we are going on tilt, it is imperative to take time-out to center ourselves. Physicians need to learn stress management techniques, build a support group, set realistic expectations for themselves, and set limits on the demands of others (gently, of course). Being overstressed impairs functioning, and once functioning has been impaired, the outcome becomes questionable. This leads to Rule 3.

Rule 3: Trouble Is Easier to Prevent Than to Fix

This concept needs little elaboration. Often a minute or two spent in explaining something or considering the consequences of a potential action can avoid extensive problems. Exploring potential outcomes and worst-case scenarios before the fact can ultimately save time and aggravation. Doing nothing is often better than doing something, especially when the data is not all in. Applying tincture of time when hasty action might precipitate an unstoppable process is an important option to consider.

Rule 4: When You Get Upset, Tune into What Is Going on with You and Go through the Three-Step Process:

1. **What am I feeling?**
2. **What do I want?**
3. **What can I do about it?**

This effective strategy for getting in touch with and managing feelings and behavior was presented in Chapter 7. It is an important skill for the physician to apply personally. Whenever there is a sense of starting to approach tilt—feeling a strong sense of being internally pressured and clearly off-balance—we recommend tuning in and labeling the feeling being experienced. It may be anger, frustration, impatience, sadness, fatigue, or something else. That is step 1.

Step 2 requires getting in touch with what is actually wanted. For example, the physician may realize: "I want the patients to stop being so demanding." "I want my receptionist to be better organized." "I want someone to take care of me, for a change." "I want someone to acknowledge that I am trying to do a good job."

Step 3 requires determining what one can do personally to accomplish what is desired. If we are more sympathetic to the patients, they may actually become less demanding. The receptionist may need some support if this is an unusual style for him or her. However, if the disorganization is chronic and unremediable, the physician may have to consider a replacement. As far as getting someone to take care of us is concerned, we may have to learn to ask for what we want—and then learn to accept it. Sometimes, there is nothing that we can do to get what we want. We cannot make it stop raining on our parade; we cannot change the past or the way in which someone else is feeling or reacting. That brings us to Rule 5.

Rule 5: If the Answer to Step 3 of Rule 4 Is "Nothing," Apply Rule 1

Rule 1, of course, states that we should not take responsibility for things we cannot control. In this case, since there is nothing we can do to get what we want, we need to accept the fact. We do not beat up on ourselves for being unable to affect something over which we have no power. Then, recycling Rule 4 usually will result in feeling sad as we keep wishing this was a more perfect world. Since there is nothing we can do to affect the situation, the result is usually a feeling of acceptance, smug satisfaction at being wise, and an appreciation of ourselves and our ability to sort out feelings. It has been our experience that when we go through this process, there is generally a strong sense of taking control. By definition, this results in a sense of competence that is mutually exclusive to feeling overwhelmed. We are fixed. We feel much better. This works for us just as it does for patients.

Rule 6: Ask for Support When You Need It—and Give Others Permission to Feel What They Feel

This simple strategy affirms the importance of accepting ourselves and others where we are, given our individual maps. We all need support sometimes, and the need does not imply weakness. Giving others permission to feel whatever emotions they feel costs nothing. It implies a recognition of the fact that if they could feel differently, they would.

Rule 7: In a Bad Situation You Have Four Options:

1. Leave it;
2. Change it;

3. **Accept it;** or
4. **Reframe it.**

This strategy was discussed at length in Chapter 8. However, we cannot emphasize too strongly the empowering effect of learning to reframe situations. If there is nothing we can do to change an uncomfortable circumstance, we can learn to give ourselves points for flowing with it, not upsetting ourselves, using the time to think about options for next time, or any other constructive attitude or behavior. Thus, we can turn the situation into a successful learning experience. In any case, a way to program small wins must be found. The small win may simply be deciding not to complain, since it is futile and may only make others uncomfortable. Finding a constructive way to look at the circumstances (changing the story) that results in a positive personal outcome is the essence of reframing.

Rule 8: If You Never Make Mistakes, You Are Not Learning Anything

Beating up on oneself for honest, unintentional mistakes is not constructive. Being human means that we cannot be perfect. If we do not own (or acknowledge) our mistakes, we cannot learn from them. Mistakes resulting from ignorance or fatigue can be reframed in the recognition that they need to be prevented (see Rule 3).

Rule 9: When a Situation Turns Out Badly, Identify the Choice Points, and Then Decide What You Would Do Differently Next Time

This rule needs little explanation. Again, the aim is to get something constructive from conditions that cannot be changed. If there is nothing that you would change, given a chance to replay the situation, it is important to acknowledge that there is no blame, since circumstances obviously did not work out as would generally be expected. However, it is usually a good idea to reexamine the original expectations and evaluate their innate reasonableness.

Rule 10: At Any Given Time, You Can Only Make Decisions Based on the Information You Have

This was also discussed in Chapter 7. It is often useful to postpone decisions when the data is not in, to apply tincture of time, and to talk things through with supportive others.

Rule 11: Life is Not Fair—and Life Is Not a Contest

Life really is not fair. Once we accept this fact, living becomes easier. We do not even have to feel guilty about talents and possessions that we have that less fortunate people lack.

Moreover, life is not a contest. (Many people live as though it were.) It helps to realize that the important things—such as love, wonder, healing, or reaching one's potential—are on a different dimension from a zero-sum game. This is because the more we allow ourselves and others to open to these experiences, the more resources become available for everyone. People who feel secure do not need to put other people down.

Rule 12: You Have to Start Where the Patient Is At

At any given time, people can only be where they are (on their maps). They are reacting to their perceptions and doing the best they can. You have to accept them "as is." If they could be any different, they would be—and so would you.

SUMMARY

In dealing with family members, power struggles must be avoided and verbal aikido used to defuse opposition. Guilt should be relieved whenever possible. When having to confront patients or families, physicians are warned to expect counterattacks, retreats, or diversions.

Training the office staff in supportive psychological strategies is effective, as is adopting enlightened expectations for oneself. A dozen rules for physician survival based on our philosophy have been presented.

REFERENCES

1. *The Holy Bible*, Luke 4:23.

2. Doherty, W. J., & Baird, M. A. *Family therapy and family medicine*. New York: Guilford Press, 1983.

3. Palmer, J. D. *Workshop on improving conflict skills*. Unpublished manuscript, 1977.

CHAPTER 11

Anticipated Outcomes

When the art of psychotherapy is incorporated into the day-to-day practice of primary care medicine, outcomes can be expected to enhance the experience of physicians, patients, patients' families, the profession, and perhaps even society as a whole.

PHYSICIAN FACTORS

Primary care physicians practicing at this particular historical moment, when the medical care delivery system is considered to be in a state of crisis, must make a choice. Either they must accept the transformed medical paradigm, finding ways to integrate new techniques and new insights into their practices, or they can try to continue functioning according to the old medical model. If they choose to accept the enriched model, after an initial period of adjustment they are likely to achieve great personal satisfaction and constructive patient outcomes, whereas if they stay with the old paradigm, they can expect large measures of frustration when both personal and patient outcomes turn out to be less than optimal.

Professional Identity Issues

When physicians use the principles outlined in this book to look at their choices and issues, they will be able to meaningfully integrate the variety of experiences that have contributed to their professional growth and development. The result of engaging in this process should be both an enhanced sense of personal coherence and increased pride in being identified as a member of the medical profession.[1] It should be possible to sort out core values and important truths that originally led to the choice of becoming a doctor. Unfortunately, the process of medical education, undergraduate and residency training, and the pressures inherent in starting a practice often cause physicians to temporarily lose sight of the original aspirations that led to the choice of medicine as a career: that is, to provide meaningful, personal care for individual patients and to enjoy a satisfying professional life. We challenge the practitioner to examine some of the underlying assumptions of the old medical model, to discard elements that are no longer useful, and then to recommit to practicing medicine with a new awareness of the positive power that is potentially inherent in the role of physician. The current upheaval in the medical care delivery system can thus be reframed to be seen as an opportunity rather than an inconvenience.

Responding to a Changed Paradigm

Buckminster Fuller's work has made it entirely clear that we cannot continue to say, "It is fortunate that the Good Lord created the universe exactly divided into the traditional academic disciplines."[2] Just as biochemistry has bridged the gap between biology and chemistry, biophysics has bridged the gap between biology and physics, and it has much to teach us about immunology. The power of imagery to affect bodily processes is demonstrated daily through biofeedback. We know now that how we think determines how we feel, and that positive thoughts contribute to positive outcomes. We also know that how we think affects our physical reactions, and that feeling either powerful or helpless affects our ability to mobilize an effective immune response.[3] The most dangerous state, for our bodies as well as for our minds, exists when we feel overwhelmed and demoralized.[4] All this new knowledge puts a traditionally trained physician into a situation of great stress. Many of the absolutes that have formed the core of his or her understanding are changing, or already have changed, drastically. Having to adapt to rapidly changing circumstances precipitates a high level of stress. How do people respond to overwhelming stress? Under extreme circumstances:

1. They intensify their usual psychological and social coping devices;
2. When these devices fail, they experience anger, which must be suppressed (or even repressed) to prevent the sources of existing support to diminish further;
3. Next, they turn on themselves, blame themselves for not managing better, internalize their aggressive impulses, and develop feelings of guilt and depression; and

4. Finally, they stop trying to cope; instead, they feel helpless, and develop symptoms.

When people give up and stop trying to cope, the prescription is to provide support, thus gratifying dependency needs without undermining self-respect.

The strategies described in *The Fifteen Minute Hour* are designed to provide support for physicians and patients alike. Our "cookbook" approach provides step-by-step instructions for applying effective techniques that can lead not only to improved patient care, but also to enhanced satisfaction, increased income, and personal growth for the physician.

Applying the Model

To start, the practicing physician can consider the following questions: How do you feel about what is going on in the medical care delivery system today? That is, how do you feel about how you are practicing medicine today? What do you want? In other words, how do you want to practice? What can you do about it? Finally, what changes do you have to make in order to be able to do this?

We recommend that the physician be very clear about the answers to these questions. If there is a desire to put things back to the way they were, there is unfortunately nothing that can be done about that. The road goes on. However, if the desire is to keep up and be productive and successful, there are many strategies in this book that will contribute to that goal—but only if put into practice.

Achieving Professional Success

As physicians develop a reputation for treating the whole person, providing acute care, preventive services and anticipatory guidance, their practices will inevitably grow. With the anticipated physician glut, those physicians who apply the biopsychosocial model and meet more patient needs will be sought out by knowledgeable patients.[5] When a practice has been developed based on continuity of care, with regular, planned visits providing anticipatory guidance to an optimally sized patient population, the predictable patient flow will provide a comfortable income level for a reasonable time commitment. By monitoring stressful events in patients' lives on an ongoing basis, problems may be caught earlier and at less complicated stages.

Also, as an increasing proportion of medical care is provided on a prepaid basis, there will be a financial incentive for keeping people well and preventing or limiting serious illnesses. The most important payoff for the physician, however, may ultimately be the satisfaction of participating meaningfully and contributing positively to the quality of patients' lives.

Personal Growth

The final payoff for physicians adopting and using our techniques of psychotherapy on a day-to-day basis will be their own personal growth. By applying the principles outlined in this book to their own life situations, physicians will feel empowered. It will become somewhat easier to juggle professional commitments, family obligations, and personal needs. Physicians will develop their own sense of coherence and incorporate a more rational, flexible, and far-sighted coping style.[6] In order to develop a coherent sense of identity, physicians need to reflect on their feelings about their careers, relationships with both patients and colleagues, personal relationships, financial and security issues, relationships to the wider community, and ultimately, the meaning of life.[7] Becoming aware of the feelings related to these issues, acknowledging personal wants, and deciding what strategies are available for satisfying them will lead to positive personal growth. As human beings, we may be organisms (affected by demands from the environment), but we are also agents (subjects who act with intentionality), as well as spiritual beings with our place in the universe.

Moving toward Self-Actualization

When needs for physical survival, security, acceptance, and achievement have been met, physicians invariably approach the part of A. H. Maslow's hierarchy of needs that he identified as self-actualization.[8] Maslow pointed out that self-actualized people make full use of their talents, capabilities, and potentialities and develop to the full stature that they are capable of attaining.

To approach self-actualization, individuals must have learned to gratify the basic emotional needs for safety, belongingness, love, respect, and self-respect, as well as intellectually met needs for knowledge and understanding.

Becoming self-actualized results in a more efficient perception of reality and more comfortable relations with the real world. Self-actualized people do not need to cling to positive illusions,[9] nor to the familiar. They are relatively comfortable with vague and indefinite perceptions, and the quest for truth assumes priority over the need for safety. They accept themselves, other people, and nature. Self-actualized people develop an increased ability to be spontaneous and an autonomous code of ethics. Self-actualized people, like good physicians, are more problem-centered than ego-centered. They exhibit a certain quality of objective detachment and have a need for privacy.

They rely on their own interpretation of situations. In other words, they have an internal locus of control.

Other desirable qualities that Maslow cited as contributing to self-actualization include a continued fresh appreciation of the richness of experience, profound interpersonal relationships, development of a democratic character structure, a sense that the means are really the ends, creativity, and friendly sense of humor.[8]

People are not born self-actualized. Rather, self-actualization is a state that is fostered by applying the type of techniques we are advocating in this book. By using these techniques and teaching them to their patients, physicians will inevitably be affected positively.

PATIENT FACTORS

Having discussed from a broad viewpoint the potential benefits likely to accrue to the physician who incorporates psychotherapeutic techniques into the usual patient visit, let us now look at the potential cumulative effects on patients.

Supporting Health Rather Than Curing Disease

When dealing with patient problems, as outlined in this book, we do not suggest that the physician is curing in the traditional sense. It may well be that there is no such thing as a specific disease in the traditional sense, or a specific cure. The therapeutic interaction with the physician that we are proposing will enhance the patient's sense of well-being. This, in turn, will support the patient's own healing powers and allow his or her immune system to function normally.[3] Moreover, from a social perspective, when the patient feels empowered, he or she will behave in ways that will result in more productive interactions with other people.

We are not claiming that we have solutions to chronic problems that have eluded other well-meaning health professionals. Our approach is simply designed to maximize positive outcomes using easily learned, proven behavioral techniques that capitalize on peoples' strengths.

For the final case example to be presented in this book, let us look at the case of Emily M., the type of patient who is characterized by an extremely thick chart.

Emily M. is a 43-year-old female, with limited education, who came in to the office two years ago complaining of chest pain. She brought prescriptions for thirteen different medications prescribed by half a dozen different doctors. She had been hospitalized numerous times for extensive workups of multiple aches and pains, for which she had gone to the Emergency Room and been admitted. Cardiologists, pulmonologists, gastroenterologists, orthopedists, otolaryngologists, and gynecologists had all run their battery of tests from computerized axial tomography (CT) scans and sigmoidoscopy to coronary catheterization, but no one was able to identify the origin of her symptoms. Each consultant added another drug to her regimen and referred her to the next specialist, until she had seen them all. Having run out of sub-specialists, she came to the Family Practice Center.

History revealed that the onset of her various acute pains would correspond with arguments with her abusive, alcoholic, unemployed (disabled) husband. Overall, she presented with the affect and vegetative signs of depression. Dr. S's clinical impression was that Emily was suffering primarily from depressive and somatization disorders. He weaned her off all her medications except sublingual nitroglycerine, taught her relaxation techniques, and started her on imipramine.

Emily was seen once a week for several months, during which time the emphasis was shifted away from her physical pains to focus on her shattered living situation and family problems. A social worker and a woman's self-help group were also involved in her case. Emily was given strict instructions to call the center when she experienced acute pain, rather than going to the Emergency Room. During her office visits, Dr. S. attended to her physical complaints without lingering on them, and then spent most of the 15 minute session listening to the precipitating factors and new stresses in her life. He offered support and sought to focus Emily on those things that she could carry out to improve matters. Intervals between visits were gradually increased until they were occurring only every four weeks. At this time, Emily showed up in the Emergency Room complaining of chest pain. However, no acute problem was found.

After that incident, visits were scheduled at intervals ranging from every two to every four weeks, and Emily improved slowly but steadily. In contrast to the multiple admissions in each of the previous five years, she has remained out of the hospital for the past two years, except for one hospitalization for hypotonic bowel with partial obstruction at the time of her sister's death. Emily continues to be seen at regular intervals, and although her living situation is no better, she is functioning at a somewhat higher level than before.

In every case, our goals involve helping patients to achieve whatever potential is reasonable for them at this time. For Emily to stay out of the hospital for two years was an enormous accomplishment. Although functioning marginally by society's standards, her current level of adaptation is nonetheless remarkable.

Patients' Realization of Their Own Potential

Rather than engaging patients in a relationship that fosters dependency, our support encourages them to maximize their own potential. We focus on their strengths and promote patients' awareness that they are exercising choices at all times by pointing out that there are always options. It is the patients' responsibility to determine what these options are. Based on the information they have, we encourage them to make the best possible choice at any given time. The implication is that the physician and the patient are on the same side—that of the patient. It is through this partnership with the physician that patients achieve the confidence to act positively in their own interest.

Enhancing Health

It is generally accepted today that a patient's health is largely determined by what he or she does: that is, by the type of life-style that the patient adopts rather than what happens during a visit to a physician's office. It is not our intention to quarrel with this statement, but rather to encourage the use of strategies and techniques to affect the patient's behavior or life-style in positive ways. When the physician provides the type of care that we are advocating, patient satisfaction, and subsequent compliance with the physician's instructions, will both be greatly enhanced.[10]

When a patient is somatizing and the physician inquires about what is going on in his or her life, some skeptics may still contend that an uninitiated patient may object to this change of focus. The following example presents one possible response.

Patient: "You mean it's all in my mind?"

Physician: "No, not at all. Your body is telling you that you are under stress and really hurting."

We want patients to start listening to their bodies: to monitor themselves and become aware of the precursors to tilt. In this way they can ease the stress themselves and not have to become sick.

In recent years, increasing numbers of patients are requesting that their physicians take a more active interest in their health and disease processes.[11] When patients are able to accept and utilize the support provided by the physician, we can expect positive health consequences. Patients' sense of well-being will be enhanced, resulting in increased resistance to stressors of all kinds. They may be less susceptible to infections of various sorts, less accident-prone, and better able to handle life's problems in constructive ways. They will also become more aware of the impact of their own reactions on others and on the things that happen to them. This type of constructive adaptation can be expected to lead to better physical and mental health.[6]

The secondary prevention implicit in our model of practice is even more obvious. Since illness itself generally upsets the balance of psychosocial well-being for patients and their families, the benefits of preventing illness complications are clear. Patients are encouraged to engage their most constructive coping mechanisms, feel supported, and get their needs met on an ongoing basis rather than forcing the physician to manage a series of catastrophes. The trust generated by being cared for and about will enhance patients' sense of basic trust in the world (the sense of coherence), resulting in improved health consequences.[6]

Improved Relationships

When patients apply the personal strategies that we have outlined, their relationships within their families, work settings, and the community in general will improve. When people feel personally powerful, they resist being exploited and also have less need to exploit others. Communication patterns become more open and direct, and problems are handled in more productive ways. This may sound utopian, but we have seen the powerful effects of small wins toward mobilizing patients. It is also amazing to see how support helps people function in their healthy, rather than neurotic, modes. When people engage their healthy maps of the world, their positive expectations of their relationships become self-fulfilling prophesies.

EFFECTS ON THE FAMILY

It is obvious from the above discussion that improved patient functioning will trickle down to other family members. Of course, this will be complicated by specific family dynamics, old conflicts, and competing (and seemingly mutually exclusive) opinions, agendas, and desires. Although family interventions are beyond the scope of this book, we recognize that the patient is a member of a (family) system. Since every part of any system reciprocally affects every other part, when the patient changes certain self-defeating behaviors, this will have significant effects on other family members. After some initial resistance, which may be quite painful, a new accommodation will be made, hopefully with healthier functioning for the entire family.

Additional Consequences of Improved Patient Functioning

By encouraging patients to communicate more clearly and directly, they and other members of their family will have less need to manipulate each other by becoming sick or engaging in various destructive behaviors. Similarly, as patients apply the practical child management techniques that we have advocated, their children can be expected to grow up with a well-formed sense of security and high self-esteem. A benevolent circle, the essence of primary prevention, will thus be engaged. People who have an enhanced sense of health and well-being can be expected to treat other people with consideration and respect. Their stories about themselves, the world, and the other people in it will be positive.

IMPLICATIONS FOR THE PROFESSION

The growing public dissatisfaction with the medical profession is no secret. Although the clamor for health care reform is currently reaching a crescendo, public dissatisfaction with the medical profession is not a new phenomenon. In fact, it was one of the major reasons for the establishment of the American Medical Association in the first place.[12] Over time, there has been some ebb and flow in the level of public satisfaction with physicians. In the middle of this century, with all the advances being made by modern medicine, there was something akin to a flood tide, resulting in a national romance with the medical profession.[13] Those were the days when numerous medical television programs and motion pictures were popular and everyone wanted Dr. Marcus Welby (Robert Young) to be their own personal physician, with Ben Casey as his consultant. Unfortunately, the love affair has become history.

Currently, there seems to be more ebb than flow in the tide of satisfaction with the medical profession. We believe, as does Engel, that much of this problem can be traced to the method of educating medical practitioners.[14] As we stressed in Chapter 1, the dualism that separates mind from body and the reductionistic approach to medical problem solving effectively isolate the disease from the patient and the patient from the physician, when in reality they are inexorably linked.

By adopting our approach, the physician demonstrates the ability to integrate the psyche and the soma in a way that will convince the patient that this physician is interested in more than just biological processes. This physician is interested in the patient as a person. There is no question that the physician must be eminently skilled in dealing with traditional biomedical problems, but to deal with only the organic is to deal incompletely with the patient. We know that by employing the techniques presented in this book, physicians will be able to respond to more of the needs that are traditionally brought by a patient to a physician. This will improve the physician's effectiveness and image. Among other benefits, this will place him or her in a much better position in our increasingly litigious society. Patients do not sue physicians with whom they have a relationship of mutual trust, respect, and caring. Improved physician-patient communication is generally seen as the most effective method of preventing malpractice claims.[15] Patients do not necessarily sue because there has been a bad outcome, rather, they sue because they feel that the physician is not willing or able to explain to them or their family how the outcome occurred. Other suits involve patient claims that they did not give truly "informed" consent.[16] One of the authors (M.S.) designed an intensive course in communication enhancement training at the request of the Medical Inter-Insurance Exchange, the physician-owned malpractice carrier in New Jersey, which teaches strategies to minimize or prevent these types of communication breakdowns.[17] *The Fifteen Minute Hour* is used as a text for this course. Norman Cousins has suggested that doctors who spend more time with their patients may have to spend less money on malpractice protection.[18] We agree, but we think the quality of the time spent with the patient is more important than the quantity.

SOCIETAL IMPLICATIONS

Achieving good health has become a professed goal for our society. As stated in a report by the U.S. Department of Health and Human Services, *Healthy People 2000: National Health Promotion and Disease Prevention Objectives*, good health means not only reducing unnecessary suffering, illness, and disability, but gaining an improved quality of life as well.[19] The three major goals to be achieved for U.S. citizens are: increasing the span of healthy life, reducing health disparities, and having all people achieve access to preventive services.

Promoting Health

Healthy People 2000 acknowledges that health promotion strategies are largely related to life-style and that personal choices people make have a powerful influence over their health. Priorities for the modification of life-styles are currently listed in the following order: physical activity and fitness; nutrition; tobacco, alcohol, and other drugs; family planning; mental health and mental disorders; violent and abusive behavior; and educational and community-based programs. All these priorities can be achieved only through behavioral change. There are many strategies in *The Fifteen Minute Hour* that will empower physicians to sucessfully engage their patients in changing behaviors that are destructive to their health.

Of course, not everyone can be healthy. Disease and disability will inevitably be experienced by all people. Predispositions based on hereditary or socioeconomic factors are, however, mediated by individual experience to include the environmental and behavioral factors capable of provoking ill health, with or without previous predisposition. Emotional stress is one of the factors cited in the report as being related to serious illnesses such as heart disease and cancer.

Control of Stress

Stress control is listed as one of the major goals of health promotion.[19] *Healthy People 2000* reports that more than one-quarter of people reporting high stress do nothing about it. Continual improvements in research methodology are expected to provide a more reliable identification of the sources of stress and the processes that mediate the transformation of stressful events in health and mental health problems. Stress management and stress reduction techniques must also be evaluated. Primary care providers are cited as having responsibility to help in these efforts. Two strategies must be employed, one to reduce actual stress and a second to modify reactions and enhance coping skills. This is seen as the responsibility of the health care professional who first sees the people at risk. The importance of starting with a clear understanding of the type of events that are most difficult for individuals to handle is cited. It is our contention that everything that we have written in this text will contribute to these efforts.

Focus on Mental Health

One of the objectives of *Healthy People 2000* is to reduce the proportion of people aged 18 and over who experience adverse health effects from stress within a given year from a baseline of 42.6 percent to less than 35 percent (p. 214).[19] We are gratified that the health planning establishment acknowledges the direct link between stress and health. This is something that physicians who are comfortable with our techniques will be able to impart to their patients along with the appropriate intervention.

Another objective from *Healthy People 2000* is to increase the percent of people with major depression who receive treatment from the current 31 percent to 45 percent (p. 215).[19] If all physicians BATHEd their patients, this objective would be easily achieved. "Most of the adult population reports experiencing personal or emotional problems in the course of a year. Half of these people say that they are unable to solve their problems" (p. 216).[19] Physicians are cited as among the most likely choices of those who seek professional help. We want physicians to feel comfortable providing it. The report further urged, "Increase to at least 75 percent the proportion of providers of primary care for children who include assessment of cognitive, emotional and parent-child function, with appropriate counseling, referral and followup, in their clinical practices" (p. 219).[19] We rest our case.

Focus on the Elderly

Healthy People 2000 underscores the importance of health promotion for the growing numbers of elderly individuals in our population. The focus is on preserving their quality of life and functional independence by changing certain risk behaviors into healthy ones (p. 587).[19] The primary mechanisms cited to reduce risk are primary prevention, strong social support, and regular primary care services. Changing certain health behaviors, even in old age, can benefit health and the quality of life. The primary care physician who incorporates psychotherapy into everyday medical practice is in a unique position to make a meaningful impact here. The aging of our population provides a strong mandate for physicians to become involved with the whole patient, provide support, and build self-confidence by helping to promote small wins.

PUTTING HEALTH PROMOTION AND DISEASE PREVENTION INTO PRACTICE

There is a clear directive for the primary care physician, as part of health maintenance functions, to screen for stress-related problems and help patients manage their reaction to the events in their lives in the most constructive way possible. We have tried to outline how this can be done effectively and efficiently. At the minimum, each patient can be BATHEd and given permission to feel whatever feelings are being experienced. Limited information about how people react to stress can be imparted, and specific suggestions can be given for managing stress effectively. Anticipatory guidance can be given to minimize the stress inherent in adjusting to expected transitions, while the ongoing relationship with the primary care physician will provide supportive therapy. Physicians must learn to ask questions that focus patients on their own strengths. Appendix A provides a dozen effective questions and three excellent responses with which to approach these goals.

SUMMING UP

A final word: Can psychotherapy, as we have proposed it be practiced, really work? It can, and it always has. It used to be called "moral treatment."

Moral treatment was practiced in the nineteenth century in the United States. This was before the time of Sigmund Freud, Carl Jung, or Alfred Adler; it was also before the time of Wilhelm Wundt, Ivan Pavlov, B. F. Skinner, Abraham Maslow, Neil Miller, Gregory Bateson, Fritz Perls, Martin Seligman, Alfred Bandura, Aaron Beck, or Albert Ellis. Moral treatment was used to prevent, treat, and correct various causes of mental disorders. Moral therapy consisted of creating a milieu in which the emphasis was on building up the self-esteem and self-control of the patient through the judicious use of "rewards and punishments in the context of a strong emotional relationship with a doctor."[20]

We think it is a great idea, both for today and into the twenty-first century, especially when we can incorporate the contributions of all those distinguished practioners and theorists cited above. Certainly, it will enhance the health of the patient and the health, happiness and image of the practicing primary care physician.

REFERENCES

1. Erikson, E. *Life history and the historical moment*. New York: Norton, 1975.

2. Fuller, R. B. *Synergistics*. New York: MacMillan, 1975.

3. Ader, R., Felton, D. L., & Cohen, N. (Eds.) *Psychoneuroimmunology*, 2d ed. San Diego, Calif.: Academic Press, 1991.

4. Kiecolt-Glaser, J. K., Glaser, R., Shuttleworth, E. C., Dyer, C. S., Ogrocki, P., & Speicher, C. E. Chronic stress and immunity in family caregivers of Alzheimer's disease victims. *Psychosomatic Medicine*, 1987, *49*, 523–535.

5. United States Department of Health and Human Services. *Summary report of the Graduate Medical Educational National Advisory Committee*. Washington, D.C.: U.S. Government Printing Office, 1980.

6. Antonovsky, A. *Health, stress, and coping*. San Francisco: Jossey-Bass, 1979.

7. Schmiedeck, R. A. The sense of identity and the role of continuity and confluence. *Psychiatry*, 1979, *43*, 157–164.

8. Maslow, A. H. Self-actualizing people: A study of psychological health. *Personality*, 1950, *symposium 1*, 11–34.

9. Taylor, S. E., & Brown, J. D. Illusion and well-being: A social psychological perspective on mental health. *Psychological Bulletin*, 1988, *103*, 193–210.

10. Ley, P. Satisfaction, compliance and communication. *British Journal of Clinical Psychology*, 1982, *21*, 241–254.

11. Fiore, N. Fighting cancer—One patient's perspective. *New England Journal of Medicine*, 1979, *300*, 284–289.

12. Starr, P. *The social transformation of American medicine*. New York: Basic Books, 1984, p. 424.

13. Lieberman, J. A., III. Family medicine and the aging patient: Clinical and educational issues. *New Jersey Family Physician*, 1984, *8*, 28–33.

14. Engel, G. L. The clinical application of the biopsychosocial model. *The American Journal of Psychiatry*, 1980, *137*, 535–544.

15. Shapiro, R. S., Simpson, D. E., Lawrence, S. L., Talsky, A. M., Sobocinski, K. A., & Schiedermayer, D. L. A survey of sued and nonsued physicians and suing patients. *Archives of Internal Medicine*, 1989, *149*, 2190–2196.

16. Annandale, E. C. The malpractice crisis and the doctor-patient relationship. *Sociology of Health and Illness*, 1989, *11*, 1–23.

17. Stuart, M. R. Communications enhancement training: Essential skills to lower the risk of malpractice suits. Seminar, 23rd Annual STFM Spring Conference, Seattle, Wash., May 1990.

18. Cousins, N. *The healing heart*. New York: Norton, 1983, p. 162.

19. United States Department of Health and Human Services, Public Health Service. *Healthy people 2000: National health promotion and disease prevention objectives*, DHHS Publication No. (PHS) 91–50212. Washington, D.C.: U.S. Department of Health and Human Services, Public Health Service, 1991.

20. Freedman, A. M., Kaplan, H. I., & Sadock, B. J. *Modern synopsis of comprehensive textbook of psychiatry II*, 2d ed. Baltimore, Md.: Williams and Wilkins Co., 1976, p. 22.

A Dozen Good Questions and Three Good Answers for All Seasons

Questions that have therapeutic value:

1. How do you feel about that?
2. What troubles you the most?
3. How are you handling that?
4. What are you feeling right now?
5. What do you want?
6. What can *you* do about that?
7. What are your options?
8. What's the best thing that can happen?
9. What's the worst thing that can happen?
10. What's in it for you?
11. What does it mean to you?
12. What, specifically, do you want from me?

Responses that have therapeutic value:

1. That must be very difficult for you.
2. I can understand *that* you would feel that way.*
3. Under the circumstances, I'm sure that you (he, she, they) did the best you (he, she, they) could!

---

*Not to be confused with "I understand how you feel." or "I know how you feel", which are not recommended, since they may lead to arguments. No one can know how another is actually feeling.

Recommended Books for Patients

FOR ANXIETY

Jeffers, S. *Feel the Fear and Do It Anyway*. New York: Fawcett Columbine, 1987.

This is an absolutely delightful, practical manual to help patients overcome the fears that limit their lives. It contains both insights and exercises, and is easy to read and apply. Patients can choose to work on certain sections and report their progress to the physician.

STRESS MANAGEMENT

Nathan, R. G., Staats, T. E., & Rosh, P. J. *The Doctor's Guide to Instant Stress Relief*. New York: Ballatine, 1987.

Inexpensive, complete, and easy to read and follow, this is a comprehensive treatment of stress management. It also includes a card that provides bio-feedback. This book will reinforce everything you teach your patients about managing stress.

Davis, M., Eshelman, E. R., & McKay, M. *The Relaxation and Stress Reduction Workbook*. 3d ed. Oakland, Calif.: New Harbinger Press, 1991.

This complete guide to relaxation techniques includes chapters on breathing, meditation, visualization, stopping stressful thoughts, time management, nutrition, and physical exercise. An effective self-help manual, it is excellent for use under a physician's supervision. New Harbinger has a whole catalog of self-help materials focusing on every imaginable topic from eating disorders (*The Deadly Diet*) to lifetime weight control.

ASSERTIVENESS TRAINING

Smith, M. J. *When I Say No, I Feel Guilty.* New York: Dial Press, 1975.

This book teaches assertiveness training with humor and great examples. Let patients read and enjoy, and then assign them exercises to put into practice.

Alberti, R. E., & Emmons, M. *Your Perfect Right.* Rev ed. San Luis Obispo, Calif.: Impact Press, 1974.

This is considered the classic on assertiveness training. It is sensibly written and easy to follow.

PARENTING GUIDANCE

Faber, A., & Mazlich, E. *How to Talk so Kids Will Listen, How to Listen so Kids Will Talk.* New York: Avon Books, 1980.

This little paperback is based on the work of Chaim Ginott and is filled with cartoons and practical suggestions. It will make parents feel as though they have a wise and loving advisor always at hand to help them to deal with normal developmental issues in good-humored ways.

Gordon, T. *P. E. T.: Parent Effectiveness Training.* New York: Penguin Books, 1975.

This classic still dispenses very good advice. It helps parents set limits and makes them feel competent in the role.

Satir, V. *Peoplemaking.* Palo Alto, Calif.: Science and Behavior Books, 1972.

Virginia Satir's philosophical approach is designed to maximize self-esteem in all members of the family. A lovely book to read and enjoy, *Peoplemaking* nonetheless casts light on the dynamics of both healthy and dysfunctional families. It should be available in all public libraries.

FOR DEALING WITH LOSS

Jewett, C. L. *Helping Children Cope with Separation and Loss.* Harvard, Mass.: Harvard Common Press, 1982.

Jewett's book presents simple techniques for adults to use to help children who have experienced loss. It contains good background material on the stages of grief and their effects on children. There is practical advice extending from how to tell children that something dreadful has happened, through the resultant shock and denial, to the anger and depression that can be expected to follow. There are also excellent suggestions for dealing with the difficult situations brought on by death, separation, divorce, hospitalizations, major moves, or other events that are traumatic for children.

Kushner, H. S. *When Bad Things Happen to Good People.* New York: Avon Books, 1981.

This is a wonderful volume to recommend to people who are dealing with tragedy. Kushner's comforting book can help people make sense of their suffering.

FOR EVERYONE

Blanchard, K., & Johnson, S. *The One Minute Manager.* New York: Berkley, 1983.

This is not just for managers. It helps focus people on what is essential, including goals, praise, and complaints, which must be formulated concisely and communicated clearly. *The One Minute Manager* will help patients to feel competent and connect with other people in positive ways.

Index

About the Editors

MARIAN R. STUART, Ph.D., is Clinical Associate Professor in the Department of Family Medicine at the University of Medicine and Dentistry of New Jersey–Robert Wood Johnson Medical School and also holds an appointment in the Department of Psychiatry. Since joining the Department of Family Medicine in 1978, she has headed the behavioral science program, developing and teaching counseling skills especially oriented to primary care physicians. Dr. Stuart's interests and publications cover a broad spectrum in medical education and behavioral science. They include faculty education, risk management, geriatrics, group dynamics, and conflict resolution. She maintains a small private practice as a clinical psychologist, but her primary commitment is to teaching the integration of mental and physical health for physicians and patients.

JOSEPH A. LIEBERMAN III, M.D., M.P.H., is Chairman of the Department of Family and Community Medicine at the Medical Center of Delaware. Before accepting this position, he was Professor of Family Medicine and Chairman of the Department of Family Medicine at the University of Medicine and Dentistry of New Jersey–Robert Wood Johnson Medical School. A frequent contributor to medical literature, Dr. Lieberman is also involved in numerous professional organizations. He is a Fellow of the American Academy of Family Physicians, and is certified by the American Board of Family Practice as well as the American Board of Medical Management.